Victor Hugo

The Destroyer of the Second Republic

Being Napoleon the Little

Victor Hugo

The Destroyer of the Second Republic
Being Napoleon the Little

ISBN/EAN: 9783337350154

Printed in Europe, USA, Canada, Australia, Japan

Cover: Foto ©ninafisch / pixelio.de

More available books at **www.hansebooks.com**

OF

THE SECOND REPUBLIC;

BEING

NAPOLEON THE LITTLE.

By VICTOR HUGO.

TRANSLATED BY A CLERGYMAN OF THE PROTESTANT EPISCOPAL CHURCH, FROM THE SIXTEENTH FRENCH EDITION.

NEW YORK:
SHELDON & COMPANY,
498 AND 500 BROADWAY.
1870.

Entered according to Act of Congress, in the year 1870,

BY SHELDON & COMPANY,

In the Office of the Librarian of Congress, at Washington.

Stereotyped by LITTLE, RENNIE & CO. Printed by the UNION PRINTING HOUSE,
646 and 647 Broadway, N. Y. 79 John Street, N. Y.

TRANSLATOR'S PREFACE.

WHEN the translator first began spending leisure hours on this book, he felt little interest, and would have spoken of his occupation in the tone of apology. He was wrong. He has almost unconsciously given to the American public a great work full of the burning genius of a great author. If this volume is not read and valued, it will not be its own fault; for if it has any fault, and it has many, the first among them appears to him to be the worthy one, that it is too keen in its delicate satire, too fine in its exquisite wit for the dull ears, or, we should rather say, the dull eyes of too many who will look into it. When judged among Victor Hugo's works, it will take rank as one of the most complete. Not possessing the sensational and popular interest of a novel, it acquires dignity from its purely historical character and intense power from the fact that its author was an eye-witness of the events which he records, and a participant in the sufferings which he resents. Seldom do we have an historical monogram of more value. When judged on its own merits, without a comparison with other works by the author, it may be said that, notwithstanding its occasional extravagance of style, and its continual use of the nominative absolute, making it hard for the reader and an affliction to the translator; and notwithstanding also its enormous French vanity, occasionally swelling to sacred allusions, which in another would be called blasphemy, the book is of value in an artistic and scientific point of view, as containing passages of incomparable eloquence, as being graphic and readable throughout, and as affording in its later portions a masterly analysis of crime. As to its moral tone, notwithstanding an occasional coarse allusion, it may be said to be everywhere high; that is, every argument is based on morals and on conscience, and never do we discover the writer yielding a vulgar homage to success. Many of its predictions* have been singularly although tardily verified, and we can read in the light of 1870 many prophesies with wonder, which in 1869 would have provoked a smile. The translator hopes that the work will be of benefit politically and morally, as well as intellectually, and as a source of recreation; although he cannot agree with all the positions taken in its pages, he does not consider any of them so far astray as to mar the general value of its conclusions. As to the character of the translation, he may have committed errors through haste, for which he will ask pardon; but as to the general plan and style in which the work has been completed, those who know what is proper in the translation of languages will see that they are correct; as to the opinion of others he is not anxious. He will add one remark, and only one, and that is, that he has endeavored to confine his work to spare intervals, and that it has not encroached seriously upon consecrated time.

* The work was first published in 1852.

HARTFORD, Conn., *Nov. 24th*, 1870.

TABLE OF CONTENTS.

BOOK FIRST.—THE MAN.

I. The 20th of December, 1848.—II. Commission of the Representatives.—III. Forced to silence.—IV. Men will awake.—V. Biography.—VI. Portrait.—VII. To make a sequel to the Panegyrics. . . . 9–50

BOOK SECOND.—THE GOVERNMENT.

I. The Constitution.—II. The Senate.—III. The Council of State and the Corps Legislatif.—IV. The Finances.—V. The Liberty of the Press.—VI. Novelties in point of legality.—VII. The Adherents.—VIII. Mens agitat molem.—IX. Omnipotence.—X. The two Profiles of M. Bonaparte.—XI. Recapitulation. 51–95

BOOK THIRD.—THE CRIME.

Chapter taken from an unpublished, book entited *The Crime of the 2d of December,* by Victor Hugo. 96–140

BOOK FOURTH.—THE OTHER CRIME.

I. Sinister Questions.—II. A Succession of Crimes.—III. What 1852 might have been.—IV. Jacquerie. 141–175

BOOK FIFTH.—PARLIAMENTARISM.

I. 1789.—II. Mirabeau.—III. The Tribune.—IV. The Orators.—V. Power of Speech.—VI. What the Orator is.—VII. What the Tribune was doing.—VIII. Parliamentarism.—IX. The Tribune destroyed. 176–199

BOOK SIXTH.—THE ABSOLUTION.
FIRST FORM: THE 7,500,000 VOTES.

I. The Absolution.—II. The Stage-coach.—III. Sifting of the Vote. The Recalling of Facts.—IV. Who really voted for M. Bonaparte.—V. Concession.—VI. The Moral Side of the Question.—VII. Explanation to M. Bonaparte.—VIII. Axioms.—IX. In what M. Bonaparte is deceived. . . . 200–231

BOOK SEVENTH.—THE ABSOLUTION.
SECOND FORM: THE OATH.

I. Upon an oath, an oath and a-half.—II. Difference of prices.—III. The oath of the men of letters and science.—IV. Curiosities of the thing.—V. The 5th of April, 1852.—VI. Oath everywhere.   232–252

BOOK EIGHTH.—THE PROGRESS INVOLVED IN THE COUP D'ETAT.

I. The quantity of Good which the Evil contained.—II. The Four Institutions which oppose the Future.—III. Slowness of Normal Progress.—IV. What an Assembly ought to have done.—V. What Providence has done.—VI. What the Ministers, the Army, the Magistracy, and the Clergy did.—VII. God's forms of government. 253–269

CONCLUSION.—FIRST PART.
Littleness of the Master, baseness of the Situation.   270–289

SECOND PART.
Mourning and Faith. 290–308

NAPOLEON THE LITTLE.

BOOK FIRST.—THE MAN.

CHAPTER I.

THE 20TH OF DECEMBER, 1848.

On Thursday, the 20th of December, 1848, the Constituent Assembly was in session, surrounded at the moment by an imposing array of troops.

A report of the representative Waldeck Rousseau, made in the name of the committee charged with giving an abstract of the vote for the election to the presidency of the Republic, had just been read. In that report one remarked this phrase, which summed up all its meaning : "It is the seal of the inviolable power of the nation, that by this perfect execution given to the fundamental law, she plants herself on the Constitution, in order to render it holy and inviolable." Following this, in the midst of the profound silence of nine hundred constituents, assembled in a mass, and almost to the entire number of the body, Armand Marrast, the President of the National Constituent Assembly, arose and said :—

"In the name of the French people :

"Seeing that the citizen Charles-Louis-Napoleon-Bonaparte, born in Paris, fulfills the conditions of eligibility prescribed by the 44th article of the Constitution;

"Seeing that in the open ballot held throughout the entire extent of this territory of the Republic, for the election of the President, he has united the absolute majority of suffrages;

"In virtue of the 47th and 48th articles of the Constitution, the National Assembly proclaims him President of the Republic, from the present day till the second Sunday of May, 1852."

A movement was seen on the benches and in the tribunes, which were full of people. The President of the Constituent Assembly added:—

"According to the terms of the decree, I invite the citizen President of the Republic to be pleased to present himself at the tribune, there to make oath."

The representatives, who were encumbering the lobby, went up to their places and left the passage free. It was about four o'clock in the evening, night was falling, and the vast hall of the Assembly was half plunged in shadow. The lights descended from the ceilings, and the attendants had just placed the lamps upon the tribune.

The President made a sign, and the door at the right opened. A man, still young, dressed in black, having on his coat the badge and the great cord of the Legion of Honor, was then seen to enter the hall and rapidly ascend the tribune. Every face turned toward the man.

A wan face, whose thin and bony angles the lamps from the skylight made peculiarly distinct; a nose thick and long; mustaches; a lock of hair curled on a narrow forehead; the eye small and without clearness; the attitude timid and ill at ease; no resemblance to the Emperor. This was the citizen Charles-Louis-Napoleon-Bonaparte.

During the kind of murmur which followed his entrance he remained several minutes with his right hand in his buttoned coat, standing, and motionless, on the tribune, whose front bore this date, 22d, 23d, 24th* of February; and above that these three words: "Liberty, Equality, Fraternity."

Before his election as President of the Republic, Charles-Louis-Napoleon-Bonaparte was a representative of the people. He had sat in the Assembly for several months, and although he rarely remained during entire sessions, he might often be seen sitting in the place which he had chosen on the higher benches of the left, in the fifth row, in that circle commonly called the "mountain," behind his old preceptor, the representative Vieillard. The man was not a new form to the Assembly, yet his entrance produced deep emotion. For all, for his friends as for his enemies, it was the future which entered, a future unknown. In the kind of immense murmur which was formed by the suppressed voices of all, his name might have been heard accompanied by remarks the most different. His antagonists recounted his adventures; his attempts; Strasbourg; Boulonge; the tame eagle and the piece of meat stuck in the little hat. His friends recalled his exile; a good book on artillery; his writings printed at Ham, which were to a certain degree liberal in spirit, democratic and socialistical; his maturer age; and to those which repeated his follies, they recalled his misfortunes.

---

* Days of the abdication of Louis Philippe, and the inauguration of the second Republic.

General Cavaignac, who, not having been named president, had just resigned power into the bosom of the Assembly, with that quiet brevity which becomes republics, seated in his habitual place at the head of the bench of ministers, to the left of the tribune, beside Marie, minister of justice, was assisting, silent, and with arms crossed, at the installation of the new man. At last silence reigned, and the President of the Assembly struck several blows with his gavel on the table. The last sound died away, and the President of the Assembly said :—

"I am about to read the form of oath."

The moment possessed something of the religious. The Assembly was no longer the Assembly, it was a temple. What added to the immense significance of this oath was that it was the only one which was taken in the whole extent of the Republic.

February had wisely abolished the political oath, and the Constitution, with equal reason, had only preserved the oath of the President. This oath had the double characteristic of necessity and grandeur. It was the executive power, which is a subordinate power, which made oath to the legislative power, which is a superior power. It was still better than that. Inverting that fiction of monarchy, according to which it is the people who make oath to the man invested with power, it was the man invested with power who made oath to the people.

The President, an officer and servant, swore fidelity to the sovereign people, bowing before the national majesty visible in the omnipotent Assembly. He received from the Assembly the Constitution, and swore obedience to it. The representatives were inviolable, and he was not. We repeat it : a citizen responsible before all citizens, he was the only man in the nation bound in this manner. On that account there was in the unique and supreme oath a solemnity which took hold of the very heart. He who writes these lines was seated in his place in the Assembly on the day on which this oath was taken. He is one of those who, taken in the presence of the civilized world, received that oath in the name of the people, and who have it yet in their hands. Here it is :—"In the presence of God, and before the French people represented by the National Assembly, I swear to remain faithful to the Democratic Republic, one and indivisible, and to fulfill all the duties which the Constitution imposes upon me."

The President of the Assembly, standing, read this majestic formula; then, all the Assembly keeping silence and riveting their attention, the citizen Charles-Louis-Napoleon-Bonaparte, raising his right hand, said in a voice high and firm, "I swear it."

The representative Boulay (from Muerthe), since Vice-president of the Republic, and one who had known Charles-Louis-Napoleon-Bonaparte from childhood, exclaimed: "He is an honest man ; he will keep his oath."

The President of the Assembly, always standing, replied, and we cite here only the words literally enregistered in the *Moniteur*, "We take God and men to witness the oath which has just been taken."

The National Assembly took action on it, ordered that it should be transcribed upon the record of proceedings, inserted in the *Moniteur*, published and posted after the manner of legislative acts.

It seemed as if everything had been done. They waited

till the citizen Charles-Louis-Napoleon-Bonaparte, thereafter President of the Republic till the second Sunday of May, should descend from the tribune. He did not descend from it. He felt the noble necessity of binding himself still further, if it was possible, and to add somewhat to the oath which the Constitution exacted of him, in order to show them to what degree this oath was free and spontaneous on his part. He asked the usual permission to speak. "You have it," said the President of the Assembly.

The attention and silence redoubled. The citizen Louis-Napoleon-Bonaparte unfolded a paper and read an address. In it he announced and installed the ministry named by him, and said :—

"I desire, as you do, citizen representatives, to re-establish society again upon its foundations, reaffirm democratic institutions, and to search out all proper means for comforting the woes of this generous and intelligent people who have just given me so distinguished a proof of their confidence."* He thanked his predecessor in the executive power, the same who could say, later on, these beautiful words, "I have not fallen from power, I have descended from it," and he extolled him in these terms : "The new administration, in entering upon affairs, must thank that which has preceded it for the efforts which it has made to transmit power intact, and for maintaining public order.† The conduct of the honorable General Cavaignac has been worthy of the loyalty of his character and of that sentiment of duty which is the first quality of the chief of a state."‡

---

* (Very good ! very good !)—*Moniteur.*
† (Marks of adhesion.)—*Moniteur.*
‡ (New marks of assent.)—*Moniteur.*

The Assembly applauded at these words; but what struck all minds, and what engraved itself deeply on all memories, and had an echo in all loyal consciences, was this *entirely spontaneous* declaration with which he began. We repeat it :—

"The suffrages of the nation and the oath which I have just taken command my future conduct. My duty is traced. I will fulfill it as a man of honor. I will see enemies of the country in all those who would try to change by illegal means what France entire has established." When he had finished speaking, the Constituent Assembly arose, and, with a single voice, sent forth this grand cry, "*Vive la République.*"

Louis-Napoleon-Bonaparte descended from the tribune, went straight to General Cavaignac, and offered him his hand. The general hesitated several moments before accepting this clasp of the hand. All who had just heard the words of Louis Bonaparte, pronounced in a tone of loyalty so profound, blamed the general.

The Constitution to which Louis-Napoleon-Bonaparte took oath on the 20th of December, 1848, "in the face of God and man," contained, among other articles, these :—

"Art. 36. The representatives of the people are inviolable.

"Art. 37. They cannot be arrested on a criminal charge, save in the case of flagrant misdemeanor; nor prosecuted except after the Assembly has permitted the prosecution.

"Art. 68. Every measure by which the President of the Republic dissolves the National Assembly, prorogues it, or places obstacles in the way of the execution of its decrees, is a crime of high treason. By this sole fact the President is suspended from his functions, the citizens are bound to refuse him obedience, the executive power passes in full right to the National Assembly. The judges of the high court shall assemble immediately, on pain of forfeiture. They shall convoke the jury in the place that they appoint, in order to proceed to the trial of the President and his accomplices. They shall declare themselves the magistrates charged with fulfilling the functions of the public ministry."

Less than three years after this memorable day, the 2d of December, 1851, at break of day, one could read, on all the corners of the streets of Paris, the following notice:—

"In the name of the French people, the President of the Republic decrees—

"ART. 1st. The National Assembly is dissolved.

"ART. 2d. Universal suffrage is re-established. The law of the 31st of May* is abrogated.

"ART. 3d. The French people are convoked in their communities.

"ART. 4th. The state of siege is decreed in the entire extent of the first military division.

"ART. 5th. The Council of State is dissolved.

"ART. 6th. The minister of the interior is charged with the execution of the present decree.

"Done at the palace of the Elysée, the 2d of December, 1851."

At the same time Paris learned that fifteen of the inviolable representatives of the people had been arrested in their homes during the night by order of Louis-Napoleon-Bonaparte.

---

* A law by which suffrage was restricted to those who had resided in a canton or precinct for three years, abrogating the old law which said six months. It practically disfranchised a million.—TR.

CHAPTER II.

COMMISSION OF THE REPRESENTATIVES.

Those who received, in deposit for the people as representatives of the people, the oath of the 20th o December, 1848; those, above all, who twice invested with the confidence of the people, saw it sworn as constituents and saw it violated as legislators, had assumed at the same time with their commission two duties.

The first was, on the day on which the oath should be violated, to arise, offer their breasts; to calculate neither the number nor force of the enemy; to cover with their bodies the sovereignty of the people, and to seize, in order to do battle with and cast down the usurper, all arms, from the law which they found in the code to the paving-stone that you pick up in the street.

The second duty was, after having accepted the struggle and all its chances, to accept the proscription and all its misery; to stand eternally upright before the traitor, with his oath in their hand; to forget their individual sufferings, their private griefs, their families distressed and crippled, their fortunes destroyed, their affections wounded, their hearts bleeding; to forget themselves. To have thereafter but one trouble, the wound of France; to cry justice! never to allow themselves to be appeased or bent; to be implacable; to seize the abominable crowned perjurer, if not with the hand of the law, at least with the pincers of the truth; to make all the letters of his oath red at the fire of history, and to brand them on his face.

He who writes these lines is of those who recoiled before nothing on the 2d of December to accomplish the first of these two great duties.

In publishing this book he fulfills the second.

CHAPTER III.

FORCED TO SILENCE.

It is time that the human conscience should awake. Since the 2d of December, 1851, an ambush has succeeded a crime odious and repulsive, infamous and unheard of, if we consider the century in which it has been committed. It triumphs and domineers; erects itself in actual theory; blooms in the face of the sun; makes laws, enacts decrees, takes society, religion, and the family under its protection; offers its hand to the kings of Europe (who accept it), and says to them, "My brother, or my cousin." This crime no one disputes, not even those who profit by it and live on it—they say only that it was necessary; nor does he who committed it dispute it—he says only that to him, the criminal, it has been *absolved!*

This crime contains all crimes; treason in the conception, perjury in the execution, murder and assassination in the struggle, spoliation, swindling, and theft in the triumph. This crime draws after it, as integral parts of itself, the suppression of laws, the violation of things made inviolable by the Constitution, arbitrary sequestration, the confiscation of goods, nocturnal massacres, shots fired in secret, commissions taking the place of the tribunals, ten thousand citizens exiled, forty thousand proscribed, sixty thousand families ruined and desperate! These things are patent. Well, this is the bitter truth. Silence is kept over this crime. It is there; one touches it; one sees it; one passes on and goes to one's affairs; the shop opens; the exchange jobs in stocks. Conscience sits down on its ballot; rubs its hands; and we also desire the moment when one is going to consider it all natural. He who measures the stuff with the ell-stick does not hear that the measure which he has in his hand speaks to him and says, "It is a false measure which governs." He who weighs a commodity does not understand that his balance lifts up its voice and says to him, "It is a false weight that reigns." Strange order that, which has for its foundation supreme *dis*order. The denial of all right! Equilibrium founded on iniquity! Let us add that which nevertheless is self-evident, that the author of this crime is a malefactor of the most cynical and base species.

At the hour which is now passing, let all those who wear a robe, a scarf, or a uniform—let all those who serve this man, know it—if they believe themselves the agents of a power, let them undeceive themselves. They are the comrades of a pirate.

Since the 2d of December there have been no more functionaries in France; there have been only accomplices. The moment has come when each man should render himself a good account of what he has done, and of what he continues to do. The gendarme who arrested those whom the man of Strasbourg and of Boulogne called insurgents has arrested the guardians of the Constitution. The judge who judged the combatants of Paris or the provinces has put on the stool the support of the law. The officer who has kept the condemned in the hold of the ship has detained the defenders of the Republic and the State.

The general of Africa who imprisons at Lambessa the transported, who are bowed down under the sun, shivering with fever, digging in the burning earth ditches which shall be their graves—this general sequesters, tortures, and assassinates the champions of right. All guards, officers, gendarmes, judges, are in full forfeiture. They have before them more than innocent heroes, more than victims—martyrs! Let them know it, then, and let them hate themselves; and as the least amends, let them break the chains. Let them draw the bolts, let them empty the hulks, let them open the gaols, since they have no longer the courage to seize the sword. Then, conscience, arise, awake, it is time. If law, right, duty, reason, equity, justice do not suffice, let them consider the future. If remorse is silent, let responsibility speak.

And let all those who, if landlords, shake hands with a magistrate; if bankers, fête a general; if peasants, salute a gendarme. Let all those who do not withdraw from the nobleman's house, where the minister is, and from the dwelling where the prefect resides, as from a lazar-house; let all those who—simple citizens, not functionaries—go to the balls and banquets of Louis Bonaparte, and do not see that the black flag is on the Elysée—let all those know it well; this kind of infamy is *contagious!* If they escape material complicity, they do not escape that which is moral. The crime of the 2d of December soils them. The present situation, which seems calm to him who does not think, is violent. Let no one be deceived on this point. When public morality is eclipsed, a shadow which affrights one is created in the social order. All guarantees depart, all props for support vanish.

Therefore, from that time forth there is no longer any tribunal in France ; no court, no judge who can render justice and pronounce a penalty in relation to anything of any character, against any one, in the name of anything. Let them bring before the assizes any malefactor whomsoever ; the thief will say to the judges, "The chief of the State has stolen twenty-five millions of francs from the bank."* The false witness will say, "The chief of State has made an oath in the face of God and man, and that oath he has violated." The man guilty of arbitrary sequestration will say, "The chief of State has arrested and detained, against all laws, the representatives of the sovereign people." The swindler will say, "The chief of State has swindled his command, swindled power, and swindled the Tuileries." The forger will say, "The chief of State has falsified a ballot." The bandit of the corner of the wood will say, "The chief of State has picked the pockets of the princes of Orleans." The murderer will say, "The chief of State has musketed, shot with grape-shot, sabred, and cut the throats of passers-by in the streets ;" and all together—swindler, forger, false witness, bandit, thief, assassin, will add, "But you judges, *you* want to *salute* this man, you want to praise him for having perjured himself, to compliment him for having done a wrong, to glorify him for having swindled, to felicitate his having stolen, and to thank him for having assassinated ! What do you want with us ?

Assuredly, such a state of things is grave. To go to sleep over such a situation is one disgrace additional. It is time, let us repeat it, that this monstrous sleep of conscience

---

* A witness saw it carted away.

should end. It is not necessary that, after this startling scandal, the triumph of crime—a scandal more startling yet should be given to men—viz., the indifference of the civilized world! If that should come to pass, history would appear one day as an avenger.* And from this moment, as lions when wounded bury themselves in solitudes, the just man veiling his face in presence of this universal abasement, would take refuge in the immensity of his contempt.

---

* Has it not to-day!

CHAPTER IV.

MEN WILL AWAKE.

But that will not be; men will awake.

This book has no other object than to shake those sleeping in this sleep.

France is *not* to adhere to this government, even by the consent of lethargy. At certain moments, in certain places, in certain shades, to sleep is to die.

Let us add, that at the present moment, France, strange to say, and yet it is the truth, knows nothing of what passed on the 2d of December and since, or knows it imperfectly, and it is that which affords an excuse.

However, thanks to several generous and courageous publications, the facts begin to *transpire*.

This book is destined to bring some of them to light, and, if it please God, to place all of them in clear day.

It is of importance that we know a little what M. Bonaparte is. At the present time, thanks to the suppression of the *Tribune*, thanks to the suppression of the press, of free speech, of liberty and truth (a suppression which has for its results to allow all liberty to M. Bonaparte, but which, at the same time, has the effect of nullifying all his acts without exception, the indescribable ballot of the 2d of December included); thanks, let us say, to this smothering of complaint and all information—no circumstance, no man, no fact, wears its own shape or carries its true name. The crime of M. Bonaparte is not crime, its name is necessity. The ambush of M. Bonaparte is not an ambush, it is called the defense of order. The thefts of M. Bonaparte are not thefts, they are termed measures of State. The murders of M. Bonaparte are not murders, they are called public safety. The accomplices of M. Bonaparte are not malefactors, they are called magistrates, senators, and counsellors of state. The adversaries of M. Bonaparte are not the soldiers of law and right, they are called jaques,* demagogues, factionists. In the eyes of France, in the eyes of Europe, the 2d of December still wears a mask.

This book is nothing else than a hand, which goes out from the shadow, which tears away the mask.

We are going to expose this triumph of order, and paint this government, so vigorous, so square and strong; this government having in its favor a crowd of young people who have more ambition than boots; which is sustained on the exchange by Fould the Jew, and in the Church by Montalembert the Catholic; esteemed by women who wish to be mistresses, and by men who wish to be prefects; propped up by a coalition of prostitutions; giving fêtes; making cardinals; wearing a white cravat, with its folding hat under its arm; gloved fresh-butter-colored, like Morney; varnished anew, like Manpas; fresh brushed, like Persigny; rich, elegant, neat, gilded, joyous—born in a pool of blood!

Yes: there will be a rewakening! Yes: men will come

---

* Insurgent peasants.

out of this stupor which, for such a people, is shame! And when France shall awake—when she shall open her eyes, and distinguish objects—when she shall see that which is before her and at her side, she will recoil—this France will—with trembling terror before this monstrous offense which has dared to espouse her in the darkness, and whose bed she has shared.

Then the supreme hour will tell. The skeptics will smile and maintain their view. They will say: "They say, hope for nothing. This reign, according to you, is the shame of France. So be it. This shame is quoted at the Bourse—hope for nothing. You are poets and dreamers if you hope. Look then at the *Tribune*, the press, intelligence, speech, thought, all which was liberty, has disappeared. Yesterday these moved, were quieted; lived; to-day they were petrified.

"Well, one is content; one accommodates himself to the petrifaction. One makes use of it; one does business with it. One sees how much as usual society continues upon it; and plenty of honest people find things go well.

"Why do you desire that the situation should change? Why do you wish that it should end? Do not delude yourself; this thing is solid; it is the present and the future!!"

We are in Russia. The Neva is frozen. They build houses on it; heavy carriages roll on its surface. It is no longer water, it is rock. The passers-by go and come on this marble which has been a river; they improvise a city; they trace out the streets; they open the shops; they sell, they buy, they drink; they eat, they sleep, they light fires on this water. They can permit themselves anything. Fear nothing; do what you please; laugh, dance—it is more solid than dry land. It actually sounds under the foot like granite. Long live winter! long live ice! There is ice, and it shall stand forever. And look at the heavens. Is it day? is it night? A gleam wan and pale crawls over the snow. One would say that the sun is dead.

No; thou art not dead, Liberty. On a day, and at the moment when they least expect it; at the hour when they had most profoundly forgotten thee, thou shalt arise. O dazzling sight! One will see thy star-like face suddenly come out from the earth and shine on the horizon. On all this snow, this ice, this hard, white plain; on this water become block, thou shalt dart thy golden arrow, thy bright and burning ray, thy light, thy heat, thy life. And then! do you hear that dull sound? Do you hear that cracking deep and dreadful? It is the breaking of the ice! It is the Neva which is tearing loose! It is the river which retakes its course!

It is the water alive, joyous, and terrible, which takes off the ice, which is hideous and dead, and crushes it. It was granite, said you; see, it splits like glass. It is the breaking up of the ice, I tell you.

It is truth, which is coming again. It is progress, which recommences. It is humanity, which again begins its march, which drifts full of fragments, which draws away, roots out, carries off, strikes together, mingles, crushes, and drowns in its waves, like the poor miserable furniture of a ruin, not only the upstart empire of Louis Bonaparte, but all the establishments and all the results of ancient and eternal despotism. Look at all this pass by. It is disappearing forever. You will never see it more. See that book half sunk ; it is the old code of iniquity. That tressel-work which has just been swallowed up is the throne! And this other tressel-work which is going off, it is—the scaffold! And for this immense engulfing, and for this supreme victory of life over death, what has been the power necessary? One of thy looks, O Sun! One of thy rays, O Liberty!

CHAPTER V.

BIOGRAPHY.

CHARLES-LOUIS-NAPOLEON-BONAPARTE, born at Paris on the 20th of April, 1808, is the son of Hortense de Beauharnais, married by the emperor to Louis Napoleon, King of Holland.

In 1831, mingling with the insurrections of Italy, where his older brother was slain, Louis Bonaparte tried to overthrow the papacy.

On the 30th of October, 1836, he endeavored to overthrow Louis Philippe. He made an abortive attempt at Strasbourg, and, having been pardoned by the king, he embarked for America, leaving his accomplices behind to be judged. On the 11th of November he wrote: "The king in his clemency has ordered that I should be conducted to America." He declared himself keenly touched at the generosity of the king, adding: "Most certainly we are all culpable toward the government in having taken arms against it, but I am the most guilty." And he closed thus: "I was guilty toward the government, and the government has been generous toward me."* He returned from America to Switzerland, had himself appointed a cap-

---

* Letter read to the Court of Assizes by the attorney Parquin, who after having read it, exclaimed, " Among the numerous faults of Louis Napoleon, we must not count ingratitude the least."

tain of artillery at Berne and burgess of Salenstein in Thurgovia, avoiding equally, in the midst of the diplomatic complications caused by his presence, to declare himself French as to avow himself Swiss; and confining himself, in order to reassure the government, to the affirmation contained in a letter of the 20th of August, 1838, "that he lived almost alone in the house where his mother died, and that his firm desire was to remain quiet." On the 6th of August, 1840, he debarked at Boulogne, making a parody of the disembarkment at Cannes.* He had on the little hat.† He carried a gilt eagle at the end of a flag-staff, and a live eagle in a cage; also plenty of proclamations. He had sixty valets, cooks, and hostlers disguised as French soldiers, with uniforms bought at the temple, and with buttons of the 42d of the line manufactured in London. He threw money to the passers-by in the streets of Boulogne, put his hat on the point of his sword, and cried with his own voice, Vive l'empereur. He shot at an officer‡ with a pistol, the bullet missing and breaking three teeth in a soldier's mouth, and he fled! He was taken. They found on him five hundred thousand francs in gold and bank-notes.§ The procurer-general, Frank Cassé, said to him, before the Court of Peers: "You have made it a practice to tamper with treason, and you have distributed money to buy it." The peers condemned him to impris-

---

* The last landing of the first emperor.

† Court of Peers. Outrage of the 2d of August, 1840, page 140. Witness: Geoffrey, a grenadier.

‡ Captain-Colonel Puygellier, who had said to him, "You are a conspirator and a traitor."

§ Court of Peers. Witness: Adam, Mayor of Boulogne.

onment for life. They shut him up in Ham. There his mind seemed to turn in on itself and ripen. He wrote and published some books of mark, in spite of a certain ignorance of France in this century, concerning democracy and progress—*The Extinction of Pauperism, The Analysis of the Question of Sugars, Napoleonic Ideas*—in which he made the emperor a humanitarian. In a book entitled *Historic Fragments*, he wrote: "I am a citizen before I am Bonaparte." Already, in 1832, in his book on political reveries, he had declared himself a "Republican." After six years of captivity, he escaped from the prison at Ham, disguised as a mason, and took refuge in England. February arrived. He hailed the Republic, and came to sit as a representative of the people in the Constituent Assembly. He mounted the tribune on the 21st of September, 1848, and said: "All my life shall be consecrated to the strengthening of the Republic." He published a manifesto which can be summed up in two lines: "Liberty, progress, democracy, amnesty, abolition of decrees of proscription and banishment." He was elected president by five million five hundred thousand votes; swore solemnly to keep the Constitution on the 20th of December, 1848, and in 1851 he destroyed it. In the interval he had destroyed the Roman Republic, and he restored in 1849 that papacy which he desired to overthrow in 1831. He had, besides, taken one does not know what part in the obscure affair, called the lottery of the ingots of gold, in the weeks which preceded the coup d'état. This sac had become transparent, and a hand resembling his own had been seen in it.

The 2d of December and the days following he seized the executive power, and made an attempt upon the legislative power; he arrested the representatives, dispersed the Assembly, dissolved the council of state, expelled the high court of justice, suppressed the laws, took twenty-five millions from the bank, gorged the army with gold, raked Paris with grape-shot, terrorized France. Since, he has proscribed eighty-four of the representatives of the people; stolen from the Princes of Orleans the property of Louis Philippe, to whom he owed his life; decreed despotism in fifty-eight articles under the title of a Constitution; garroted the Republic; made the sword of France a gag in the mouth of liberty; stock-jobbed in the railroads through brokers; rifled the pockets of the people; regulated the budget by ukase; transported to Africa and Cayenne ten thousand Democrats; exiled in Belgium, in Spain, in Piedmont, in Switzerland, and in England forty thousand Republicans; placed in all souls grief, and on all foreheads blushes.

Louis Bonaparte thought to mount a throne. He does not perceive that he is mounting the post.

CHAPTER VI.

PORTRAIT.

LOUIS BONAPARTE is a man of about the middle height; he is cold, pale, slow, and has the air of one who is not entirely awake. He has published, as we have already recalled, a treatise on artillery, which has been well received, and he is thoroughly acquainted with the maneuvering of cannon. He rides well. He has a slight German accent. What he has of the buffoon about him has appeared at the tourney of Eglington. He has a thick mustache, covering up his smile, like the Duke of Alba, and a dim eye like Charles IX. If one should judge him disconnected from what he calls his "necessary acts," or his "great acts," he is a personage vulgar, puerile, theatrical, and vain.

The persons invited by him in the summer at St. Cloud, receive at the same time with the invitation the order to bring a morning as well as an evening toilet. He likes bombast, the top-knot, the tuft, embroidery, spangles, and shirt-pins. He has also a fondness for large words, great titles, things that sound, things that shine, and all the glassware of power. In his character as kinsman of the battle of Austerlitz, he dresses as general.

It makes little difference to him whether he is respected. He contents himself with the imitation of respect. This man would tarnish the second plane of history; he soils the first. Europe laughed from the other continent,* as she looked at Hayti, when she saw this white Soulouque appear.† There is now in Europe, evident even to strangers, a profound stupor in the depths of all minds, and, as it were, the feeling of a personal affront; for the continent of Europe, whether she wish it or not, is bound up with France, and what abases France humiliates Europe.

Before the 2d of December, the leaders of the right freely said of Louis Bonaparte, "The man is an idiot." They were mistaken. Assuredly his brain is muddy. It has gaps, but one can decipher in it in places several coherent thoughts, sufficiently linked together. It is a book with many pages torn out. Louis Bonaparte has one fixed idea. But a fixed idea is not idiocy. He knows what he desires, and he travels toward it, over justice, over law, over reason, over honesty, over humanity; but he goes toward it. A man who does this is not an idiot. It is one who belongs to another age indeed. He seems absurd and insane, because he is badly matched. Transport him to the sixteenth century and to Spain, and Philip II. will recognize him; to England, and Henry VIII. will smile on him; to Italy, and Cæsar Borgia will throw his arms around his neck. Or even do no more than place him outside of European civilization; put him, in 1817, at Janina, Ali Tepeleni will offer him his hand. There is something of the middle ages and the lower empire‡ about him. What he does has an altogether pure resemblance to

---

* That is, Europe which had emigrated to America.

† Soulouque was a negro emperor of Hayti, who had treated that island as Louis Napoleon has treated France.

‡ The Roman empire, from the fall of the Empire of the West to the aking of Constantinople.

Michel Ducas, to Romain Diogène, to Nicephorus Botoniate, to the eunuch Narses, to the vandal Stilicon, to Mahomet II., to Alexander VI., to Ezzelin of Padua,* and, above all, it most purely resembles himself—only he seems to forget or he ignores that in the times in which we live his actions will have to cross those great rivers of human morality cleared by our three centuries of literature and by the French Revolution, and that in the midst of these his actions will take their true shape, and will appear what they are—hideous.

His partisans—he has some—freely place him on a par with his uncle, the first Bonaparte. They say, one did the 18th of Brumaire, the other the 2d of December. They are both ambitious: the first Bonaparte desired to re-establish the Empire of the West, make Europe a vassal, rule the continent with his power, and dazzle it with his greatness; to take an arm-chair, and give stools to kings, and make history say, "Nimrod, Cyrus, Alexander, Hannibal, Cæsar, Charlemagne, Napoleon;" in fact, to be a master of the world. He *was* one. That is why he made the 18th Brumaire.† This Napoleon wants to have horses and girls, to be called "My lord," and to enjoy good living. That is why he made the 2d of December.

These are two ambitious men; the comparison is just.

Let us add, that like the first, this one also wishes to be emperor;‡ but what calms a little these comparisons is, that

---

* Various scoundrels well known in history.

† Coup d'état of the First Napoleon.

‡ The Constitution which declared Louis Bonaparte emperor bears the date of December 25th, 1852, and consequently had not been enacted when this book was first published. He was then dictator, elected for ten years.

there is perhaps a little difference between conquering an empire and cheating one's way into one.

Be that as it may ; what is certain, and what nothing can veil, not even that dazzling curtain of glory and misfortune on which one reads Arcold Lodi, the Pyramids, Elau, Friedland, Saint Helena ; what is certain, for our part, we affirm, is that the 18th of Brumaire* is a crime, whose stain on the memory of Napoleon the 2d of December has enlarged.

M. Louis Bonaparte allows himself freely to be suspected of socialism. He thinks that it affords a sort of waste field, susceptible of being cultivated by ambition. As we have said, he passed his time, during his imprisonment, in creating for himself a quasi reputation as a Democrat.

One fact describes him. When he published his book on the Extinction of Pauperism, during his confinement at Ham, a book apparently having for its sole and exclusive object to probe the wound of the miseries of the people and to point out methods of relief, he sent the work to one of his friends, with this note, which has passed under our eyes: "Read this work on pauperism, and tell me if you think that it is calculated *to do me good.*"

The great talent of M. Louis Bonaparte is silence.

Before the 2d of December he had a council of ministers, which, as it was responsible, imagined itself to be something. The president presided. He never, or almost never, took part in the discussions ; while Messrs. Odilon, Barrol, Passy, Tocqueville, Dufaure, or Faucher were speaking, he was constructing, with profound interest, prostitutes out of paper, or designing boon companions on the

---

* Day of Napoleon the Great's coup d'état.

backs of the documents. To make death, that is his art. He remains mute and motionless, looking in the other direction from that in which his purpose lies, until the hour arrives; then he turns his head and descends on his prey. His policy appears to you, abruptly, at an unexpected turning; the pistol or the fist "*ut fur.*" Till then, the least motion that is possible.

At one moment, in the three years which have just flown by, one sees him abreast of Changarnier,* who is also, on *his* side, meditating an enterprise. "*Ibant obscuri,*" as Virgil says. France was observing these two men with considerable anxiety. What is there between them? Is one of them thinking of Cromwell and the other pondering Monk?

People were questioning themselves and watching them. About both there was the same mysterious manner, the same tactics of motionlessness. Bonaparte did not say a word, Changarnier did not make a gesture. One did not stir, the other did not breathe; both seemed to tilt at which could be the most a statue.

As for this silence, however, Louis Bonaparte broke it sometimes; then he did not speak, he lied. This man lies as other men breathe. He announces an honorable intention, take care; he affirms something, suspect him; he makes oath, tremble.

Machiavelli made some disciples; Louis Bonaparte is one of them.

To announce an enormity at which the world exclaims; to disown it with indignation; to swear by the Great God; to declare himself a man of honor, and then—at the moment when one has reassured himself, and when one is

---

* Former candidate for the presidency.

laughing at the possibility of the enormity in question—to *do* it. This he has done to accomplish the coup d'état; this, for the decrees of proscription; this, for the robbery of the Orleans princes; this he will do for the invasion of Belgium or Switzerland, and for the rest. This is the way in which he proceeds. Think of what you will, it serves his purposes; he thinks well of it, it is his affair. He will have to clear it up with history. One is of his intimate circle; he will allow you to catch a glimpse of a project which seems not immoral; one does not look at it so closely; but it seems senseless and dangerous to himself. One raises objections; he listens, does not answer; yields sometimes for two or three days, then he takes up his plan again and does as he pleases. There is often at his table, in his cabinet at the Elysée, a drawer, half open; he draws from it a paper, reads it to a minister. It is a decree. The minister approves or opposes. If he opposes, Louis Bonaparte throws the paper back into the drawer, where there is a good deal more waste paper, dreams of men who are all-powerful, shuts the drawer, takes the key, and goes out without saying a word. The minister bows and retires, charmed with his deference. The next morning the decree is in the *Moniteur*, sometimes with the signature of the minister. Thanks to this style of doing things, he has always at his service the unexpected—a great force; and not meeting in himself any interior obstacle in that which other men call conscience, he pushes his purpose, it makes little difference over what, and he attains his object.

He recoils sometimes, not before the moral, but the material effect of his acts. The decree for the expulsion of eighty-four representatives, published on the 9th of January in the *Moniteur*, shocked public sentiment. Well as France was bound, one felt the start. One was still very near the 2d of December. Every excitement may have its danger. Louis Bonaparte understood it. The next day, the 10th, a second decree of exile was to appear, containing eight hundred names. Louis Bonaparte had the proof-sheet of the *Moniteur* brought to him. The list filled fourteen columns of the official journal. He crushed the proof, threw it into the fire, and the decree did not appear. The proscription continued without a decree!

In these enterprises he wants assistants and fellow-laborers. He needs that which he calls himself "men." Diogenes looked for them, holding a lantern; he, however, looks for them, holding a bank-note. Certain aspects of human nature each produce one entire species of personages, of whom that aspect is the natural center, and who group themselves necessarily around it, according to that mysterious law of gravitation which governs the moral being not less than the material atom. To undertake the 2d of December, to execute it, and to complete it, he needed men. He had them. To-day he is surrounded with them. These men form his court and retinue. He mingles their radiation with his. At certain epochs of his history there are galaxies of great men, at others there are galaxies of vagabonds. However, not to confound this epoch, the minute of Louis Bonaparte with the nineteenth century, the poisonous toad-stool shoots up at the foot of the oak; but it is not the oak.

M. Louis Bonaparte has succeeded. He has hereafter on his side, money, the exchange, the bank, the bourse, the counting-house, the strong-box, and all those men who pass so easily from one boundary to the other, when there is nothing to stride over but shame. He has made a dupe of M. Changarnier, a mouthful of M. Thiers, an accomplice of M. de Montalembert, of power a den, of the budget his farm. They are engraving at the mint a medal called the medal of the 2d of December, in honor of the manner in which he keeps his oaths. The frigate "Constitution" has changed her name. She is called the "Elysée."* He can, whenever he may desire it, have himself anointed by M. Sibour, and exchange the couch of the Elysée for the bed of the Tuileries. In the mean while, for seven months, he has been making great display. He has harangued, triumphed, presided at banquets, given balls, danced, reigned, paraded, and strutted. He has bloomed in his ugliness at an opera-box. He has had himself called prince-president; he has distributed flags to the army, and crosses of the Legion of Honor to the commissaries of police. And when the question of choosing a symbol was agitated, he stood in the background and took the eagle; the modesty of the sparrow-hawk.

---

* Name of his palace.

CHAPTER VII.

TO MAKE A SEQUEL TO THE PANEGYRICS.

He has succeeded. Consequently apotheosis does not fail him. Panegyrists! he has more of them than Trajan.

One thing, however, strikes me; it is that, in all the qualities that they recognize in him since the 2d of December, in all the eulogiums which they address to him, there is not one word which goes beyond these: cleverness, composure, audacity, address; enterprises admirably prepared and conducted; times well chosen; secrets well kept; measures well taken; false keys well made—all these are there. When these things are said, all is said, except a few phrases on clemency. And yet, did they not praise the magnanimity of Mandrin, who sometimes did not take all the money; and of Jean l'Ecorcheur, who sometimes did not kill all the travelers? When it endowed M. Bonaparte with twelve millions, plus four millions, for the maintaining of chateaux, the Senate endowed by M. Bonaparte with a million, felicitates M. Bonaparte on having "saved society," very much as a personage in a comedy felicitates another on having looked out for the cash.

As for me, I have still to find in the adulations which his most ardent apologists make toward M. Bonaparte, one commendation which would not apply equally well to Cartouche and Poulailler* after a good stroke at their trade; and I blush sometimes for the French language and the

---
* Brigands.

name of Napoleon, on account of the terms—truly a little crude, too little veiled, and too appropriate to the facts—in which the magistracy and the clergy felicitate this man for having stolen power by disobeying the Constitution, and for having evaded his oath by working in the dark.

After all the infringements and all the thefts of which the success of his policy has been composed were accomplished, he took back his true name. Everybody then recognized that this man was a lord. It was M. Fortoul, let us say it to his honor, that perceived it first.* When one measures the man and finds him so little, and then measures the success and finds it so great, it is impossible not to feel surprise; one asks himself, how has he done it; one analyzes the adventure and the adventurer, and laying out of question the influence which he derives from his name, and certain external facts by which he aided himself in climbing the ladder, one only finds at the bottom of the man and his deeds two things—cunning and money.

Cunning. We have already characterized this great phase in the character of Louis Bonaparte, but it is useful to dwell upon it.

The 27th of November, 1848, he said to his fellow-citizens in his manifesto:—

"I feel myself bound to make you acquainted with my feelings and my principles. *There is no necessity for any equivocation between you and me. I am not an ambitious man.* Educated in *free* countries, at the school of misfortune, *I will remain always faithful* to the duties which your suffrages

---

* The first report addressed to M. Bonaparte, or in which M. Bonaparte is spoken of as *Monseigneur*, is signed Fortoul.

and the wishes of the Assembly shall lay upon me. *I will pledge my honor to leave to my successor*, at the end of four years, power strengthened, liberty intact, and real progress accomplished."

On the 31st of December, 1849, in his first message to the Assembly, he wrote :—"I wish to be worthy of the confidence of the nation, and maintain the Constitution to which I have sworn." The 12th of November, 1850, in his second annual message to the Assembly, he said :—"If the Constitution includes errors and dangers, you are all free to expunge them in the eyes of the people. I only, *bound by my oath*, *I* must confine myself within the strict limits which that Constitution has traced."

On the 4th of September of the same year, he said, at Caen :—"Since prosperity seems to be receiving new life everywhere, he would be exceedingly guilty who would try to arrest its flight by *the changing of the situation of things as they exist to-day*." Sometime before the 22d of July, 1849, at the time of the inauguration of the St. Quentin Railroad, he had gone to Ham. He smote his breast at the recollections of Boulogne, and pronounced these solemn words : —"Since, to-day having been elected by entire France, I have become the legitimate chief of this great nation, I cannot be proud of a captivity which had for its cause *an assault upon a regular government*. When one has seen how much evil the most just revolutions cause, one can scarcely comprehend the audacity of one's being willing to assume the responsibility of a change. I do not complain, then, that I expiated here, by an imprisonment of six years, my temerity against the laws of my country ; and it is with pleasure that, in these very scenes where I suffered, I propose to you a toast in honor of men who are determined in spite of their convictions to respect the institutions of their country." All the while that he was saying that, he was cherishing, at the bottom of his heart, this thought, written by him in this very prison at Ham:—"Rarely do great enterprises succeed at the first attempt." And after his own fashion he has proved it. Toward the middle of November, 1851, the representative F., an elyséan,* was dining with M. Bonaparte.

"What do they say in Paris and at the Assembly?" asked the President of the representative.

"Eh, prince!"

"Well?"

"They are always talking."

"Of what?"

"Of the coup d'état."

"And does the Assembly believe in it?"

"A little, prince."

"And you?"

"I? not at all."

Louis Bonaparte seized both M. F——'s hands, and said to him with emotion :

"I thank you, Monsieur F., you at least do not believe me a rascal."

This took place fifteen days before the 2d of December. At this period, and at this very moment, according to the avowal of the accomplice Maupas, they were preparing Mazas.†

---

* *i. e.*, a frequenter of the palace.

† A prison in Paris where criminals awaited trial. The representatives and others were imprisoned there.

Money is the other power of M. Bonaparte. Let us speak of the facts proved legally in the proceedings at Strasbourg and Boulogne. At Strasbourg, on the 30th of October, 1836, Colonel Vaudrey, the accomplice of M. Bonaparte, charged the quarter-masters of the fourth regiment of artillery to "divide among the cannoneers of each battery two pieces of gold."

On the 5th of August, 1840, in the packet-boat, "City of Edinburgh," chartered by him at sea, M. Bonaparte called around him the sixty poor devils, his servants, whom he had cheated into believing that he was going to Hamburg on an excursion of pleasure, and harangued them from the top of one of his carriages fastened on deck; he declared to them his project; threw down to them their disguises, which were uniforms of soldiers, and gave them one hundred francs a-head. Then he made them drink. A little drunkenness does not hurt great enterprises. "I saw," said the witness Hobbs,* bar-keeper, before the Court of Peers, "I saw in the room a good deal of money. The passengers seemed to me to be reading printed papers. The passengers passed the night eating and drinking." After the bar-keeper, hear the captain.

The Judge asked Captain Crow: "Did you see the passengers drink?"

Crow: "With excess. I never saw anything like it."†

They disembark. They light upon the custom-house post of Wimereux. M. Louis Bonaparte gives the lead

---

* Court of Peers. Depositions of witnesses, p. 94.

† Court of Peers. Depositions of witnesses, p. 78. See also, pp. 84 and 88 to 94.

by offering the lieutenant of customs a pension of twelve hundred francs.

The Judge: "Did you not offer to the commandant of the port a sum of money if he would march with you?"

The Prince: "I offered it to him, but he refused it."*

They arrive at Boulogne; his aides-de-camp (he had some at the time) carried suspended around their necks rouleaux of white iron full of gold pieces.

Others followed with bags of money in their hands.† They threw the money to the fishermen and peasants, inviting them to cry: "*Vive l'empereur.*" "It is enough, for three hundred bawlers," said one of the conspirators.‡ Louis Bonaparte accosted the 42d, which were in barracks at Boulogne. He said to the voltigeur, George Koehly: "I am Napoleon; you will have promotions and decorations." He said to the voltigeur, Antoine Gendre: "I am the son of Napoleon; let us go to the Hôtel du Nord and order a dinner for ourselves." He said to the voltigeur, Jean Meyer: "You will be well paid."§ He said to the voltigeur, Joseph Meny: "You will come to Paris; you will be well paid." An officer beside him held his hat in his hand, full of five-franc pieces, which they distributed to the curious, saying, cry "*Vive l'empereur.*"‖ The grenadier Geoffroy, in his deposition, characterizes in these terms the attempt made on his mess by an officer and a sergeant in

---

* Court of Peers. Cross-questioning of those implicated, p. 15.
† Court of Peers. Depositions of the witnesses, p. 105, 185, etc.
‡ The President: "The children who cried, were they not the three hundred bawlers at Strasbourg whom you asked for in a letter?"
§ Court of Peers. Depositions of witnesses, p. 143.
‖ Court of Peers. Depositions of witnesses. Witness: Febivre Voltigeur, p. 142.

the plot: "The sergeant carried a bottle, and the officer had a saber in his hand." These two last lines describe the 2d of December. Let us go on. "The next day, the 17th of June, the commandant Mésonan, who I thought had gone, entered my office, announced, as always, by my aide-de-camp. I said to him: 'Commandant, I thought you had gone.' 'No, general, I have not gone; I have a letter to deliver to you.' 'A letter, and from whom?' 'Read, general.' I bade him sit down; I took the letter; but the moment I opened it I perceived that the direction ran: to M. Commandant Mésonan. I said to him: 'But, my dear commandant, it is for you, it is not for me.' 'Read it, general.' I opened the letter and read:—

"'My dear Commandant,—There is the greatest necessity that you should see the general in question immediately. You know that he is a man of action, and one on whom one can count. You know also that he is a man whom I have marked to be one day a marshal of France. *You will offer him one hundred thousand francs* in my name, and you will ask him at the office of what banker or notary he wishes that I shall leave three hundred thousand francs counted out to him in case he loses his command.' I stopped, indignation overcoming me. I turned the leaf and I saw that the letter was signed *Louis Napoleon*. I handed the letter back to the commandant, telling him that it was a ridiculous and hopeless game."

Who speaks thus? General Magnan. Where? In open court, the Court of Peers. Before whom? Who is the man seated on the stool? the man that Magnan covers with ridicule, the man toward whom Magnan turns his indignant face? Louis Bonaparte!

Money, and together with it drunkenness; that was his plan of action in his three enterprises: at Strasbourg, at Boulogne, and at Paris; two failures, one success.

Magnan, who refused at Boulogne, sold himself at Paris. If Louis Bonaparte had been conquered on the 2d of December, they would have found the twenty-five millions belonging to the Bank at the Elysée, just as they found on his person at Boulogne the five hundred thousand francs belonging to London.

There is, then, in France—it is necessary to come to plain statements on these matters—there is in France, in this land of the sword, of knights; in this land of Hoche, of Drouot, and of Bayard—there has been a day when one man, surrounded by five or six Greek* politicians, experts at ambushes, and jockeys of coups d'état, leaning on his elbows in a gilded office, with his feet on the andirons and his cigar in his mouth, has made out a tariff of military honor, has weighed it in a scale like provisions, as a thing to be bought and sold, and valued the general at a million and the soldier at a louis, and has said of the conscience of the French army: it is worth so much.

And this man is the nephew of the Emperor. Nevertheless, this nephew is not proud. He knows how to adapt himself to the necessities of his adventures. He takes easily and without rebellion any turn of destiny whatsoever. Put him in London, and let it be his interest to please the English Government; he will not hesitate, and with the very hand with which he desires to seize the scepter of Charlemagne he will grasp the club of the policeman.

---

* Filled with Greek trickery.

If I were not Napoleon I would like to be Vidocq. And now thought is arrested. And this is the man by whom France is governed! What do I say, governed? Owned as if by sovereign authority! And every day and every morning, by his decrees, by his messages, by his harangues, by all the unheard-of follies that he displays in the *Moniteur*, this emigrant, who does not know France, gives lessons to her, and this scoundrel tells France that he has saved her! And from whom? From herself! Before him Providence has only made blunders. The good God has waited for him to put all things in order. At last he has come! For thirty years there have been all sorts of pernicious things in France— that uproar, that tribune; that hubbub, the press; that insolent thing, thought; this crying abuse, liberty. But he has come; and he has put in the place of the tribune, the Senate; in the place of the press, the censorship; in the place of thought, platitude; and in the place of liberty, the saber; and by the saber, the censorship, by folly, and by the Senate, France is saved! Saved! Bravo! And from whom? I repeat it, from herself; for what was France, if you please? She was a tribe of pillagers, thieves, assassins, and demagogues. It has been necessary to bind her, this mad woman, this France; and it is M. Bonaparte—Louis—who has put the manacles on her. Now she is in a dungeon; on bread and water; punished, humiliated; tied fast under good guard; be quiet; M. Bonaparte, policeman at the Elysée, answers to Europe; he has done his duty by her; this miserable France will have the strait-jacket the moment she stirs. Ah! what is this sight? what is this dream, this nightmare? On one side a nation, the first of nations, and on the other a man, the last of men. And see! there is what this man does to this nation. What? He tramples her under his feet; he laughs in her face; he mocks her; he defies her; he forbids her; he insults her; he scoffs at her. What? He says there is only I. What? In this land of France, where one could not slap a man's face, one can slap the people's face. What an abominable shame! Every time that M. Bonaparte spits, all faces must be wiped. And it is possible that this can last; and you tell me that it WILL last! No! no! no! by all the blood which we all have in our veins, no! it shall not last! Ah! if it should last, it would be, in fact, as if there were no God in heaven, or as if there were no France on earth!

BOOK SECOND.—THE GOVERNMENT.

CHAPTER I.

THE CONSTITUTION.

Roll of drums; clowns, attention!

"The President of the Republic, considering that all laws restrictive of the liberty of the press have been repealed; that all laws against colportage have been abolished; that the right of assemblage has been fully re-established; that all unconstitutional laws and all measures resorting to martial law have been suppressed; every citizen having it in his power to say what he pleases through all the channels of publication—in the journals, by posting, by electoral assemblage; seeing that all engagements which have been assumed, especially the oath of the 20th December, 1848, have been scrupulously kept; all facts having been examined; all questions asked and cleared up; all candidateships having been publicly debated, so that no one can allege that the least violence has been done against the least citizen; that is to say, in one word, in liberty the most complete; the sovereign people, interrogated by the following question:—Do the French people intend to place themselves, bound hand and foot, in the discretionary power of M. Louis Bonaparte? have answered YES, by seven million five hundred thousand suffrages—(interruption of the author; we shall speak again of these seven million five hundred thousand suffrages)—promulges the Constitution, whose tenor is as follows :—

"Article first.—The Constitution recognizes, confirms, and guarantees the great principles proclaimed in 1789, and which are the foundation of the public rights of Frenchmen.

"Articles second and others.—The tribune and the press, which fetter the march of progress, are replaced by the police and the censorship, and by the secret discussions of the Senate, Corps Legislatif, and Council of State.

"Article last.—That thing which they call human intelligence is suppressed.

"Done at the palace of the Tuileries, January the 14th, 1852.

"Louis Napoleon.

"Examined, and sealed with the great seal, by the keeper of the seals, minister of justice.

"E. Rouher."

M. Bonaparte has been evidently and happily inspired with this Constitution, which boldly proclaims and affirms the Revolution of 1789 in its principles and consequences, and which only abolishes liberty, by an old post-bill of a country theater, which it is à propos to recall :—

TO-DAY:

GRAND REPRESENTATION OF

THE WHITE LADY.

OPERA IN THREE ACTS.

Note.—The music which embarrassed the ease of the action will be replaced by a lively and piquant dialogue.

CHAPTER II.

THE SENATE.

THE lively and piquant dialogue is between the Council of State, the Corps Legislatif, and the Senate. There is, then, a Senate? Without doubt. This "great body," this "balancing power,"* this "supreme moderator," is even the principal splendor of the Constitution. Let us dwell on it. A Senate; of what Senate do you speak? Is it of the Senate which deliberated on the sauce with which the Emperor would eat his turbot? Is it of the Senate of which Napoleon said, on the 5th of April, 1814: "A sign was an order to the Senate; it always did more than one asked of it?" Is it of the Senate of which Napoleon said, in 1805: "The cowards were afraid to displease me?"† Is it of the Senate which almost extorted the same cry from Tiberius: "Ah the wretches! more slaves than one can wish?" Is it of the Senate which made Charles the Twelfth say, "Send my boot to Stockholm." "For what, sire?" asked the minister. "To preside at the sessions of the Senate?" No, we are not joking, they are eighty this year; next year they will be one hundred and fifty. They have all to themselves, and in full possession, fourteen articles of the Constitution, from the nineteenth to the thirty-third; they are "guardians of the

---

* Appeal to the People.
† Thibaudeau, *Hist. du Consulat et de l'Empire.*

public liberties;" their functions are gratuitous (article twenty-second); in consequence they have from fifteen to thirty thousand francs a year; they have the monopoly of taking care of their own interests and this property; "they do not oppose themselves to the promulgation of laws;" they are all illustrations. This is not a would-be Senate, like that of the other Napoleon; this is a serious Senate. The marshals belong to it, the cardinals belong to it, M. Lebœuf belongs to it. "What are you doing in this country?" one asks of the Senate. "We are charged with the duty of guarding the public liberties." "What are you doing in this city?" asks Jack Pudding of Harlequin? "I am ordered to comb the bronze horse."*

One knows what the *esprit de corps* is. That spirit will impel the Senate to augment its power by all instrumentalities. "It will destroy the Corps Legislatif, and if the occasion presents, it will tamper with the Bourbons." Who said that?" The first Consul. Where? At the Tuileries, in April, 1804. "Without title, without power, and in violation of all principles, it has betrayed the country and completed its ruin; it has been the plaything of high intriguers. I do not know a body which ought to be recorded in history with more ignominy than the Senate." Who said that? The Emperor. Where? At St. Helena. There is, then, a Senate in the "Constitution of the 14th of January;" but frankly, it is a fault. One is

---

* "All the illustrations of the country." Louis Bonaparte's appeal to the people, 2d of December, 1857.

"The Senate has been nullified in France; one does not like to see people well paid for doing nothing." The words of Napoleon, memorial of St. Helena.

accustomed, now that the care of the public health has made such progress, to see the public roads better kept than that. Since the senate of the empire, we did not believe that people would deposit any more senates along constitutions.

CHAPTER III.

THE COUNCIL OF STATE AND THE CORPS LEGISLATIF.

THERE is also the Council of State and the Corps Legislatif. The Council of State, cheerful, paid, chub-faced, rosy, fat, fresh; the eye quick, the ear red, the voice high, with its sword at its side, with stomach, embroidered in gold; the Corps Legislatif, pale, gaunt, sad, embroidered in silver. The Council of State goes, comes, enters; goes out, comes back, rules, disposes, decides, cuts off; sees Louis Napoleon face to face. The Corps Legislatif walks on tip-toe, turns its hat around in its hands, puts its finger on its lips, smiles humbly, sits in the corner of its chair, does not speak unless it is asked a question; its words being naturally obscene, there is an excuse given to the journals for not making the least allusion to them. The Corps Legislatif votes the laws and the taxes (article 39), and when believing itself in need of instruction—some details, some figures, some explanation—it humbly presents itself at the door of the ministries to speak to the ministers. The attendant waits upon it in the ante-chamber, and bursting out laughing, gives it a blow over the nose. Such are the rights of the Corps Legislatif. Let us grant that this melancholy situation commenced, in June, 1853, to draw several sighs from certain elegiac individuals who took part in the affair. The report of the commission of the budget will remain in the memory of men as one of the most heart-rending *chef-d'œuvres* of the plaintive kind. Let

us repeat its sweet words. "Formerly, you know, neces-
"sary communications in some cases were held directly
"between the commissioners and the ministers. It was to
"the latter that one addressed himself to obtain the docu-
"ments indispensable to the scrutiny of affairs. They
"came themselves, with the chief of their different ser-
"vices, to give verbal explanations sufficiently often to
"prevent all further discussion; and the resolutions
"which the commission of the budget stopped, after
"having heard them, were submitted directly to the
"Chamber. To-day we cannot have conference with the
"government, except through the Council of State,
"which, in its secrets and organ of its thought, has the
"sole right to transmit documents to the Corps Legis-
"latif, which the latter in its turn is forced to send back
"by the hands of the ministers. In a word, for written
"reports, as for verbal communications, the commis-
"sioners of the government* replace the ministers, with
"whom they ought previously to have an understanding.
"As to the modifications which the commission may wish
"to propose, whether in consequence of the adoption of
"amendments presented by the deputies, or following
"their own examination of the budget, they ought, before
"you are called upon to deliberate on them, to be sent
"back to the Council of State, and there to be discussed.
"There (it is impossible not to call attention to it) they,
"that is, the reports, etc., have no interpreters, no official
"defenders. This mode of procedure seems to be derived
"from the Constitution itself, and if we speak of it, it is
"solely to show you that it is certain to cause delays in

---

* That is, the Council of State.

"the accomplishment of the task of the commission of the budget."*

One cannot be more tender in reproach. It is impossible to receive with more chastity and grace what M. Bonaparte calls, in his autocratic style, "guarantees of calm,"† and what Molière, in his liberty as a great writer, calls "kicks . . . . !"‡

There is, then, in the shop in which laws and budgets are manufactured, a master of the house, the Council of State, and a servant, the Corps Legislatif. According to the terms of the Constitution, who is it that names the master of the house? M. Bonaparte. Who is it that names the servant? The nation. That is well.

---

* Report of the Commission of the Budget from the Corps Legislatif.
† Preamble of the Constitution.
‡ Crument. See the Cheat of Scapin.

CHAPTER IV.

THE FINANCES.

LET us note that in the shadow of these "wise" institutions, and, thanks to the coup d'état, which, as one knows, has re-established order, the finances, security, and public prosperity—the budget, according to the avowal of M. Gouin—closes with a deficit of a hundred and twenty-three millions.

As to commercial movements since the coup d'état, as to the prosperity of interests, as to the renewal of business, it is sufficient, in order to appreciate them, to abandon words and take to figures.

Make figures of it. Here is one which is official and decisive. The discounts of the Bank of France only produced, during the first half-year of 1852, 589,502 francs 62 centimes, for the central cash office; and the profits of the branch offices have only reached 651,108 francs 7 centimes. The bank itself accords with this in its semi-annual statement.

Nevertheless, M. Bonaparte does not restrain himself within the bounds of the taxes. Some fine morning he will awake, yawn, rub his eyes, take a pen, and decree— What? The budget! Achmet III. once wished to levy taxes at his own fancy. "Invincible lord," said his vizier, "thy subjects cannot be taxed beyond the limits prescribed by the law and the prophet."

This same M. Bonaparte, while he was at Ham, wrote:— "If the sums levied every year upon the masses are employed in modes that are unproductive, as for instance, *in creating useless places, raising barren monuments, in maintaining in the midst of a profound peace an army more expensive than that which conquered at Austerlitz*, the tax becomes a crushing weight, it drains the country, it takes everything and gives nothing." *A propos* of this word, budget, one observation occurs to us. To-day, in 1852, the bishops and councilors of the Court of Appeals have fifty francs a-day; the archbishops, the councilors of state, the chief presidents,* and the procurors-general have each sixty-nine francs per day; the senators, the prefects, and the division-generals receive eighty-three francs a-day; the presidents of the sections † of the Council of State have two hundred and twenty-two francs a-day; the ministers two hundred and fifty-two francs a-day; my lord, the Prince - President, comprising in his allowance the sum necessary to maintain the royal *chateaux*, touches daily forty-four thousand four hundred and forty-four francs forty-four centimes. They made the revolution of the 2d of December against the twenty-five francs.

---

* Presidents of Corps Legislatif and Senate.
† They are six.

CHAPTER V.

THE LIBERTY OF THE PRESS.

WE have just seen what the legislature, the administration, and the budget are. And justice—what they called formerly the Court of Appeal's—is no longer anything but the recorder's office for the registering of courts-martial. A soldier goes out of the guard-house, and writes on the margin of the law-book, *I will*, or *I will not*. Throughout, the corporal orders and the magistrate countersigns. "Come, tuck up your robes; march, or if not! . . . ." Hence these judgments, these arrests, these abominable condemnations! What a sight is this troop of judges, with their heads down and their backs bent, led with the crosier on their loins into iniquities and baseness.

And the liberty of the press! what shall I say of it? Is it not laughable simply to pronounce the word? This press free, an honor to the French mind, light brought to bear from all points at the same time on all questions; perpetual watch of the nation? Where is it? What has M. Bonaparte done with it? It is where the *Tribune* is. In Paris twenty journals annihilated; in the departments eighty; a hundred journals suppressed. That is to say, when you only look at the material side of the question, the bread taken out of the mouths of innumerable families. That is to say, remember it, bourgeois, a hundred houses confiscated, a hundred farms taken from their owners, a hundred coupons of the funds torn out of the great book.

Profound identity of principles! Liberty suppressed is property destroyed! Let the idiotic egotists who are applauders of the coup d'état reflect on this.

For a law regulating the press, a decree resting on it; a fet-fa; a firman* dated from the imperial stirrup; the régime of fulmination! One recognizes it, this régime; one sees it every day at work. It needed these people to invent this thing. Never has despotism shown itself more clumsily insolent than in this kind of censorship of the morrow, which precedes and announces the suppression, and which gives the bastinado to a journal before suppressing it. In this government the silly corrects the atrocious and tempers it. Every decree on the press can be summed up in one line: "I permit you to speak, but I enact that you shall hold your tongue." Who then is reigning? Is it Tiberius? Is it Schahabaham? Three-quarters of the republican journalists transported or proscribed, the rest driven by the mixed commissions, dispersed, wandering, hidden; here and there in four or five surviving journals, in four or five independent journals, but watched, and with the cudgel of Maupas hanging over their heads, fifteen or twenty writers, courageous, serious, pure, honorable, generous, who write with the chain about their neck and the ball at their foot. Talent between two sentries, independence gagged, honesty guarded under the eye, and Veuillot† crying: I am free!

---

* Persian term.
† A bigotted Catholic writer.

CHAPTER. VI.

NOVELTIES IN POINT OF LEGALITY.

THE press has the right of being censured, the right of being warned, the right of being suppressed; it has even the right of being judged. Judged? By whom? By the tribunals. What tribunals? The correctional tribunals.

And this excellent picked jury, what is it? Progress is far outrun. The jury is far behind us. We return to the government judges. "Suppression is more rapid and efficacious," as Master Rouher* says. "And then it is better. Call the causes, police correctional Sixteenth Chamber; first matter of business: the man named Roumage, swindler; second affair, the man named Laumenais,† writer. This has a good effect, and accustoms the Bourgeois to say indiscriminately a writer and a swindler. Assuredly there is an advantage in that, but in a practical point of view, from the point of view of "the repression." Is the government altogether sure of what it is doing in this thing. Is it entirely sure that the Sixteenth Chamber will be worth much more than that good Court of Assizes in Paris, which had such abjects to preside over it as Partarrieu-Lafosse, and men as low as Suins and as dull as Mongis to harangue it?

Can it reasonably hope that the correctional judges will be still more cowardly and contemptible than that? These

---

* Late President of the Senate.
† A Liberal, formerly a Roman Catholic priest.

judges, all paid though they be, will they work better than that small knot of a jury which had the public minister for corporal and which pronounced condemnations and gesticulated verdicts with the precision of the charge in twelve time, so well that Carlier, the prefect of police, said good-naturedly to a celebrated advocate, M. Desm : "The jury! What a blockhead of an institution! When one does not make it, it never condemns; when one does make it, it condemns always."

Let us lament this honest jury that Carlier made and that Rouher unmade. This government feels itself hideous. It does not desire any portrait, much less any looking-glass; like the osprey, it takes refuge in the night. If one saw it, it would die of it. But it wishes to live. It does not hear that they are speaking of it, nor what they say of it. It has imposed silence on the press of France. We have just seen how. But they make the press of France keep silence; that is only a half success. They want to make foreigners hold their tongues. They tried lawsuits in Belgium. A lawsuit against the *Bulletin Français* and one against *La Nation*. The loyal Belgian jury brought in a verdict of acquittal. That was inconvenient. What shall one do? They take the Belgian journals by the purse. You have subscribers in France; if you discuss us you shall not come in. Do you want to enter? be pleasant. They try to take hold of the English journals by fear. "If you discuss us (decidedly one does not wish to be discussed!) we will drive your correspondents out of France." The English press broke out into a roar of laughter. But this is not all. There are French writers outside of France. They are proscribed—that is to say, free!

If they are going to speak, these people; if they are going to write, these demagogues (they are quite capable of it), we must stop them; how shall we do it? Gag them at a distance? That is not so easy. M. Bonaparte has not an arm long enough for that. Let us try, however, and have a lawsuit brought against them where they are. So be it. The juries of free countries will understand that the proscribed represent justice, and that the Bonapartist government is iniquity. These juries will do what the Belgian juries did. They will acquit. Let us pray friendly governments to expel these expelled men; to banish these banished. So be it. The proscribed will go elsewhere. They will always find a corner of the earth free, where they can speak. What shall be done to reach them? Rouher clubs with Baroche,* and between them both they have hit upon this: fasten a law on crimes, committed by Frenchmen abroad, and slip in among these crimes, offensive publications. The Council of State said yes, and the Corps Legislatif did not say no. To-day the thing is in force. If we speak outside of France, they judge us in France. Prison in the future in case of need; fines and confiscations. So be it still. This book on which I write will then be judged in France, and the author duly sentenced. I expect it, and I confine myself to anticipating the individuals, whoever they may be, calling themselves magistrates, who in black robes or in red robes shall plot the thing, by saying, the case having come up, the condemnation to the utmost limit of the law having been handsomely and well pronounced, that nothing can equal my disdain for the judgment, except my contempt for the judge. That is my plea.

* Lately Minister of Justice and Worship.

CHAPTER VII.

THE ADHERENTS.

WHO are grouped about the establishment? We have said; the bosom heaves as we reflect on it. Ah! these men of the government of to-day, we the proscribed of the moment, we remember them when they were the representatives of the people. Only a year ago and they were going and coming in the lobbies of the Assembly, with their heads up, and with expression of independence, and with the gait and air of men who belonged to themselves. How proud, and how bold they were, and how they put their hands upon their hearts and cried: Vive la République; and if, on the tribune, any terrorist, any man of the mountain,* if any "reds" made allusion to a coup d'état arranged by conspiracy, of an empire which had been projected, how they shouted at him, "You are a slanderer;" how they shrugged their shoulders at the suggestion of the Senate. The empire to-day, cried the one, it would be mud and blood: you slander us, we will never have a hand in it. Another affirmed that he only held the office of minister of the President for the purpose of devoting himself to the defense of the Constitution and the laws. Another glorified the tribune as the palladium of the country. Another recalled the oath of Louis Bonaparte, and said, "Do you doubt that he is an

---

* Extreme revolutionist, named from the mountain, a certain row of seats in the Corps Legislatif.

honest man?" These two last went so far as to vote and sign his forfeiture the 2d of December in the mayoralty of the tenth district. Another sent on the 4th of December a note to him who writes these lines to felicitate him on having dictated the proclamation of the left, which outlawed Louis Bonaparte.

And there they are, senators, councillors of state, ministers; laced, galloon-laced, gilded wretches! Before embroidering your sleeves, wash your hands.

M. Quentin Bauchart goes to find M. Odilon Barrot and tells him: "Can you comprehend the coolness of this Bonaparte? Has he not dared to offer me a place as master of requests?" "You have refused?" "Assuredly." The next day an offer of a place as councillor of state—twenty-five thousand francs—the indignant master of requests becomes a softened councillor of state. M. Quentin Bauchart accepts.

One class of men rally en masse: the imbecile. They compose the *sane* part of the Corps Legislatif. It is they to whom the chief of the state addresses this clap-trap:—

"The first trial of our Constitution, which is entirely French in its origin, ought to have convinced you that we possess the elements of a government which is strong and free. Registration is accurate; discussion is free; and the vote on taxes decisive. There is in France a government animated by good faith and by a love of the right; which reposes on the people, who are the source of all authority; on the army, the source of all force; on religion, the source of all justice. Assure yourselves of the character of my opinions."

These excellent dupes we know also. We have seen a good number of them on the benches of the majority at the

Legislative Assembly. Their chiefs, clever operators, had succeeded in terrifying them, a sure means of leading them wherever they wished : these chiefs having been no longer able to employ the old scarecrows, the words Jacobin and san-culottes,* which had been decidedly too much used, had reinstated the word *demagogue*. These ring-leaders, brought up to underhand dealings and maneuvers, speculated upon the word "the mountain" with success. They worked this terrifying and munificent souvenir seasonably. With these few letters of the alphabet, grouped in syllables and accented suitably—Demagogues, Mountain-men, Socialists, Communists, Reds—they bleared the eyes of the silly. They had found means to pervert the brains of their innocent colleagues to the extent of encrusting on them, so to speak, kinds of dictionaries, in which each of the expressions which the orators and writers of the Democracy made use of should be found translated. For humanity, read ferocity ; universal welfare, read overthrow ; republic, read terrorism ; socialism, read pillage ; fraternity, read massacre ; gospel, read death to the rich.

So that when an orator of the left said, for example : "We wish the suppression of war and the abolition of the death penalty," a crowd of poor people on the right distinctly heard : "We wish everything put to fire and sword," and shook their fists with fury at the orator. After a speech, in which there had been no other question than liberty, universal peace, welfare by means of work, unity, and progress, one saw the representatives belonging to that set which we have described become excited at these allusions, rise pale as ashes ; they were not

---

* Expression for extreme revolutionaries.

very sure that they were not going to be guillotined, and went away to look for their hats in order to see if they still had their heads on their shoulders.

These poor, horrified creatures did not sell their adhesion on the 2d of December. It was on their account that the sentence, "Louis Napoleon has saved society," was especially invented. And these everlasting prefects, these eternal mayors, these eternal aldermen, these eternal worshipers of the rising sun or of the lighted lamp-post, who come the day after success to the conqueror, or the man enjoying a triumph, to the master, to his majesty Napoleon the Great, to his majesty Louis XVIII., to his majesty Alexander I., to his majesty Charles X., to his majesty Louis Philippe; to the citizen Lamartine, to the citizen Cavaignac; to my lord the prince-president; on their knees, smiling, merry, carrying on plates the keys of their cities, and on their faces the keys of their consciences!

But the imbeciles are an old story; imbeciles have always made a part of institutions, and they are almost an institution themselves. And as to the prefects and capitouls,* as to the adorers of all to-morrows, insolent with good luck and dullness that is seen in every age. Let us do justice to the régime of the 2d of December. It has not only such partizans as these, it has adherents, and creatures which belong to it alone. Nations do not always know how rich they are in the matter of rogues. There is needed this kind of overthrow, this sort of removing, to make them see the truth. Then people are filled with wonder at what comes out of the dust! It is splendid to contemplate. A man who wore

---

* Municipal officers of Toulouse.

shoes and clothing, and had a reputation such as to make all the puppies in Europe cry after him, springs up an ambassador. This other, within sight of Bricêtre and La Roquette,* wakes up a general and great eagle of the Legion of Honor. Every adventurer has an official coat on his back, accommodates himself with a pillow crammed with bank-notes, takes a sheet of white paper and writes on it, "End of my adventures. You know such a man well? Yes; he is in the galleys? No; he is a minister."

---

* Prisons.

CHAPTER VIII.

MENS AGITAT MOLEM.

IN the center is the man; the man of whom we have spoken; the Carthaginian,* the fatal man; attacking civilization in order to arrive at power; looking for one knows not what ferocious popularity, elsewhere than among the true people; speculating on those traits of the peasant and the soldier which still remain savage; trying to succeed by coarse egotisms, by brutal passions, by awakened envies, excited appetites; something like Marat, a prince, to hit the nail almost on the head, who in Marat's house was great, and who in Louis Bonaparte's is little? The man who kills, transports, exiles, expels, proscribes, and plunders, this man with languid gesture, with glassy eye, who walks with a preoccupied air in the midst of the horrible things which he has done like a sort of sinister somnambulist. They said of Louis Bonaparte, perhaps with a good, perhaps with an evil meaning, for these beings have strange flatterers: "He is a dictator, he is a despot, nothing more."

He is that in our opinion, and he is also something else.

The dictator was a magistrate. Titus Livius,† and Cicero,‡ call him *prætor maximus;* Seneca § calls him

---

* Allusion to Punic faith, proverbially bad.
† Lib. vii. cap. 34. ‡ *De Republica*, lib. i. cap. 40.
§ Ep. 108.

magister populi. What he decreed was held as a decree from above. Titus Livius* says, *pro numine observatum.* In those days of incomplete civilization, the rigidity of ancient laws not having foreseen everything, his function was to provide for the safety of the people. He was the product of this text, *Salus populi suprema lex esto.* He had the twenty-five axes, which were the signs of the power of life and death, brought before him. He was above and outside of the law, but he could not touch the law. The dictatorship was a veil behind which the law remained entire. The law was before the dictatorship and after the dictatorship. She seized the man again as he went out of office. He was appointed for a very short time—six months. "*Semestris dictatura,*" says Titus Livius, lib. vi. cap. 1. Habitually, and as if this enormous power, although freely assented to by the people, always ended by weighing a man down like remorse, the dictator abdicated before the end of the term. Cincinnatus went out of office at the end of eight days. The dictator was forbid to dispose of the public moneys without authority from the Senate; also to leave Italy. He could not ride without the permission of the people. He might be a plebeian. Marcus Rutilus and Publius Philo were dictators. They appointed dictators for various reasons—to establish fêtes on the occasions of holidays, to drive a sacred nail into the walls of the temple of Jupiter, once to name the Senate. Republican Rome had eighty-eight dictators. This intermissive institution lasted one hundred and sixty-three years, from the 552d to the 711th year of Rome. It commenced with

---

* Lib. iii. cap. 5.

Servilius Geminus, and reached to Cæsar submitting to Sulla. With Cæsar it expired. The dictatorship was made to be repudiated by Cincinnatus and married by Cæsar. Cæsar was five times dictator in five years, from 706 to 711. This magistracy was dangerous. It finished by devouring liberty.

Is M. Bonaparte a dictator? We do not see any inconvenience in answering—yes. Is he Prætor-Maximus, general-in-chief? The flag salutes him. Is he Magister Populi, master of the people? Ask the cannons pointed on the public squares. *Pro numine observatum*—held to be God? Ask M. Troplong. He has nominated the Senate; he has instituted holidays; he has provided for the safety of society; he has driven a sacred nail into the wall of the Pantheon, and he has hung on this nail his coup d'état. Only he makes and unmakes the law at his caprice. He puts his hand familiarly, and without authority from the Senate, into the pocket of the public; he rides without permission; and as to six months, he takes a little longer time. Cæsar took five years—he takes twice it. That is correct. Julius Cæsar five; Louis Bonaparte ten. Proportion is well preserved.

From the dictator let us pass to the despot. It is the other title almost accepted by M. Bonaparte. Let us use the language of the lower empire a little. It suits the subject. The Despotés came after the Basileus. He had among other powers that of general of infantry and cavalry, *magister utrinsque exercitus*. It was the Emperor Alexis, surnamed the Angel, who created the dignity of despotés. The despotés was less than the emperor and above the Sebastocrator, or Augustus, and above Cæsar. One sees that he is this, also, to some degree. M. Bonaparte is despotés when you admit, which is perfectly easy, that Magnan is Cæsar, and that Maupas* is Augustus.

Despotés, dictator? It is admitted. All this great éclat, all this triumphant power, cannot prevent the bringing into notice little incidents like the following, happening in Paris—incidents which honest Cockneys, witnesses of the fact, relate to you most pensively :—Two men are walking along the street, talking of their affairs and their trades. One of the two speaks of some rogue or other of whom he thinks he has cause to complain. "He is a wretch," says he, "a swindler, a beggar." An agent of the police hears these last words. "Sir," says he, "you are speaking of the President. I arrest you."

Now, will M. Bonaparte be or will he not be Emperor?† Beautiful question! He is master, he is cadi, mufti, bey, dey, soudan, grand-khan, grand-lama, great-mogul, great-dragon, cousin to the sun, commander of believers, schah, czar, sophi, and caliph. Paris is no longer Paris, it is Bagdad, with a Giafar who is called Persigny,‡ and a Scheherazade who risks having her neck cut off every morning, and whose name is the *Constitutionnel*.§ M. Bonaparte can do whatever he pleases with goods, with families, and persons. If French citizens wish to know the depth of the government into which they have fallen, they have only to ask a few questions of each other. Let us see. Judge—he tears off your robe and sends you to

---

* Prefect of police.
† He had not yet been declared Emperor.
‡ Minister of the Interior, and now a duke.
§ A Bonapartist newspaper.

prison. What then? Let us see. Senate, Council of State, Corps Legislatif—he seizes a shovel and makes a heap in the corner of you. After that? You, landlord, he confiscates your summer house and your winter house, with courts, stables, gardens, and dependencies. After that? You, father, he takes your daughter; you, brother, he takes your sister; you, bourgeois, he takes your wife with authority, by main force. After that? You, passer-by, your countenance displeases him, he shoots you through the head with a pistol, and goes back into his house. After that? All these things having been done, what results from them? Nothing. My lord the prince-president has taken his usual drive in the Champs Elysées to-day, in a barouche, à la Daumont, drawn by four horses, accompanied by a single aide-de-camp. That is what the journals will say. He has erased from the walls Liberty, Equality, Fraternity. He was right. Ah, Frenchmen, you are no longer either free (the strait-jacket is there), nor equal (the military man is everything), nor brothers (civil war hatches martial under this lugubrious peace law). Emperor? Why not? He has a Maury,* who is called Sibour;† he has a Fontanes,‡ a Faciuntasinos, if you like it better, which is called Fourtoul; he has a La Place, who answers to the name of Leverrier, but who did *not* write the *Mécanique Céleste*. He will easily find Esmenards and Luce de Lancivals. His Pius VII. is at Rome, in the cassock of Pius IX. His green uniform they saw at Strasbourg; his eagle—they saw it in Boulogne; his

---

* A play on the word which literally means " they make asses."
† Archbishop of Paris.
‡ Tools of the First Emperor.

gray overcoat—did he not wear it at Ham? casaque, or redingate,* it is all one. Madame de Staël has just made him a call. She has written *Lelia*. He smiles on her while he is waiting to exile her. Are you expecting an arch-duchess? Wait a moment; he will have one. *Tu felix Austria nube.* His Murat calls himself St. Amand,† His Talleyrand, Morny.‡ His Duke d'Enghieu§ is called the right. See, what does he lack? Nothing; scarcely anything; scarcely Austerlitz and Marengo. Resign yourself to it; he is emperor in heart. One of these mornings he will be it in the face of day. It only lacks one entirely trifling formality to sanctify and crown at Notre Dame his false oath. After which it will be fine. Hold yourself in readiness for an imperial play; expect caprices; expect surprises, stupors, wonderings, alliances of words the most unheard of, jarring sounds the most fearless; expect Prince Troplong, Duke Maupas, Duke Mimerel, Marquis Lebœuf, Baron Baroche! In line, courtiers! hats low, senators! The stable opens; my lord, the horse is consul. Let them have the oats of his highness Incitatus gilded. Everything will hang down: the gulf of the public will be prodigious; all enormities will pass; the antique flycatcher will disappear, and will make room for the whale-catcher.

For us who speak, from the present time the empire

---

* Two kinds of overcoats.
† Minister of War.
‡ At one time Minister of Interior.
§ Arrested and murdered by the First Napoleon outside of the limits of France. The other names just mentioned are those of prominent men in the employ of the First Emperor.

exists, and without expecting the proverb of the Senatus-Consultum, and the comedy of the Plebiscitum, we send this circular note to inform Europe that the treason of the 2d of December is confined with the empire. Mother and child are doing badly.

CHAPTER IX.

OMNIPOTENCE.

LET us forget this man's 2d of December. Let us forget his origin. Let us see what he is as to political capacity. Do you want to judge him for the eight months that he has reigned? Look at his power on the one hand, and his acts on the other.

What can he do? Everything. What has he done? Nothing. With this full power during eight months, a man of genius might have changed the face of France, of Europe perhaps.

He could not assuredly have effaced the crime of his setting out, but he might have covered it up. By dint of material ameliorations he might have succeeded in masking from the nation his moral abasement. Even, it is necessary to confess, even for a dictator of genius the thing was not hard. A certain number of social problems, elaborated in these last years by several robust minds, seemed ripe, and could have received, to the great profit and contentment of the people, both actual and relative solutions. Louis Bonaparte did not himself appear to doubt of it; he has come up with—he has caught a glimpse of none. He has not even found again at the Élysée a few of the old remnants of the socialistic meditations in which he indulged at Ham.

He has added several crimes to his first crime, and in that he has been logical. These crimes excepted, he has produced nothing. Omnipotence complete, initiative none. He has taken France and does not know what to do with her. In truth, one is tempted to pity this eunuch struggling with omnipotence. Assuredly this dictator bestirs himself, let us do him this justice; he does not remain a moment quiet; he feels with fear that he is surrounded with darkness and solitude. Those who are afraid in the dark sing, but he moves about. He turns everything topsyturvy; he touches everything; he runs after projects; not being able to create, he decrees; he tries to mislead as to his nothingness; it is perpetual motion; but, alas! that wheel turns empty. The conversion of the rentes, where is the profit of them to this day? A saving of eighteen millions; be it so. The rente-holders lose them, but the President and the Senate, with their two endowments, pocket them; benefit to France: zero. Landed credit? the cash does not arrive. Railroads? one decrees them and then one withdraws them. He is in all things as he was in the working-men's cities. Louis Bonaparte subscribes, but he does not pay. As to the budget—as to this budget checked by the blind men who are in the Council of State, and voted by the dumb men who are in the Corps Legislatif, the abyss opens beneath it. Nothing was possible or could have been efficacious but the greatest economy in the army: two hundred thousand soldiers left in their homes, two hundred millions saved. Come, then, try to touch the army. The soldier, who will become once more free, will applaud; but what will the officer say? And in reality it is not the soldier, it is the officer that one caresses. And then, it is necessary to guard Paris, and Lyons, and all the cities; and later, when one shall be emperor, it will be quite necessary to make a little war in Europe·

See the gulf! If from financial questions one passes to political institutions, oh! there the neo-Bonapartists brighten up; there are creations! What creations? Good God! A Constitution of the style of Ravrio, we have just viewed her, decked with palmettoes, swans' necks, carried to the Elysée with old arm-chairs in the carriages of the yeomen of this store; the Senate, the conservative force, sewed up again, re-gilded; the Council of State of 1806, dressed and re-trimmed with a few new laces; the old Corps Legislatif, repaired and re-painted, with Lainé away and Morny added. For the liberty of the press, the bureau of the public mind; for individual liberty, the minister of police. All these institutions (we have passed them under review) are nothing else in the world but an old piece of parlor furniture belonging to the Empire. Beat the dust, take out the cobwebs, splash the whole with stains of French blood, and you have the establishment of 1852. This odds and ends governs France. These are the creations! Where is good sense? Where is reason? Where is truth? There is not a sane part of contemporaneous intellect which is not run foul of, not a righteous acquisition of the century which has not been cast to the earth and shattered. Every extravagant device has become possible. What we see since the 2d of December, is a mediocre man, who has been seized with a freak, galloping across the absurd. These men, the malefactor and his accomplices, have an immense power, incomparable, and absolute, and unlimited, and sufficient, we repeat it, to change the face of Europe. They make use of it in enjoying themselves. To amuse one's self, and to enrich one's self, that is their "socialism." They have stopped the budget on the high road; the coffers lie there open; they fill their saddle-bags; they have money, do you wish some? there is some. All salaries are doubled and tripled. We have given some of the figures above. Three ministers, Turgot (there is a Turgot in this affair), Persigny, and Maupas have each a million of secret funds; the Senate has a million; the Council of State a half-million; the officers of the 2d of December have a Napoleonic month, that is to say, some millions; the soldiers of the 2d of December have medals, that is to say, some millions. M. Murat wishes millions and has them; a minister gets married, speedily, a half-million; M. Bonaparte, QUIA NOMINOR POLEO, has twelve millions, plus four millions, sixteen millions. Millions, millions! This régime is called Million. M. Bonaparte has three hundred useless and costly horses, the fruits and vegetables of the national castles and of the parks and gardens which were royal in days of yore; he overflows; he said the other day, "*All my carriages*," as Charles V. said, "All my Spains," and as Peter the Great said, "All my Russias." The nuptials of Gamache are at the Elysée. The steaks turn night and day before the bonfires; they consume there; these bills are published; they are the bulletins of the new empire—six hundred and fifty pounds of meat a day. The Elysée will soon have a hundred and forty-nine cooks like the château de Schœnbrunn; they drink, they eat, they laugh, they banquet: a banquet at the houses of all the ministers, a banquet at the Ecole Militaire, a banquet at the Hotel de Ville, a banquet at the Tuileries, a monstrous fête on the 10th of May, a fête still more monstrous on the 15th of August. One swims in all the abundance and in all the drunkenness. And the man of the people, the poor day-laborer, whose work has failed, the workman in rags, with naked feet, to whom the summer brings no bread and the winter no wood, whose aged mother lies languishing upon a foul straw mattress, whose young daughter prostitutes herself at the corners of the streets to live, whose little children shiver with hunger, fever, and cold, in the paltry lodging-houses of the Faubourg Saint-Marceau, in the garrets of Rouen, in the cellars of Lisle, do they think of him? What becomes of him? What do they do for him? Die, dog!

CHAPTER X.

THE TWO PROFILES OF M. BONAPARTE.

THE curious thing is, that they should wish that one should respect them. A general is venerable, a minister is sacred. The Countess de Audl——, a young lady of Brussels, was in Paris in March, 1852. She happened one day to be in a drawing-room in the Faubourg St. Honoré. M. de P. entered; Madame de Audl——, wishing to leave the place, passed before him, and it happened that while she was probably thinking of something else she raised her shoulders. M. de P. perceived it; the next day Madame de Audl—— is notified that henceforth, under pain of expulsion from France, as a representative of the people, she must abstain from all signs of approbation or disapprobation when she sees ministers. Under this corporal government, and under this constitution of instructions, all marches with military precision. The French people go to the order to see how they are to rise, lie down, dress themselves, in what toilet they can go to a trial at the tribunal or to the soirée of the prefect. A prohibition against making mediocre verses; a prohibition against wearing a beard, the shirt-frill, and the white cravat, are laws of the State. Regulation, discipline, passive obedience, the eyes cast down, silence in the ranks, such is the yoke under which the nation bows down at this moment—the nation of leadership and liberty, great revolutionary France. The reformer will only stop when France shall be enough a barrack for the generals to say, "Very well," and sufficiently a seminary for the bishops to say, "It will do!" Do you like the soldier? They have put him everywhere. The municipal council of Toulouse gives in its resignation; the prefect, Chapuis Montlaville, replaces the mayor by a colonel, the first assistant by a colonel, and the second assistant by a colonel.*

The warriors take the wall. "The soldiers," says Mably, "thinking themselves to be in the place of the citizens who had formerly made the consuls, dictators, censors, and tribunes, associated the government of emperors with a kind of military democracy." Have you a shako on your skull? Do what you like. A young man, returning from a ball, passes down Richelieu Street before the door of the Bibliothèque; the sentinel takes aim at him and kills him; the next day the journals say, "The young man is dead," and that is all. Timour-Beig accorded to his companions-in-arms, and to their descendants to the seventh generation, the right of impunity for any crime whatsoever, except the delinquent had committed the crime nine times. The sentry of Richelieu Street has eight more citizens to kill before being delivered over to a court-martial. It pays well to be a soldier, but it does not pay to be a citizen. At the same time they dishonor this unfortunate army. The 3d of September they decorated the commissioners who arrested its generals and representatives. It is true that it received itself two louis a-man. O shame on all sides! Money to the soldiers and the cross to the spies.

---

* These three colonels are Messrs. Galhassou, Dubarry, and Polycarp.

Jesuitism and corporalism, that is this régime complete. All the political expediency of M. Bonaparte is composed of two hypocrisies. A soldier's hypocrisy directed toward the army, a Catholic hypocrisy directed toward the clergy. When it is not Fracasse, it is Basile. Sometimes it is both together. In this fashion he succeeds in enrapturing at the same time Montalembert, who does not believe in France, and St. Arnaud, who does not believe in God.

Does the dictator smell the incense? Does he smell the tobacco? Examine; he smells the incense and the tobacco. O France, what a government! The spurs submit to the cassock, the coup d'état goes to mass, belabors the common soldiers, reads its breviary, embraces Catin,* tells its beads, empties the pots, and receives the sacrament at Easter. The coup d'état affirms what is dubious, viz., that we have returned to the epoch of jacqueries; what is certain, is, that it has taken us back to the time of the Crusades. Cæsar takes the cross for the pope. Diex el volt.† The Elysée has the faith of the templar, and the thirst too. To enjoy and live well let us repeat it, and to eat the budget, to believe nothing, to turn everything to profit, to compromise at once two holy things, military honor and religious faith; to stain the altar with blood, and the flag with holy-water; to make the soldier ridiculous, and the priest somewhat ferocious; to mingle with this grand political swindle which he calls his power, the church, and the nation, Catholic consciences, and patriotic consciences. That is the method of Bonaparte the Little.

All his acts, from the most enormous to the most puerile,

---

* Throws a kiss to the girls.
† Motto on the Crusader's shield.

from that which is hideous to that which is laughable, are stamped with this double dealing. For example, the national solemnities annoy him, the 24th of February and the 4th of May; he then has troublesome recollections which return obstinately on the day fixed. An anniversary is an intrusion. Let us suppress the anniversaries. Be it so. Let us only keep one feast, our own. Admirably well. But with one feast, only one, how can we satisfy both parties? the soldier party and the priest party. The soldier party is Voltairian, at what Canrobert will smile at, Riancy will greet with a grimace. What shall be done? You shall see. Great jugglers are not embarrassed at such a trifle. The *Moniteur* declares one fine morning that there shall be henceforth only one national fête, the 15th of August. At this, as semi-official commentary, the two masks of the dictator set themselves to remark :—The 15th of August, says the mouth-Ratapoil,* the day of St. Napoleon.—The 15th of August, says the mouth-Tartuffe,† the fête of the Holy Virgin ! On one side, the 2d of December inflates its cheeks, swells its voice, draws its great saber, and cries "Sacre bleu," grumblers, let us fête Napoleon the Great ! On the other, it casts down its eyes, makes the sign of the cross, and mutters : My very dear brethren, let us adore the Sacred Heart of Mary ! The government for the time being—a hand soaked in blood which dips its finger in holy-water.

---

* A general. † A hypocrite.

CHAPTER XI.

RECAPITULATION.

But they tell us, "don't you go rather far? are you not unjust? concede him something. Has he not in a certain measure made socialism?" and they put again upon the tapis the landed credit, the railroads, the falling of the funds, etc. We have already appreciated those measures at their just value; but in admitting that this was socialism you would be simple in attributing the merit of it to M. Bonaparte. It is not he who made socialism, it is time. A man swims against a rapid current, he wrestles with unheard-of efforts, he strikes the wave with his fist, with his forehead, with his shoulder, with his knee. You say he will make headway; a moment after, you look at him—he has lost ground. He is much further down the river than he was at the time of his setting out. Without knowing it, or having a suspicion, at every effort which he makes he loses ground. He imagines he is getting up again and he is always going down. He thinks that he is gaining and he loses. Landed credit, as you say, fall of the funds, as you say, M. Bonaparte has already made several of those decrees that you wish so much to characterize as socialistic, and he will make more. If M. Changarnier had triumphed instead of M. Bonaparte, he would have made them. If Henry the Fifth* would return tomorrow he would make some. The Emperor of Austria is

---
* Candidate of the legitamists, the Count of Chambord.

making some in Gallicia, and the Emperor Nicholas in Lithuania. In short, and after all, what does this prove? That this current, which is called Revolution, is stronger than the swimmer, who is called Despotism. But this same socialism, M. Bonaparte, what is it? That socialism? I deny it. Hatred of the Bourgeoisie, be it so. Socialism? No! See the ministry which was socialistic par excellence, the ministry of agriculture and commerce, he has abolished it. What does he give you in compensation? The ministry of the police. The other socialistic ministry is the ministry of public instruction; it is in danger; one of these mornings they will suppress it. The point of departure of socialism is education; it is gratuitous and obligatory teaching,—it is light. It is to take the children and make men of them, to take the men and make citizens of them, —citizens intelligent, honest, useful, and happy.

Intellectual progress at first, moral progress at first, material progress follows. The two first progresses of themselves and irresistibly bring on the last. What does M. Bonaparte do? He persecutes and stifles instruction everywhere. There is an outcast in our France to-day; it is the school-master. Have you never reflected on what a schoolmaster is to that magistracy to which tyrants formerly flew for refuge like criminals to the temple seeking a place of asylum? Have you ever considered what the man who teaches the children is? You enter the house of a cartwright; he is making wheels and poles; you say that he is a useful man. You enter the house of a weaver; he is making cloth, and you say that is a valuable man. You enter the house of a smith making mattocks, hammers, and ploughshares; you say that is a necessary man. These men, these good works, you salute. You enter the house of a school-master, make a lower bow. Do you know what he is making? He is making minds. He is the cartwright, the weaver, the forger of that work in which he aids God, the future. Well, to-day, thanks to the reigning party of priests, how little necessary it is that the school-master should work on this future, and how necessary it is that the future should be made of shadow and of brutishness, and not of intelligence and light.

Do you want to know in what fashion they make this humble and grand magistrate, the school-master, work? He serves mass, sings at the chorister's desk, sounds vespers, arranges the chairs, renews the bouquets before the Sacred Heart, and furbishes the chandeliers before the altar, dusts the tabernacle, folds the copes and chasubles, keeps in order and keeps an account of the linen of the sacristy, puts oil in the lamps, beats the cushions of the confessional, sweeps the church and sometimes the presbytery. The time which remains to him he can, if it seems good to him, make the little children spell A, B, C, on condition that they shall pronounce none of these three words of the demon, Country, Republic, Liberty. M. Bonaparte strikes instruction above and below, below to please the curates, above to please the bishop; at the same time that he tries to shut up the village school he mutilates the college of France; he throws down, or he upsets with a kick, the chairs of Quinet and of Michelet. One fine morning he declares by decree, that Greek and Latin letters are suspected, and he interdicts as much as he can the intercourse of intelligence with the old poets and historians of Athens and of Rome, scenting in Æschylus and in Tacitus, a vague odor of demagogueism. He puts physicians, for example, with one stroke of the pen, outside of literary learning, instruction, which made Dr. Serres say, "There we are dispensed by decree from the obligation of knowing how to read and write." New taxes; sumptuary taxes; vestry taxes; *nemo audeat comedere præter duo fercula cum potagio;* taxes on the living; taxes on the dead; taxes on successions; taxes on carriages; taxes on paper. Bravo, yells the beadle party, the less books; taxes on dogs, the collars will pay; taxes on senators, the coats of arms will pay. I am the man who is going to be popular, says M. Bonaparte, rubbing his hands; he is the socialistic emperor, roar the trusty ones in the faubourgs. It is the Catholic emperor, murmur the bigots in the sacristies. How happy he would be if he could pass here for Constantine, and therefore Babœuf.* Words of order repeat themselves. The adhesion declares itself; enthusiasm gains gradually; the Ecole Militaire designs his number with bayonets and pistol-barrels; the Abbé Gaume and the Cardinal Gousset applaud; they crown his bust at the market with flowers. Nanterre dedicates rose-trees to him. The social order is decidedly saved; property, the family, and religion, breathe again, and the police erect him a statue of bronze? Pshaw! that will do for the uncle! Of *marble*, tu-es Pietri super hanc pietram,† ædificabo effigiam meam.‡

---

* An outlaw.

† The commission appointed by the employees of the prefecture of police thought that bronze was not worthy to reproduce the image of the prince, it will be cut in marble. On the marble they will have the following inscription engraved in the luxuriant magnificence of the stone: "Souvenir of the oath of fidelity to the prince-president, taken by the employees of the prefecture of police, the 20th of May, before

That which he attacks, and that which he pursues, and that which they all pursue with him; that on which they set, that which they wish to crush, burn, suppress, destroy, annihilate, is it this poor, obscure man that they call primary teacher? Is it this square of paper that they call a journal? Is it this bundle of leaves that they call a book? Is it this engine, machine of wood and iron, that they call a press? No, it is thou, thought; it is thou, reason of man; it is thou, nineteenth century; it is thou, providence; it is thou, God. We who resist them; we are the "eternal enemies of order;" we are the demagogues. In the language of the Duke of Alva, to believe in the sanctity of the human conscience, to resist the inquisition, to have the faggot for one's faith, to draw the sword for one's country, to defend one's worship, one's city, one's house, one's family, one's God, that is called beggary; in the language of Louis Bonaparte, to struggle for liberty, for justice, for the right; to battle for the cause of progress, of civilization, of France, of humanity; to wish the abolition of war, and of the death penalty; to take as serious the brotherhood of men; to believe in the sworn oath; to arm one's self for the Constitution of one's country; to defend the laws, that is to be a demagogue. One is demagogue in the nineteenth century as one was beggar

---

M. Pietre, prefect of police." The subscription among the employees, whose zeal it has been necessary to moderate, will be thus divided: the chief of division, ten francs; the chief of bureaux, six francs; employees at eighteen hundred francs, three francs; at fifteen hundred francs, two francs; finally, at twelve hundred francs, two francs. They calculate that this subscription will rise higher than six thousand francs.

‡ You read in a Bonapartist correspondence.

in the sixteenth. It being granted that the dictionary of the Academy no longer exists; that it is dark in full noon; that a cat is no longer called a cat, and Baroche is no longer called a rogue; that justice is a chimera; that history is a dream; that the Prince of Orange was a beggar, and the Duke of Alva a just man; that Louis Bonaparte is identical with Napoleon the Great; that those who violated the Constitution are saviors; and that those who have defended it are brigands; in a word, that human honesty is dead. Be it so, then I admire this government; it suits me well, it is a model of its kind; it compresses, it represses, it oppresses, it impresses, it exiles, it mows down with grapeshot, it exterminates and even pardons, it makes authority by cannon-shots, and clemency by blows with the flat of a saber.

Nurse your indignation at your ease, repeat a few incorrigible bravos of the party of order, sneer, weep, spit, it's all the same to us. Vive stability! All this constitutes, after all, a solid government. Solid? We have not yet had an understanding on this solidity. Solid! I admire this solidity. If it snowed journals in France for only two days, on the morning of the third one would not know what had become of M. Louis Bonaparte. It makes no difference. The man weighs on the entire epoch; he disfigures the nineteenth century; and there will be perhaps in this century two or three years on which, by one cannot tell what ignoble trace, one will recognize that Louis Bonaparte has been seated.

This man, sad to say, is now the question of all men. At certain epochs of history the entire human race, from all points of the earth, fixes its eyes on one mysterious place from which it seems that the destiny of all is about to issue. There have been hours when the world looked at the Vatican: Gregory VII., Leo X., had there their throne. There have been other hours when they contemplated the Louvre: Philippe-Auguste, Louis IX., Francis I., Henry IV., were there; Saint Just: Charles V. considered it; Windsor: Elizabeth the Great reigned there; Versailles: Louis XIV., surrounded by stars, shot forth his rays there; the Kremlin: one caught a glimpse of Peter the Great there; Potsdam: Frederick II. shut himself up there with Voltaire. . . . . To-day, hang your head, history, the universe is looking at the Elysée! That kind of bastard gate, guarded by two sentry-boxes, painted ticking color, at the end of the Faubourg St. Honoré, that is what the age of the civilized world is contemplating to-day with a kind of profound anxiety. . . . Ah! what is that place from which there has not issued one idea which is not a trap? not one action which is not a crime? What place is that where all that is cynical dwells with all that is hypocritical? What is that place where bishops elbow Jeanne Poisson on the staircase, and, as a century ago, bow down to her to the earth; where Samuel Bernard laughs in a corner with Laubardemont; where Escobar enters with Gusman d'Alfarache on his arm; where, frightful rumor, in a thicket in the garden they dispatch with the bayonet, as they say, men whom they do not wish to judge; where one hears a man say to a woman who intercedes and who weeps: "I allow you your loves, allow me my hatreds!" What is that place where the orgy of 1852 importunes and dishonors the grief of 1815? Where Cæsarion,* with his arms crossed or with his hands

---
* The pigmy Cæsar.

behind his back, walks under those very trees, in those very paths which the indignant specter of Cæsar still haunts? This place, it is the stain of Paris; this place is the dirt-spot of the century; this gate, from which all sorts of joyous sounds issue—flourishes of trumpets, the playing of bands, laughter, clashing of glasses—this gate, saluted in the day by battalions which pass, illuminated by night, all wide open with an insolent confidence, it is a sort of public wrong always present. The center of the world's shame is there. Ah! what is France dreaming of? Assuredly, it is necessary to wake up this nation; it is necessary to take its arm and shake it, and speak to it; it is necessary to travel all over the fields, to enter the villages, enter the barracks; to speak to the soldier, who no longer knows what he has done; to speak to the laborer, who has an engraving of the Emperor* in his cottage, and who votes whatever they wish for that reason; it is necessary to take away from them the radiant phantom which they have before their eyes! The whole situation is nothing but an immense and fatal mistake. It is necessary to throw light on this mistake; to go to the bottom and to disabuse the people, the people of the surrounding country; to startle them; to agitate them; to stir them up; to show them empty houses, open graves; to make them touch with their fingers the horror of this régime. These people are good and honest. They will understand. Yes, peasant, they are two—the great and the little, the illustrious and the infamous, Napoleon and Naboleon!†

Let us give a summary of this government. Who is at

---

* First Emperor.
† Spoken with German accent.

the Elysée and the Tuileries? Crime. Who sits at the Luxembourg? Baseness. Who sits at the palace of the Bourbons? Imbecility. Who sits at the d'Orsay palace? Corruption. Who sits at the palace of Justice? Prevarication. And who are in the prisons, in the forts, in the cells, in the casemates, in the hulks, at Lambessa, at Cayenne, in exile? Law, honor, intelligence, liberty, right. Proscribed men, of what do you complain? you have the best part.

BOOK THIRD.—THE CRIME.

But this government, this horrible government, hypocritical and stupid; this government which makes one hesitate between a shout of laughter and a sob; this gibbet of a Constitution on which all our liberties hang; this huge universal suffrage and this little universal suffrage; the first naming the president, and the last naming the legislators; the little saying to the huge: my lord, receive these millions; the huge saying to the little: receive the assurance of my regards; this Senate, this Council of State; from whence do all these things emerge? My God! Have we already come to that strait that it is necessary to call it to recollection. From what does this government emerge? Look! it flows still; it smokes still, it is blood. The dead are far, the dead are dead. Ah! frightful thing to think of and to say. Shall one never give attention to it again? Can it be a fact that because one eats and drinks; because driving flourishes; because you, navvy, have work at the Bois de Boulogne; because you, mason, earn four sous a day at the Louvre; because you, banker, have made money on the metalliques of Vienna, or on the obligations of Hope & Co.; because the titles of nobility are re-established; because one can address others Monsieur le Compte, or Madame la Duchesse; because processions march on the Fête Dieu; because one is amused; because one laughs; because the walls of Paris are covered with the post-bills of fêtes and of plays—will one forget that there are corpses beneath it all?

Because one has been at the ball at the Ecole Militaire; because one has returned home with eyes dim, head fatigued, dress torn, bouquet faded, and because one has thrown one's self on one's bed, and gone to sleep, dreaming of a certain handsome officer, shall one no longer remember that there is there, under the sod, in an obscure grave in a deep hole, in the inexorable shadow of death, motionless, stiff, and terrible, a multitude of human beings, already become shapeless, whom the worms are devouring, whom decomposition is consuming, who are beginning to mingle with the earth, who lived, worked, thought, loved, and who had the right to live, and—whom they have slain? Ah! if one remembers it no longer, let us recall it to those who have forgotten it. Awake! ye who sleep. The dead are about to defile before your eyes.*

---

* Extract from an unpublished book, entitled the *Crime of the Second of December*. By Victor Hugo. This book will be published soon. It will be a complete narration of the infamous event of 1851. A great part is already written. The author is gathering in at this moment materials for the rest. He believes it *a propos* to enter at present on a few details on the subject of that work which he has imposed on himself as a duty.

The author must do himself the justice to say, that in writing this narrative, the austere occupation of his exile, he has unceasingly in mind the high responsibility of the historian. When it shall appear, this narrative will certainly provoke numerous and violent complaints. The author expects it. One does not hew with impunity into the living flesh of a contemporaneous crime, and in the hour in which it is all-powerful. However that may be, whatever may be the objections, more or less interested and finally for the especial purpose that one may judge in advance of the merit of these objections, the author believes that he ought to explain in what style, with what scrupulous care of the truth, this history shall have been written, or to speak more correctly, the verbal record has been drawn up.

This recital of the Second of December will contain, besides the general facts of which no one is ignorant, a very great number of unknown facts which will be brought to light in it for the first time. Several of these facts the author himself has seen, touched, crossed. Of the latter he can say: *quæque ipse vidi et quorum pars fui.* The members of the Republican left, whose conduct has been so intrepid, have seen these facts as he has, and their evidence shall not be wanting. For all the rest the author has proceeded to a veritable judicial inquest. He has constituted himself, so to speak, examining magistrate, in the matter. Every actor in the drama, every combatant, every victim, every witness, has come to depose before him; for all doubtful facts he has consulted the words, and, when necessary, the persons. In general, historians speak to dead facts; they touch them in the tomb with their judicial rods, make them arise, and question them. But *he* speaks only to living facts. All the details of the Second of December have thus passed before his eyes. He has them all registered, he has them all weighed; none can escape him.

History may be able to complete this recital, but not to make it void. The magistrates failing of their duty, he has done it for them. When direct evidence from the living voice has failed him, he has sent on the spot one what could call a real judicial commission. He could cite similar facts for which he has laid down veritable question-books of questions according to which he has been minutely answered. He repeats it, he has submitted the Second of December to a long and searching examination. He has carried the torch as far forward as he has been able. He has, thanks to this inquest, nearly two hundred documents in his possession out of which this book will issue. There is not a fact in this recital to which, when the work shall have been published, the author could not put a name. The public will comprehend that he abstains from it; they will comprehend that he even substitutes sometimes for the correct names, and even for certain indications of places, designations as little transparent as possible in presence of impending proscriptions.

He does not wish to furnish a supplementary list to M. Bonaparte. Assuredly the author will not be more impartial, as one is accustomed to cry when one wishes to praise an historian, in the sketch of the Second of December than he is in the present volume. Impartiality!

strange virtue that Tacitus does not possess. Evil to him who could remain impartial before the bleeding wounds of liberty. In presence of the fact of December, 1851, the author feels all the human nature rise up within him; he does not conceal it; and one ought to perceive it in reading him. But with him passion for the truth equals passion for the right. The indignant man does not lie. This history of the second of December, then, he declares it, at the moment of citing a few pages from it, will have been written, as one has just seen, giving particulars with the most absolute exactness. We deem it useful to detach from it, for the present, and to publish here a chapter which we think will strike attention, in that it throws new daylight on the success of M. Louis Bonaparte. Thanks to the reticence of the official historiographers of the second of December, one does not know how near the coup d'état was to ruin, and one ignores altogether by what means it was saved. Let us place this last fact especially under the eye of the reader.

THE DAY OF THE FOURTH OF DECEMBER.

CHAPTER I.

THE COUP D'ÉTAT AT BAY.

RESISTANCE had assumed unexpected proportions; the fight had become threatening. It was no longer a fight, it was a battle, and one in which the engagement extended on all sides. At the Elysée, and in the ministries, men grew pale. They had wanted barricades, they made them. All the center of Paris covered itself with improvised forts. The barricaded quarters formed a sort of immense uneven square, formed between the Halles* and Rambuteau-street on one side, and the Boulevards on the other, and bounded on the east by Temple-street, and on the west by Montmartre-street. This vast network of streets, cut into all kinds of redoubts and intrenchments, gathered hour by hour a more terrible aspect, and became a sort of fortress. The combatants of the barricades pushed their advance guards even upon the quays. On the outside of the irregular oblong which we have just described, the barricades went up, we have said, to the Faubourg St. Martin and to the grounds around the canal. The school quarter, where the committee of resistance had sent the representative Le Flotte, was more stirred up still than the evening

---

* Great markets.

before. The outskirt took fire; they beat the roll-call at the Batignolles; Madier de Montjau agitated Belleville. Three enormous barricades were constructed at the Chapel St. Denis. In the trading streets the bourgeois delivered up their guns, the women made lint; B * * * cried to us, coming in to the committee of resistance, all radiant, "Things are advancing, Paris is divided!"*

From moment to moment the news was arriving to us, all the lodges of the different quarters were in communication with us. The members of the committee were deliberating and dispatching their orders and instructions concerning the battle on all sides. It was a moment of enthusiasm and of joy, and these men, again placed between life and death, embraced each other. "Now," cried Jules Favre, "let a regiment turn or a regiment retire, and Louis Napoleon is lost." "To-morrow, the Republic will be at the Hôtel de Ville," said Michel (from Bourges).

All the city was fermented, and all was boiling over. In the most peaceable quarters they were tearing down the post-bills and the decrees. In Beaubourg-street, while they were constructing a barricade, the women at the windows cried "Courage!" The agitation reached even the Faubourg St.

---

* A committee of resistance, charged with the duty of centralizing the action and directing the combat, which had been nominated the 2d of December, in the evening, by the members of the left, assembled at the house of the representative Lafou, Quai Jemmapes, No. 2. This committee, which was destined to change its place of asylum twenty-seven times in four days, and which remained in session after some fashion night and day, did not cease for a single instant to act during the different crises of the coup d'état. It was composed of the representatives Garnot, De Flotte, Jules Favre, Madier de Montjau, Michel (from Bourges), Schoelcher, and Victor Hugo.

Germain. At the Hotel of Jerusalem-street, the center of that great spider's net which the police stretch over Paris, everything was trembling. The anxiety was deep; one caught a glimpse of the Republic victorious. In the courtyards, in the committees, in the lobbies, between clerks and sergeants of police, they began to speak with tenderness of Canssidière.* If it is necessary to believe in what has transpired from that den, the prefect Maupas, so keen the night before, and so odiously aggressive, began to draw back and grow faint. He seemed to listen with terror to that sound of rising tide which the insurrection was making, the holy and legitimate insurrection of the right. He stuttered and stammered, the word of command died on his lips. "That little young man has got the colic," said the old Prefect Carlier as he left him. In this alarm Maupas hung on Morny. The electric telegraph was in perpetual dialogue from the prefecture of police to the minister of the interior, and from the minister of the interior to the prefecture of police. All the most disturbing news, every sign of panic and disorder arrived, from the prefect to the minister, blow following blow. Morny, less frightened, and a man of mind at least, received all these shocks in his office. They say that at first he said—Maupas is ill; and to this question—What must be done? he had answered by the telegraph—Go to bed! At the second he still answered, Go to bed. At the third he lost all patience, he replied,—Go to bed, j... f.....† The zeal of his agents gave out; commenced to turn its coat.

---

* Who had constructed the barricades.
† An obscene insult.

A fearless man, sent by the committee of resistance to excite the Faubourg St. Marceau, was arrested in Fossé-Saint-Victor-street, with his pockets full of the proclamations and decrees of the left. They had him led off toward the prefecture of police; he expected to be shot. As the squad who were taking him off were passing before the dead-house, St. Michael's quay, gun-shots rattled in the city; the sergeant who was leading the party said to the soldiers, "Go back to your posts, I will take care of the prisoner." As soon as the soldiers were out of the way he cut the cords which bound the wrists of the prisoner, and said to him, "Be off—I save your life; do not forget that it is I who set you at liberty. Look at me well, so as to recognize me."

The principal military accomplices held council. They discussed the question, whether it would not be necessary for Louis Bonaparte to quit immediately the Faubourg Saint Honoré, and betake himself either to the Invalides or the Luxemburg palace, two strategic points, easier to defend together than the Elysée. Some gave their opinion for the Invalides, others for the Luxemburg.

An altercation broke out upon this subject between two generals. It was at this moment that the late King of Westphalia, Jérome Bonaparte, seeing the coup d'état totter, and looking out for the future, wrote this significant letter to his nephew :—

"My dear Nephew,—French blood has flowed, stop its effusion by a serious appeal to the people. Your meaning is misunderstood. The second proclamation, in which you speak of the plebiscite, is badly received by the people, who do not consider it an establishment of the right of suffrage. Liberty is without guaranty if an assembly does not take part in maintaining the constitution of the Republic. The army has the upper hand. Now is the moment to complete the material victory by a moral one; and what a government cannot do when it is defeated, it ought to do when it is victorious. After having crushed the old parties, complete the restoration of the people. Announce that universal suffrage, sincere and acting in harmony with the greatest liberty, will be established, and that it will appoint the President of the Constituent Assembly to save and restore the Republic. It is in the name of the memory of my brother, having his horror of civil war, that I write you. Trust to my long experience, and consider that France, Europe, and posterity will be called to judge your conduct.

"Your affectionate Uncle,

"JÉROME BONAPARTE."

On Madeleine-square, the two representatives, Fabvier and Crestin, met and accosted each other. General Fabvier drew the attention of his colleague to four pieces of limbered cannon which turned bridle, left the Boulevard, and took the direction of the Elysée at a gallop. "Is the Elysée already on the defensive?" said the general; and Crestin, pointing to the front of the palace of the assembly, on the other side of Revolution-square, replied, "General, to-morrow we shall be there." From the top of a certain roof which overlooked the court-yard of the stables of the Elysée might have been seen, since morning, three traveling-carriages standing harnessed and loaded, with the postilions in their saddles, ready to set off. The impulse had actually been imparted, the shock of anger and hatred was becoming universal, the coup d'état seemed lost. One shock more and Louis Bonaparte was overthrown. Let the day end as it had began, and the tale would have been told. The coup d'état touched despair. The hour of supreme resolution had come; what are they going to do? It was necessary to strike a great blow; an unexpected blow, a frightful one. The situation was reduced to this—to perish, or to save one's self frightfully. Louis Bonaparte had not left the Elysée. He kept himself in an office on the ground-floor in the neighborhood of that splendid gilt saloon, where, a child in 1815, he had assisted at the second abdication of Napoleon. He was there, alone; the order was given to allow no one to be admitted to him. From time to time the door was set ajar, and the gray head of General Roguet, his aid-de-camp, appeared. General Roquet was the only person permitted to open that door and enter. The general kept bringing news more and more disturbing, and entered frequently with these words: "The thing is not working," or "the thing goes badly." When he had finished, Louis Bonaparte, who was leaning with his elbow upon a table, resting his feet on the andirons before a large fire, half turned his head upon the back of his arm-chair, and in a tone of voice the most phlegmatic, and without visible emotion, invariably answered these *five* words: "Let them execute my orders." The last time General Roguet entered with bad news in this way, it was near one o'clock. He himself has subsequently related these details to the honor of the impassibility of his master. He says he informed the prince that the barricades in the central streets held their own and were multiplying; that on the Boulevards the cries: "Down with the dictator," (he did not dare to say, down with Soulouque) and the hisses resounded everywhere, whenever troops went by; that before the Galerie Jouffroy, an adjutant-major had been chased by the mob ; and that at the corner of the Café Cardinal a captain of the staff had been torn from his horse. Louis Bonaparte half rose from his arm-chair and calmly said, while he looked at the general, fixedly : " Well, let them tell St. Arnaud to execute my orders."

What were those orders ?

You are going to see.

Here we recoil, and the narrator puts his pen to the sheet with a sort of hesitation and anguish. We have come up with that sudden and abominable change of this dismal day of the fourth ; that monstrous deed, out of which the success of the coup d'état issued, all covered with blood. We are about to unveil the most sinister of the plans of Louis Bonaparte ; we are going to reveal in detail what the historians of the 2d of December have concealed ; what General Magnan has carefully omitted from his report ; what in Paris itself, where the things were seen, one dares scarcely whisper in the ear. We enter the horrible. The 2d of December is a crime covered with night ; a coffin closed and silent, from the crevices of which there come out streams of blood. We are going to open this coffin.

CHAPTER II.

SINCE morning—for here let us insist on this point, premeditation cannot be denied—since morning strange postbills had been posted on all the corners of the streets. We have transcribed them; people remember them. Since the cannon of the Revolution thundered sixty years ago on certain days in Paris, when now and then it occasionally happened that the threatened authorities recurred to desperate resources, nothing equal to it had been seen. These notices announced to the citizens that all crowds of any kind whatsoever would be dispersed by force, *without summons.* In Paris, the central city of civilization, one hardly believes that a man can go to the extreme of crime; and the public only saw in these notices a hideous and savage and almost ridiculous means of intimidation.

They were mistaken. These notices contained in germ the plan of Louis Bonaparte. They were serious. A word on what is going to be the theater of the unheard act, prepared and perpetrated by the man of December. From the Madeleine to the Faubourg Poissonnière the Boulevard was clear; from the theater of the Gymnasium to the theater of the Port St. Martin it was barricaded, as well as Bondy-street, Meslay-street, La Lune-street, and all the streets which border on or come out at the St. Denis and St. Martin gates. On the other side of the St. Martin gate the Boulevard became again free, up to the Bastille, near which a barricade had been thrown up as high as the

Château d'Eau. Between the two gates, St. Denis and St. Martin, seven or eight redoubts cut the pavement from point to point. A square of four barricades enclosed St. Martin's gate. That one which faced the Madeleine, and which was to be the first to receive the shock of the troops, was constructed at the culminating point of the Boulevard, the left resting upon the angle of La Lune-street, and the right on Mazagnan-street. Four omnibuses, five furniture wagons, the desk of the inspector of hacks upset, the demolished Vespasian columns, the benches of the Boulevard, the flag-stones of the staircase of La Lune-street, the iron balustrade of the sidewalk torn off entire, and with one effort, by the formidable grip of the multitude — these formed the heap which was scarcely enough to bar the Boulevard, which was too wide in this place. There were no paving-stones, for the street was macadamized. The barricade did not even reach from one kirb of the Boulevard to the other, and left a wide space open on the side of Mazagnan-street. There was a house in course of erection at this spot. Seeing this gap, a young man, well dressed, mounted the scaffold, and alone, and quietly, and without taking his cigar out of his mouth, cut all its cords. From the neighboring windows they applauded him with laughter. A moment afterward the scaffold fell with a great crash, and in one mass, and this completed the barricade.

While this redoubt was in course of construction, a score of men entered the Gymnasium by the Actors' gate, and came out a few moments afterward with guns and a drum which they had found in the store-room of costumes, and which made part of what they call in the language of theaters, "the accessories." One of them took the drum and began to beat the roll-call; the others, with the Vespasian columns which had been thrown down, with carriages which had been laid on their sides, with Venetian blinds and shutters unhooked from their hinges, and with old scenery of the theater, built as high as the Bonne-Nouvelle station—a little advanced barricade, or rather a lunette, which looked out toward the Boulevards Poissonnière and Montmartre and Hauteville-street. The troops had since morning evacuated the guard-house. They took the flag of the guard-house and planted it on the barricade. That is the flag which has since been declared by the journals of the coup d'état the red flag. Fifteen men or so installed themselves in this advanced post. They had guns, but few or no cartridges. Behind them the grand barricade, which covered the St. Denis gate, was occupied by a hundred combatants, in the midst of which you might have remarked two women, and an old man with white locks, supporting himself with a cane which he held in his left hand, while he held a gun in his right. One of the two women carried a saber, slung over her shoulders. In helping to tear off the balustrade of the sidewalk she had cut off three of her fingers in the angle of a bent bar of iron. She held up her mutilated hand to the crowd, and cried out, "Vive la République!" The other woman mounted on the top of the barricade, and leant on the staff of the flag, escorted by two men in blouses, armed with guns, and presenting arms, and read in a high voice the call of the representatives and of the left to arms; the people applauded. All this happened between noon and one o'clock. An immense population on this side of the barricaded streets covered the pavements on both sides of the Boulèvard—silent at some points, at others crying, "Down with Soulouque! Down with the traitor!"

At intervals lugubrious processions crossed this multitude. They were files of hand-barrows carried by hospital attendants and soldiers. At their head marched men holding long staves, from which hung blue pennants, on which were written in great letters, "Service of the military hospitals." On the screens of the barrows you read : The wounded : Ambulances. The weather was somber and rainy. At this moment a crowd collected at the Bourse. The porters were pasting there on all the walls dispatches announcing the adhesion of the departments to the coup d'état. The Exchange agents, all pushing for a rise, laughed and shrugged their shoulders before these placards.

All of a sudden a well-known speculator, and a man who had greatly applauded the coup d'état for two days past, came up all pale and gasping, like a man who was flying for his life, and said, "They are sweeping the Boulevards with grape-shot!" This is what was taking place.

CHAPTER III.

A LITTLE after one o'clock, a quarter of an hour after the last order given by Louis Bonaparte to General Roguet, the Boulevards throughout their entire length from the Madeleine, were suddenly covered with cavalry and infantry. The Carrelet division, nearly entire, composed of the five brigades of Cotte, Bourgon, Canrobert, Dulac, and Reybell, and presenting an effective force of sixteen thousand four hundred and ten men, had taken position, and were placed in échelon from the Rue de la Paix to the Faubourg Poissonnière. Each brigade had its battery with it. One could count on the Boulevard eleven pieces of cannon; two, which turned their backs to each other, had been pointed, one at the entrance of Mont Martre-street, the other at that of the Faubourg Mont Marte. No one could imagine why they were so placed, as the street and the Faubourg did not show even the sign of a barricade. The curious crowds on the sidewalks and at the windows looked on with amazement. It was one closely packed mass of gun-carriages, sabers, and bayonets. "The troops were laughing and talking," says a witness. Another witness says "the soldiers had a strange air; the greater part had their gun-stocks on the ground, and were leaning on their pieces, and seemed half reeling with weariness or *something else*." One of those old officers who have had long practice in inspecting troops, and had the habit of looking them in the depths of the eyes, General L***, said, as he passed before café Frascate, "*They are drunk.*"

Symptoms were manifesting themselves. At one time, when the crowd cried to the troops, Long live the Republic, down with Louis Bonaparte, an officer was heard to say in a low tone, "This will soon turn into the pork-butcher's business." A battalion of infantry debouched by Richelieu-street, before the Cardinal Café; they were received with a unanimous cry of Vive la République. A writer who was there, editor of a conservative journal, added also, "À bas, Soulouque!" The staff-officer who was leading the detachment, struck at him with his saber; the blow, avoided by the writer, cut one of the shrubs of the Boulevard. As the First Lancers, commanded by Colonel Rochefort, arrived at the head of Taitbout-street, a numerous group covered the composition pavement of the Boulevard. They were the residents of the quarter, the traders, artists, journalists, and among them a few women holding young children by the hand. As the regiment passed by, men, women, all cried, "Vive la Constitution," "Vive la Loi," "Vive la République." Colonel Rochefort, the same who had presided on the 31st October, 1851, at the banquet given by the First Lancers, at the Ecole Militaire, and who in this banquet had pronounced this toast, "To Prince Napoleon, the Chief of the State; he is the impersonation of the order of which we are all the defenders." This colonel, at the perfectly legal cry, sent forth by the crowd, dashed his horse into the middle of the group, across the chairs of the sidewalk, the lancers rushed after him, and men, women, and children, *all were sabered!* "A good number of them remained on the spot," says an apologist of the coup d'état, who adds, "It was the affair of a moment."* Toward two o'clock they pointed two howitzers at the end of the Boulevard Poissonnière, at one hundred and fifty paces from the little barricade-lunette of the Bonne-Nouvelle station. In placing their pieces in battery, the soldiers of the train, little accustomed, however, to false maneuvers, broke the pole of a caisson. "You see plainly that *they are drunk*," cried a man from among the people. At half-past two o'clock, for it is necessary to follow step by step this hideous drama, the fire opened against the barricade gently, and as it were without purpose. It seemed as if the military chiefs had their minds on anything but a battle. We are going to see what they were actually dreaming of. The first cannon-shot, badly aimed, passed above all the barricades and almost all the windows. The projectile struck and killed a young boy who was pouring out water into a basin in a distant house.

The shops were closed, and almost all the windows. One window, however, remained open in the higher story of the house which formed the corner of du Sentier-street. The curious continued to flock, principally on the south sidewalk. It was a crowd and nothing more: men, women, children, and old men; for them the barricade, little attacked, little defended, had the effect of a sham fight. This barricade was a play, until it became a pretext. There was about a quarter of an hour that the troops fired, and the barricade responded, without there being one wounded man on either side, when suddenly, as if by an electric shock, an extraordi-

---

* Captain Mauduit. Military Revolution of the Second of December, page 217.

nary and terrible movement took place, first in the infantry, then in the cavalry. The troops suddenly changed front. The historians of the coup d'état have related that one shot directed against the soldiers was fired from the open windows at the corner of du Sentier-street. Others said from the top of the house which formed the corner of Notre Dame de Recouvrance and Poissonnière streets. According to others the shot was a pistol-shot, and was shot from the high house which marks the corner of Mazagnan-street. This shot is disputed; but what is not contested is that for having fired this questioned pistol-shot, which was, perhaps, nothing but the violent shutting of a door; a dentist residing in the next house was shot. In short, was a pistol or gun shot heard coming from one of the houses on the Boulevard? was it? is it true? is it false? a crowd of witnesses deny it. If the pistol-shot was fired, it remains to be cleared up whether it was a cause, or whether it was a *signal*. Be that as it may, suddenly, as we have just said, the cavalry, the infantry, the artillery, wheeled their front to the crowd massed on the sidewalks, and without any one being able to divine why, abruptly, without motive, "without summons," as the infamous postbills had declared in the morning, from the Gymnasium to the Chinese baths, that is to say, in all the length of the richest Faubourg, the most stirring and joyous of Paris, a slaughter commenced. The army set itself to work shooting the people at the muzzles of their guns. It was a sinister and inexpressible moment; the cries, the arms raised to heaven, the surprise, the terror, the crowd flying in all directions, a hail of balls raining up and down from the pavements to the roofs, in one minute the dead strewing the pavement;

young men falling with cigars in their mouths; women in velvet dresses killed stone dead by the iron balls; two booksellers musketed on the thresholds of their shops, without having known what the matter was; gun-shots fired down the ventholes of cellars, and there killing it made no difference whom, the bazar riddled with bullets and shell; the Hôtel Sollandrouze bombarded; the Maison d'Or covered with grape-shot; Tortoni taken by assault; the hundreds of corpses; Richelieu-street a stream of blood. Let the narrator be here again permitted to interrupt himself.

In presence of these nameless facts, I who write these lines, I declare, I am a recorder, I register the crimes, I call up the cause, that is all my function; I cite Louis Bonaparte, I cite St. Arnaud, Maupas, Morny, Magnan, Carrelet, Canrobert, de Cotte, Reybell, his accomplices, I cite still others whose names will be found elsewhere; I cite the executioners, the murderers, the victims, the witnesses, the warm cannon, the smoking sabers, the drunkenness of the soldiery, the mourning of families, the dying, the dead, the horror, the blood, and the tears, to the bar of the civilized world. The narrator alone, whoever he might be, one would not believe. Let us then give speech to living facts, to bloody facts. Let us listen to the witnesses.

CHAPTER IV.

We will not print the names of the witnesses; we have said why; but you will recognize in them the sincere and poignant tone of truth.

One says: "I had not taken three steps on the pavement "before the company which were defiling stopped sud- "denly, made the right about face, lowered their pieces, " fired on the distracted crowd with a simultaneous move- "ment. The fire continued without interruption during " twenty minutes; accompanied from time to time by a few "cannon-shots. At the first fire I cast myself on the "ground and dragged myself like a reptile on the pavement " to the first half-open door which I could reach. This was " the shop of a wine-merchant, situated at No. 180, beside the " Bazaar of Industry. I was the last that entered. The mus- " ketry firing continued uninterruptedly. There were in this "shop nearly fifty persons, and amongst them five or six "women, and two or three children. Three unfortunate men "had entered, wounded; two died at the end of a quarter "of an hour, in horrible sufferings; the third was still living " when I left the shop, at four o'clock. A few women, two "of whom have just bought in the quarter, provisions for "their dinner; a little cryer-clerk, sent on business by his " master; two or three habitués of the Exchange; two or "three landlords; a few workmen: few, or none, dressed " in blouses. One of the unhappy refugees in this shop " produced a vivid impression on me. He was a man

"about thirty years old, of light complexion, with a gray
"paletot on. He was returning with his wife to the Fau-
"bourg Montmartre to dine with his family, when he was
"stopped in the Boulevard by the passage of a column of
"troops. In the first moment, and at the first discharge,
"he and his wife fell. He rose up, was drawn into the
"wine-merchant's shop; but he no longer had his wife on
"his arm, and his despair cannot be described. He tried
"with all his strength, and in spite of our representations,
"to get the door open, and run to search for his wife in
"the midst of the volleys that swept the street. We had
"the greatest difficulty in keeping him back for the space
"of an hour. The next day I learned that his wife had
"been killed, and that the corpse had been recognized at
"the city Bergère. Fifteen days afterward I learned that
"this unfortunate, having threatened to make M. Bonaparte
"suffer vengeance, had been arrested and transported to
"Brest, to be sent ultimately to Cayenne. Almost all the
"citizens assembled in the wine-merchant's shop held mon-
"archical opinions; and I did not meet among them but
"one, a former compositor of the *Reforme* newspaper, of
"the name of Meunièr, and one of his friends, who avowed
"themselves Republicans. Toward four o'clock I went out
"of that shop."

A witness—one of those who thought he heard the gunshot sent from Mazagnan-street, adds: "The gunshot was
"the signal for the troops to direct a continuous fire on
"all the houses and the windows, the rattling of which
"lasted at least thirty minutes. It was kept up simultane-
"ously from the St. Denis gate to the café of the Grand-

"Balcon. The cannon soon mingled its roar with the "musketry."

One witness says: "At half-past three o'clock a singular "movement took place. The soldiers, who were facing the "St. Denis gate, effected instantaneously a change of front, "resting on the houses from the Gymnasium, the house of "Pont du Fer, the Hôtel Saint-Phar; and, at the same time, "a rolling fire was directed on the houses and on the people "who were on the other side, from St. Denis-street to Riche-"lieu-street. A few minutes were enough to cover the "sidewalk with corpses. The houses were riddled with "balls, and this furious action kept up its paroxysm during "three-quarters of an hour."

A witness says: "The first cannon-shot, directed on the "barricade Bonne-Nouvelle, had served as a signal for the "rest of the troops, who had fired almost at the same time "on all who were found within gunshot."

A witness says: "Words cannot describe such an act of "barbarism. It is necessary to have been a witness in order "to venture to relate it, and to give evidence of the truth "of so indescribable a deed. Musket-shots were fired by "thousands—it is inappreciable*—by the troops on all the "inoffensive people, and that without any necessity; they "desired to produce a strong impression—that is all."

A witness says: "When the excitement was very great in "the Boulevard, the line, followed by the artillery and cav-"alry, arrived. A gunshot was soon fired in the midst of "the company, and it was easy to see that it had been fired "in the line by the smoke which arose perpendicularly."

---

* The witness meant to say incalculable. We have desired to avoid changing anything in the text.

That, therefore, was the signal to fire, "without summons to disperse," and to charge bayonets on the people. This is significant, and proves that the troops wished to have the semblance of a motive for commencing the massacre which followed.

A witness relates : "The cannon, charged with grape-"shot, hacked the fronts of the houses, from the Magazin "du Prophète to Montmartre-street; from the Boulevard "Bonne-Nouvelle they were to fire also with bullets on "Billecoq-house, for it had been hit at the corner from the "side of Aubusson, and the bullet, after having pierced the "wall, penetrated to the interior."

Another witness—one of those who deny the gunshot—says : "They have tried to extenuate this fusilade and these "assassinations by pretending that they had fired on the "troops from a certain house. In addition to the fact that "General Magnan's report seems to give the lie to this re-"port, I affirm that the volleys were instantaneous from the "St. Denis gate to the Montmartre gate, and that there "had not been, before the general discharge, a single shot "fired alone, either from the windows or by the troops, "from the Faubourg St. Denis to the Boulevard des "Italiens."

Another, who did not hear the gunshot any more than the other, says : "The troops defiled before the staircase of "Tortoni, where I was, about twenty minutes before; "when, before any sound of a gunshot reached us, they "moved. The cavalry took a gallop, the infantry the double-"quick ; all of a sudden we saw a fringe of fire come from "the side of the Boulevard Poissonnière, and extend and "gain rapidly, the fusilade being begun. I can guarantee

"that no explosion had preceded it, that not a gunshot was
"sent from the houses between the Café Frascati to the
"place where I was standing. At last, we saw the muzzles
"of the guns which were before us lower and threaten us.
"We took refuge in Taitbout-street, under a porte cochère.
"At the same moment the balls passed above us and around
"us. A woman was killed within ten paces of me, at the
"moment when I was hiding myself under the coachway.
"There was neither barricade there nor insurgents, I can
"make oath. There were hunters and the game which
"tried to escape them. That was all."

That image, "hunters and game," is that which comes first to the mind of those who saw the terrible thing.

We shall find the image again in the words of another witness : —

"The gendarmes were seen at the foot of my street, and I
"know that there were some likewise in the neighborhood,
"holding their guns, and holding themselves in the attitude
"of hunters who were waiting for the rising of the game, that
"is to say, with the gun near the shoulder, so as to be more
"prompt in placing and firing it. Also, in order to lavish
"the best care to the wounded who should fall in Mont-
"martre-street, near the gates, one saw from point to point
"doors open, and an arm shoot out and draw in the corpse
"or the dying, whom the balls still contended for."

Another witness again uses the same image : "The
"soldiers in ambuscade at the corner of the streets were
"waiting for the citizens who should pass, as hunters lie in
"wait for their game, and as soon as they saw them occupied
"in the street, they fired on them as on bulls' eyes in a tar-
"get. Numbers of citizens were killed in this manner in

"Du Sentier and Rougemont streets, and the Faubourg "Poissonnière. . . . 'Go off!' said the officers to the "inoffensive citizens who asked protection from them. At "this order the latter drew off quietly and with confidence; "but it was only a word of command which meant death, "and, actually, scarcely had they taken a few steps before "they fell."

"At the moment when the fire commenced on the Bou-"levards," says another witness, "a bookseller in the "neighborhood of the carpet-house was hastening to close "his front, when the fugitives, trying to enter, were sus-"pected by the troops, or the gendarmes, I don't know "which, of having fired on them. The troops broke into "the bookseller's house. The latter desired to make "some explanation. He was alone before his own door, "and his wife and daughter had only time to cast them-"selves between him and the soldiers before he fell dead. "The wife received a ball through the thigh, and the "daughter was saved by the busk of her corset."

Another witness says: "The soldiers entered the two "bookstores which are before the Maison du Prophète "and that of M. Sallandrouze. Murders are averred to "have taken place. They cut the two booksellers' throats "on the sidewalks; the other prisoners were slaughtered "in the house." Let us end with these extracts, which one cannot transcribe without shuddering.

"In the first quarter of an hour of this horror," says a witness, "the fire, for a moment less active, made a few "citizens who were only wounded believe that they could "rise. Amongst the men lying before the Prophète two "rose up. One took to flight toward Du Sentier-street,

"from which a few yards only separated him. He then
"came in the midst of balls, which carried away his cap.
"The second could only place himself on his knees, and
"with joined hands beg the soldiers to spare him ; but he
"fell instantly, shot. The next day one could see beside
"the staircase du Prophète a space scarcely more than a
"few feet in diameter where more than a hundred balls
"had struck."

Another says : "At the entrance of Montmartre-street
"up to the fountain, a space of about sixty paces, there
"were sixty corpses—men, women, ladies, children,
"young girls. All these unfortunates had fallen victims
"of the first shots fired by the troops and the gendarmes,
"placed facing them on the opposite side of the Boule-
"vard. All those who fled at the first report took a few
"more steps, then at last fell to rise no more. A young
"man was seeking refuge in the frame of a closed coach-
"way, and was sheltering himself under the projection of
"the wall at the side of the Boulevards. *He served for a
"target to the soldiers.* After ten minutes of unsuccessful
"shooting he was hit, in spite of all his efforts to make
"himself thinner by stretching himself up ; and they saw
"him fall to rise no more."

Another : "The glasses and the windows of the Maison
"du Pont de Fer were broken. A man in the courtyard
"became crazy from terror. The cellars were full of women
"who had taken refuge there uselessly. The soldiers fired
"into the shops and down the ventholes of the cellars.
"From Tortoni to the Gymnase it was like that. It lasted
"more than an hour."

CHAPTER VI.

LET us stop these extracts here, and close this mournful appeal. It is enough for proofs. The *accursed character* of the deed is apparent. One hundred other sheets of evidence, which we have here before our eyes, repeat almost the same facts in almost the same words. It is certain, from henceforth it is proved, it is without doubt and without question. It is as visible as the sun, that on Thursday, the 4th of December, 1851, the inoffensive people of Paris, the population not mingled with the riot, were mowed down with grape-shot, without summons, and massacred for the simple purpose of intimidation, and that there is no other sense to give to the mysterious words of M. Bonaparte, "Let them execute my orders." This execution lasted till nightfall. During more than an hour there was on the Boulevard an orgy of musketry and artillery. The cannonade and the pelting of balls crossed each other at hazard. At one particular moment the soldiers killed each other. The battery of the 6th regiment of artillery, which formed part of the brigade Canrobert, was dismounted; the horses rearing in the midst of the balls broke the fore carriages, the wheels and the poles of the whole battery; in less than a minute, there remained but one piece that could roll. An entire squadron of the First Lancers was obliged to take refuge in a shed in St. Fiácre-street. They counted the next day seventy bullet-holes in the pennants of the lances.

Madness had seized the soldiers. At the corner of Rougemont-street, in the midst of the smoke, a general threw up his arms as if to restrain them. A surgeon aide-major of the 27th just escaped being killed by soldiers whom he was trying to moderate. A sergeant said to an officer who arrested his arm, "Lieutenant, you are committing treason." The soldiers had no longer any self-possession. They were as if made insane by the crime which they had been made to commit. There comes a moment when the very abomination of what we do makes us redouble our blows. Blood is a sort of horrible wine; slaughter makes one drunk. It seemed as if a blind hand were launching death from the depth of a cloud. The soldiers were nothing more than projectiles. Two pieces were pointed from the pavement of the Boulevard on a single house-front, that of the Sallandrouze warehouse, and fired on the front to the death, in full volley, at a few paces distance. This house, an old hotel, built of freestone, and remarkable for its almost monumental staircase, split by the bullets as if by wedges of iron, opened and cracked from top to bottom. The soldiers redoubled their efforts. At each discharge a crack was heard. Suddenly an artillery officer arrived at a gallop and cried, "Stop! stop! the house is leaning forward, a bullet more and it will fall on the cannons and the cannoneers." The cannoneers were so drunk that, no longer knowing what they did, several allowed themselves to be killed by the recoil of the guns. Balls came at the same time from the St. Denis gate, from the Boulevard Poissonnière, and from the Boulevard Montmartre. The artillerymen, who heard them whistle on all sides, lay down on their horses. The men on the carriages took refuge under the caissons and behind the wagons. One saw soldiers in Notre Dame de Réconasance-street letting their képi fall and fly distracted. The dragoons, losing their self-command, fired their carbines in the air; others dismounted and took shelter behind their horses. Three or four loose horses galloped back and forth wild with terror. Frightful jests mingled with the slaughter. The skirmishers of Vincennes were established on one of the barricades of the Boulevard, which they had taken at the point of the bayonet. There they were practicing as at a mark on distant passers-by. They heard from the neighboring houses these hideous dialogues: "I lay a wager that I drop that fellow." "I say no;" "I say yes," and the shot sped on its way. If the man fell, it was announced by a loud shout of laughter. When a woman was passing by, "Fire at the woman!" cried the officer, "fire at women!" That was one of the words of command. On the Boulevard Montmartre a young captain of the staff cried, "Prick the women!" A woman thought she could cross St. Fiácre-street. She had a loaf of bread under her arm. A skirmisher brought her down.

On Jean-Jacques-Rousseau-street they did not go to those lengths. A woman cried, "Vive la République!" She was only lashed by the soldiers. But let us return to the Boulevard. A passer-by, an usher, was hit in the forehead. He fell on his hands and knees, crying "Mercy!" He received thirteen other balls in the body. He survived. By an unheard-of accident no wound proved mortal. The ball in the forehead had ploughed through the skin, and gone around the skull without piercing it. An old man of eighty-five years of age, found squatting somewhere or other, was taken before the staircase of the Prophète and shot. He fell. "He will not give himself a bump on the head," said a soldier. The old man had fallen on a heap of corpses. Two young men of Issy, married a month before, and who had married two sisters, were crossing the Boulevard coming from their business. They saw themselves aimed at. They threw themselves on their knees, and cried, "We have married two sisters!" They were killed. A cocoa-seller, named Robert, and living at No. 97, Faubourg Poissonnière, was flying down Montmartre-street, with his fountain on his back. They killed him.* A child, thirteen years old, a saddler's apprentice, was passing on the Boulevard before the Vachette coffee-house. They took aim at him. He uttered desperate cries. He was holding in his hand a bridle. He waved it, saying, "I am going on an errand." They killed him. Three balls bored through his breast. All the length of the Boulevard one heard the howling and the movements of agony made by the wounded, whom the soldiers covered with bayonet-wounds, and left without even dispatching. A few bandits took the time to steal. A cashier of a company, whose office was in Bank street, left his office at two o'clock; went to Bergère-street to cash a check;

---

* One can name the person who saw this deed. He is proscribed. It was Versigny, a representative. He says: "I see yet, at the head of Du Croissant-street, an unfortunate coffee-house keeper, walking along, with his fountain of white iron on his back. He staggered, then sank, bending down, and fell dead against the front of a shop. He alone, his only arms being his bell, had had the honor of a volley." The same witness adds: " The soldiers swept with gunshot places where no paving-stone had been touched, and where there was no combatant."

was returning with the money when he was killed on the Boulevard. When they raised the body it had on it neither purse nor watch, nor the sum of money which he had been carrying back. Under the pretext of gunshots fired on the troops, they entered ten or twelve houses, here and there, and put to the bayonet all whom they found in them. There are on all the houses of the Boulevard iron waste-pipes, by which the refuse-water is emptied into the stream. The soldiers, without knowing why, held every house which was shut up from top to bottom, and silent and gloomy, to be uttering defiance, for, like all the houses of the Boulevard, they seemed inhabited, though silent. They knocked at the doors, which opened. They entered. A moment afterward a red and smoking wave might have been seen coming out of the mouths of the waste-pipes. It was blood. A captain, with his eyes starting out of his head, cried to the soldiers: "No quarter!" A chief of battalion shrieked: "Enter the houses and kill all!"

You might have heard the sergeants say—"Hit the bèdouins, steady on the bèdouins!" "From the time of the uncle, relates a witness, "the soldiers called the citizens pèkins; really we are bèdouins. When the soldiers massacre the people, it is a cry of—*now then, down on the bèdouins.*" At the circle of Frascati, where several habitués, among others an old general, were assembled, they heard this thunder of musketry and cannonade, and they could not believe that they were firing with ball. They laughed and said—"It is only blank cartridge! What a get-up! What a comedian that Bonaparte is!" They believed themselves at the circus. Suddenly the soldiers entered furious, and wanted to kill everybody. They did not have sufficient misgiving of the danger to run; they kept on laughing. One witness says, "We thought that this made part of the farce." However, the soldiers kept threatening. At last they understood. "*Let us kill all*," said they. A lieutenant who knew the old general kept them from it. Yet a sergeant said: "*Lieutenant, let us be; it is not your business, it is ours.*" The soldiers killed for the sake of killing. A witness says they killed even the horses and dogs in the courtyards of houses.

In the house which formed with that of Frascati the corner of Richelieu-street, they wanted tranquilly to kill even the women and children; they were already heaped together for it in front of a platoon, when a colonel came up. He suspended the murder, penned up these poor trembling creatures in the Passage of Panoramas, had the gratings of it shut, and saved them. A distinguished writer, M. Lireux, having escaped the first balls, was led about during two hours from guard-house to guard-house, to be shot. It took miracles to save him. The celebrated artist, Sax, who happened to be in the music-store of Brandus, was going to be shot there, when a general recognized him. Everywhere in other places they were killing at hazard.

The first man who was killed in this butchery (history also preserves the name of the first massacred on St. Bartholomew's day) was called Theodore Debaecque, and lived in the house on the corner of Du Sentier-street, near which the carnage commenced.

CHAPTER VII.

THE slaughter ended,—that is to say, the night having set in,—they had commenced in full day,—they did not raise the corpses; they were so packed, that before a single shop—that of Barbedienne—they counted thirty-three of them.

Every square of earth, cut in round the trunks of the trees on the Boulevard, was a reservoir of blood. "The "dead," says another witness, "were crowded in heaps, "one on top of another; old men, children, blouses, and "paletots, together in an indescribable pell-mell, with "heads, arms, legs, mixed together." Another witness, who describes a group of three persons, "two were thrown "down on their backs; a third, being caught in their legs, "had fallen on them." Separate corpses were rare; people remarked them more than the others. A young man, well dressed, was seated with his back to the wall, with his legs apart, and his arms half crossed; he had a sprig of green in his right hand, and seemed to be looking at it. He was dead.

A little further on the balls had nailed against a shop a youth in pantaloons of cotton velvet, who was holding in his hand proofs from the press. The wind moved these bloody leaves on which the wrist of death was contracted. A poor old man, with white hair, was stretched in the middle of the street, with his umbrella beside him. He almost touched the elbow of a young man in varnished boots and yellow gloves, who was lying with his eye-glass yet in his eye. At a few paces from him was lying, with her head on the sidewalk and her feet on the pavement, a woman who had been flying, with her child in her arms. The mother and the child were dead, but the mother had not let go the child. Ah! you will tell me, M. Bonaparte, that you are very sorry for it, but that it was an accident; that in presence of Paris almost risen it was necessary to do something; that you had been forced to do it, since it was necessary; and that as to the coup d'état, you had debts, and your ministers had debts, and your aid-de-camps, and your foot-servants, and that you were responsible for all; that one is not prince,—what, the devil!—not to consume from time to time a few millions too much; that it is very necessary to amuse one's self and enjoy life; and that it was the fault of the Assembly, who did not understand matters, and who wished to condemn you to something like two meager millions a year, and what is more, to force you to go out of power at the end of four years, and to carry out the Constitution; that, above all, one could not go out of the Elysée to enter Clichy; that you had in vain had recourse to the little expedients foreseen by the 405th article; that scandals were approaching, and the demagogue press were prating that the affair about the ingots of gold was going to make a noise; that you owed respect to the name of Napoleon, and that, faith! having no other choice, rather than be one of the vulgar swindlers of the code, you have preferred to be one of the great assassins of history.

Then instead of defiling you, this blood has washed you clean! Very well. I continue.

CHAPTER VIII.

WHEN it was finished, Paris came to see ; the crowd flowed in upon these terrible places ; they let them go where they pleased. It was the object of the slaughterers. Louis Bonaparte did not do this thing to hide it. The south side of the Boulevard was covered with the paper of torn cartridges. The sidewalk on the north side had disappeared under the plaster dug by the balls from the fronts of the houses, and was all white, as if it had snowed ; the pools of blood made large blackish spots in this snow of ruins. The foot only avoided a corpse to encounter the splinters of glass, plaster, and stones. Certain houses were so crushed in with grape-shot and bullets, that they seemed to sink ; among others the Sallandrouze house, of which we have spoken, and the mourning-store at the corner of the Faubourg Montmartre. "Billecoq-house," says a witness, "is still to-day propped by strong sticks of timber, "and the front will be in part rebuilt. The carpet-house "is shot through and through, so as to let in the daylight in "several places." Another witness says, "All the houses, "from the Circle of Strangers to Poissonnière-street, are "literally riddled with bullets, on the right side of the "Boulevard throughout. One of the great windows of "the La Petite Jeannette warehouse had alone received "certainly more than two hundred of them. There was "not a window which did not have some ; one breathed "an atmosphere of saltpetre. Thirty-seven corpses were

"heaped in the city Bergère, the passers-by could count
"them through the grating. A woman had stopped at the
"corner of Richelieu-street, she was looking on; suddenly
"she perceived that she had her feet wet, 'I declare,' said
"she, 'it has been raining a good deal; my feet are in the
"water.' 'No, Madame,' a passer-by said to her, 'it is not
"water.' She had her feet in a pool of blood."

In Grange-Batelière-street, three corpses entirely naked might have been seen in a corner. During the killing, the barricade of the Boulevard had been taken away by the Bourgon brigade. The corpses of the defenders of the barricade of the Saint Denis gate, of which we spoke when we began this recital, were crowded before the gate of the Jouvin-house. "But," says a witness, "it was nothing compared with the heaps which covered the Boulevard." Two steps from the theater of the Varieties, the crowd stopped before a cap, full of brains and blood, hung up on the branch of a tree. A witness says: "A little beyond
"the Variétés, I came upon a corpse, with the face toward
"the ground; I wished to lift it up, helped by a few per-
"sons; some soldiers prevented us. A little farther there
"were two bodies, a man and a woman, and then a single
"one, a workman, * * * * (we abridge). From Mont-
"martre-street to Du Sentier-street one *literally walked in*
"*blood :* it covered the sidewalks in many places, to the
"depth of several lines, and without hyperbole, without
"exaggeration, precautions were necessary in order not to
"step into it; I counted there thirty-three corpses. This
"sight was too much for my strength, I felt great tears
"furrow my cheeks. I asked to cross the street to enter my
"house, which was accorded to me." A witness says: "The

"aspect of the Boulevard was horrible ; *we literally walked* "*in blood.* We counted eighteen corpses within a length "of twenty-five paces." A witness, a shopkeeper of Du Sentier-street, says : "I made the tour from the Boulevard "du Temple to my house ; I entered with an inch of "blood on my pantaloons." The representative Versiquy relates, "We perceived at a distance, near the St. Denis " gate, the immense bivouac fires of the troops ; these "were, with a few scattered lamps, the only light which "permitted one to find his way in the midst of this fright-"ful carnage. The battle of the day was nothing beside "these corpses, and this silence. R. and I were utterly crushed." A citizen came passing along ; at one of my exclamations he approached, took me by the hand and said, "You are a Republican, I was what they call a friend of "order, a reactionary ; but a man would be abandoned "by God, not to abhor this terrible orgy. France is dis-"honored ! And he quitted us sobbing." A witness, who permits us to name him, a Legitimist, the honorable M. de Cherville, declares : " In the evening I wished to " recommence these sad investigations ; I met in Lepel-" letier-street Messrs. Bouillon and Gervais, (from Caen ;) " we took several steps together, and I slipped ; I caught "myself by Mr. Bouillon ; I looked at my feet, I had trod "into a large pool of blood. Then M. Bouillon "narrated to me, that in the morning, when he was at " his window, he had seen an apothecary, whose shop "he showed me, occupied in shutting up its door. A "woman fell. The apothecary rushed out to lift her "up ; at the same instant, a soldier took aim at him, " at ten paces, and struck him down with a ball through

"his head. M. Bouillon, indignant and forgetting his own
"danger, cried to the people who stood there : 'You will
"give evidence, all of you, as to what has just happened.'"

Toward eleven o'clock, when the bivouacs were lighted throughout, M. Bonaparte permitted them to amuse themselves. There was on the Boulevard a sort of night fête. The soldiers laughed and sang, while they kept up the fires with the débris of the barricade ; and then, as at Strasbourg and Boulogne, came the distribution of money. Let us listen to what a witness says : "I saw at the St. Denis
"gate, an officer of the staff deliver two hundred francs to
"the chief of a detachment of twenty men, saying to him,
"'The prince has charged me to deliver this money to
"you, to be distributed to your brave soldiers ; and he
"will not confine the proofs of his satisfaction to this.'
"Each soldier received ten francs." On the evening of Austerlitz the Emperor said : "Soldiers, I am satisfied
"with you!" Another adds : "The soldiers, with cigars
"in their mouths, bantered the passers-by, jingling the
"money which they had in their pockets." Another says :
"The officers broke the rouleaux of Louis like sticks of
"chocolate." The sentinels only permitted women to pass ; if a man presented himself, they cried to him :
"Off." The tables were set in the bivouacs ; officers and soldiers were drinking there. The flames of the quick clear fires were reflected on all their joyous countenances. The corks and white tops of the champagne bottles swam in the gutters, which were red with blood. From bivouac to bivouac, they were calling each other with loud shouts, and obscene jokes. They hailed each other with Vive les gens-d'armes ! long live the lancers ! and all added : Long

live Louis Napoleon ! One heard the clashing of glasses and the sound of breaking bottles.—Here and there, in the shade, with a yellow wax candle or a lantern in their hands, women were roaming among the corpses, looking at the pale faces one after another, this one trying to find her son, that one her father, a third her husband.

CHAPTER IX.

Let us get through these frightful details at once.

The day following, the fifth, at the Montmartre cemetery, a shocking object could be seen. A vast space which had remained vacant till this day, was "made useful" for the temporary burial of a few of the slaughtered. They were buried with their heads out of the ground so that their families might recognize them. The greater part with the feet out also, and they had only a little earth on their breasts. The crowd came there; the flow of the curious pushed you on; you wandered among graves; every moment you felt the earth bend in under your feet; you had trodden on the stomach of a corpse. You turned around, you saw boots, wooden shoes, women's buskins, come out of the earth; on the other side of you was the head that your pressure on the body had made start up.

An illustrious witness, the great statuary David, to-day proscribed and a wanderer outside of France, says: "I "saw at the Montmartre cemetery forty corpses with their "clothes still on; they had placed them side by side; a few "shovelfuls of earth hid them up to the head, which they "had left exposed so that their relations might recognize "them. There was so little earth that one saw the feet still "uncovered, and the public walked on these bodies; it was "horrible! There were noble heads of young men there, "bearing the stamp of courage; in the midst was a poor "woman, the servant of a baker, who had been killed "carrying bread to the customers of her master, and beside "her a beautiful young girl who had sold flowers on the "Boulevard. Those who were looking for persons who had "disappeared were obliged to trample on the feet of bodies "so that they might get a view of their faces. I heard a "common man say, with an expression of horror : One "walks as if he were walking on a spring-board."

The crowd continued to collect at the different places where victims had been deposited, especially the city Bergère, so much so that the same day, the fifth, as the multitude increased and became troublesome, and it was necessary to keep off the curious, one could read on a great bill at the entrance these words, in capital letters : *There are no more corpses here.*

The three naked corpses of Grange Batelière-street were not taken away till the evening of the fifth. You plainly saw, we emphasize it, that at first; and for the capital which it hoped to make out of it, the coup d'état did not try the least in the world to hide its crime ; shame did not come to it till later ; on the contrary, the first day they made a display of it. Atrocity did not satisfy, cynical audacity was necessary. To slaughter was only the means, to terrify was the end.

CHAPTER X.

WAS this object attained? Yes. Immediately, from the evening of the 4th of December, the effervescence of public feeling ceased, stupor froze Paris. The indignation which raised its voice before the coup d'état became suddenly mute in the presence of the carnage. This no longer resembled history. One feels as if one was dealing with the unknown.

Crassus crushed the gladiators; Herod cut the children's throats; Charles the Ninth exterminated the Huguenots; Peter of Russia the Strélitz; Mahomet-Ali the Mamelukes; Mahmoud the Janezaries; Danton massacred the prisoners. Louis Bonaparte has invented a new mode of slaughter, the massacre of passers-by.

It ended the struggle. There are hours when that which ought to exasperate the people fills them with consternation. The population of Paris felt that it had the foot of a bandit on its back. They struggled no longer. This same evening, Mathieu (from la Drôme) entered the place where the committee of resistance were in session, and said to us:—"We are no longer at Paris, we are no longer the Republic; we are at Naples, and in the house of King Bomba." From this moment, notwithstanding the efforts of the committee of the Republican representatives and their courageous helpers, there was further resistance at a few points only, for example, at the barricade of the Petit-Carreau, where Denis Dussoubs, the brother of the representative, fell so heroically; but it was a resistance which was less a struggle than the last convulsions of despair. All was over.

The next day, the fifth, the victorious troops were parading on the Boulevards. One saw a general show his naked saber to the people and cry: "The Republic? there it is!" Thus an infamous butchery, the massacre of passers-by, was what the "measure" of the 2d of December involved as a supreme necessity. To undertake it, it was necessary to be a traitor; to make it succeed, it was necessary to be a murderer. It was by this proceeding that the coup d'état conquered France and Paris! Yes, Paris! One has to repeat it to himself. It is at *Paris* that this thing took place! Great God! the baskirs entered Paris with the lance lifted and singing their savage chant, Moscow had been burned; the Prussians entered Paris, they had taken Berlin; the Austrians entered Paris, they had bombarded Vienna; the English entered Paris, the camp of Boulogne had menaced London; they arrived at our boundaries, these men of all nations, with drums beating, with clarions in front, with flags displayed, with sabers drawn, cannon rolling, matches lighted, drunk, enemies, conquerors, avengers, shouting with fury before the domes of Paris the names of their capitals, London, Berlin, Vienna, Moscow. Well, from the time that they put foot on the soil of this city, from the time that the hoofs of their horses rang on the pavements of our streets, Austrians, English, Prussians, Russians, all, in entering Paris, saw in these walls, in these buildings, in this people, something predestinated, venerable and august; all felt the holy honor of the sacred city, and understood that they did not have there before them the city of a people, but of the human race; all lowered the sword!

Yes, massacre the Parisians, treat Paris like a place taken by assault, put to the sack a quarter of Paris, violate the Second Eternal City, murder civilization in its shrine, mow down old men, children, and women with grape-shot in this great enclosure, this light-house of the world. What Wellington forbade to his half naked mountaineers, what Schwartzenburg refused to his Croats, what Blucher did not permit his landwehr to do, nor Platow dare to have done by his Cossacks, thou hast made French soldiers do, wretch!

BOOK FOURTH.—THE OTHER CRIMES.

CHAPTER I.

SINISTER QUESTIONS.

WHAT is the total of the dead? Louis Bonaparte, perceiving history approach, and imagining that Charles the Ninths are able to extenuate St. Bartholomews, has published, by way of justification, a statement of the "deceased persons," called "official." One remarks in this "alphabetical list"* allusions such as these: Adde, bookseller, Boulevard Poissonnière, 17, killed in his house; Boursier, child, 7 years and a half old, killed in Tiquetonne-street; Belval, cabinet-maker, La Lune-street, No. 10, killed in his house; Coquard, freeholder at Vire (Calvados), killed, Boulevard Montmartre; Debaecque, merchant, Du Sentier-street, 45, killed at his house; De Convercelle, florist, St. Denis-street, 257, killed at his house; Labilte, jeweler, boulevard Saint Martin, 63, killed at his house;

---

* The employee who prepared this list we know as a scientific and exact statistician; he prepared it in good faith, we do not doubt. He verified what they showed him, and what they allowed him to ascertain; but he was able to arrive at no certainty about what they hid from him. The field remains open to conjecture.

Monpelas, perfumer, St. Martin-street, 181, killed at his house; Grellier, spinster, working-woman, Faubourg St. Martin, 209, killed Boulevard Montmartre; Guillard, shop-woman, Faubourg St. Denis, 77, killed Boulevard St. Denis; Garnier, confidential business woman, Boulevard Bonne-Nouvelle, No. 6, killed Boulevard St. Denis; Ledaust, working-woman, Passage du Cassé, 76, at the dead-house; Frances Noel, waistcoatmaker, Des Fosse, Montmartre-street, 20, dead at the Charity; Count Poninski, annuitant, De la Paix-street, 32, killed Boulevard Montmartre; Radoisson, mantua-maker, dead at the Maison Nationale de Santé; Vidal, 97, Temple-street, dead at the Hôtel-Dieu; Séquin, embroiderer, St. Martin, 240, dead at Beaujon hospital; Miss Leniac, shop-girl, Temple-street, 196, dead at the Beaujon hospital; Thirion de Montauban, landlord, de Lancry-street, 10, killed at his door; etc., etc.

Let us abridge. Louis Bonaparte, in this document, *avows one hundred and ninety-one assassinations.*

This registered statement taken for what it is worth, what is the true total? What is the real number of victims? With how many corpses is the coup d'état of December strewed? Who can tell? Who knows? Who will ever know? As we have seen above, one witness deposes: "I counted there thirty-three corpses." Another, at another point on the Boulevard, says: "We counted eighteen corpses within a length of twenty or twenty-five paces." Another, standing elsewhere, says: "There were, within sixty paces, more than sixty corpses." The writer, so long time threatened with death, told us ourselves: "I saw with my own eyes more than eight hundred dead throughout all the length of the Boulevard." Now search, calculate, what broken skulls and chests plowed with grape-shot are necessary to cover, literally with blood, a quarter of a league of boulevard. Do as the wives did, as the sisters did, as the daughters did, as the despairing mothers did: take a torch, go away into this night, feel on the ground, feel the pavement, the wall; pick up the corpses, question the specters, and count if you can the number of victims! One is reduced to conjectures. It is a question which history reserves. As for us, we assume the duty of examining it to its depths at a future time. The first day, Louis Bonaparte made a show of his slaughter. We have said why: it was useful to him. After which, having drawn from the thing all the advantage which he desired, he hid it. They gave the order to the newspapers in his interests to keep quiet about it, to Magnan to omit it, to the historians to ignore it. They interred the dead after midnight, without torches, without processions, without chants, without priests,—furtively. They forbade the families to weep too loud. And there was not only the massacre on the Boulevard, there was the rest—summary fusillades, unpublished executions.

One of the witnesses whom we interrogated asked a major of the gendarmerie mobile, which distinguished itself in these slaughters: "Well, let us see! The number? Is it four hundred?" The man shrugged his shoulders. "Is it six hundred?" The man shook his head. "Is it eight hundred?" "Add twelve hundred," said the officer, "and you will not be beyond it." To the present hour nobody knows exactly what the 2d of December is, what it did, what it dared, whom it has killed, whom it has shrouded, whom it has buried. Since the morning of the crime the printing-offices have been put under seal, speech has been suppressed by Louis Bonaparte, the man of silence and of night. The 2d, 3d, 4th, 5th, and since, the truth has been taken by the throat and strangled at the moment when it was about to speak. It has not even been able to utter a cry. He has tried to thicken obscurity over his ambush and he has partially succeeded. Whatever may be the efforts of history, the 2d of December will be plunged, perhaps for a long time yet, in a sort of frightful twilight. This crime is composed of audacity and darkness; on one side it spreads itself out cynically in full day; on the other it undresses itself and goes away into the fog. An effrontery oblique and hideous which hides one knows not what monstrosities under its mantle! What one catches a glimpse of is enough. On a certain side of the 2d of December all is darkness, but one sees tombs in this darkness. Under this grand outrage one distinguishes confusedly a *crowd* of outrages.

Providence desires it thus. He attaches necessities to treasons. Ah! you perjure yourself! you violate your oath! you infringe right and justice! Well! take a cord, for you will be forced to strangle; take a poignard, for you will be forced to stab; take a club, for you will be forced to crush; take shadow and night, for you will be forced to hide yourself. One crime necessitates another; horror is full of logic. One does not stop, one does not hesitate. Go! this first; well. And then that, and then still that; advance always! the law is like the veil of the temple; when it is torn, it is from the top to the bottom. Yes, let us repeat it, in what they call the 2d of December one finds crime at every depth. Perjury on the surface, assassination at the bottom. Individual murders, slaughters en masse, volleys of grape-shot in full day, volleys of musketry by night, a vapor of blood issues from all parts of the coup d'état. Search in the public graves of the cemeteries, search under the pavements of the streets, under the slopes of the Champs de Mars, under the trees in the public gardens, look in the bed of the Seine! Few revelations.

It is perfectly plain. Bonaparte has had the monstrous art to bind to himself a crowd of miserable men in the offices of the nation, by I know not what universal complicity. The stamped paper of the magistrates, the ink-horns of the recorders, the cartridge-boxes of the soldiers, the prayers of the priests, are his accomplices.

He has cast his crime around him like a net, and the prefects, the mayors, the judges, the officers, and the soldiers are taken in it. The complicity descends from the general to the corporal, and re-ascends from the corporal to the president. The policeman feels himself as much compromised as the minister. The gendarme, whose pistol is at the ear of an unfortunate, and whose uniform is splashed with human brains, feels himself as guilty as the colonel. Above, atrocious men gave orders which were executed below by ferocious men. Ferocity keeps the secret with atrocity.

Hence this hideous silence.

Between this ferocity and this atrocity, there is even a strife and emulation, what escapes the one, the other seizes again. The future will not be able to believe these prodigies of animosity. A workman was passing by on the Pont-au-Change, some marching gendarmes arrested him, they smelt his hands. He smells of powder, said a gendarme. They shoot the workman; four balls passed through his body. Throw him into the water, cries a sergeant. The gendarmes take him by the head and feet and throw him over the balustrade of the bridge. The man shot and drowned goes away down the river. However, he is not dead; the icy cold of the river revives him; he is past making a movement, his blood flows into the water from four wounds, but his blouse sustains him. He comes ashore under the arch of a bridge. There the harbor people find him, they pick him up, they carry him to the hospital, he gets well; and when convalescent he goes out. The next day they arrest him, and bring him before a court-martial. Death having refused him, Louis Bonaparte takes him back. The man is to-day at Lambessa! What the Champs de Mars especially has seen, the frightful nocturnal scenes which have terrified and dishonored it, history can no longer tell. Thanks to Louis Bonaparte, this august field of the federation must be henceforth called Aceldama!

One of the miserable soldiers whom the man of December has transformed into an executioner, relates with horror and below his breath, that in a single night the number of those shot was not less than eight hundred. Louis Bonaparte has dug a grave in haste, and cast his crime into it. A few shovelfuls of earth, the holy-water of a priest, and all was told. Now, the imperial carnival dances over it. Is that all? Is it finished? Does God permit and accept such shrouding? Do not believe it. Some day, between the marble pavements of the Elysée and the Tuileries, this grave will re-open suddenly, and one will see all the corpses come forth with their wounds one after the other. The young man stabbed to the heart, the old man shaking his old head pierced by a ball, the mother sabered with her slain infant in her arms, all standing, livid, terrible, and fixing on the assassin their bloody eyes! Awaiting that day, and from the present moment, history commences your trial, Louis Bonaparte. History rejects your official list of the dead and your justifying statements. History says that they lie, and that you lie. You have put a bandage over the eyes of France and a gag in her mouth. Why? Is it that you may do loyal actions? No, crimes. Who fears the light does evil. You have shot people by night, at the Champs de Mars, at the Prefectures, at the Palais de Justice, on the squares, on the quays, everywhere. You say no. I say yes. With you, one has the right to suppose, to suspect, to accuse, and when you deny, one has the right to believe; your denial is recognized as an affirmation. Your 2d of December is pointed at by the public conscience. No one thinks of it without a secret shudder. What did you do in that shadow there? Your days are hideous, your nights are suspected. Ah, what a man of darkness you are! Let us return to the butchery of the Boulevards, to the words: "Let them execute my orders," and to the day of the 4th. Louis Bonaparte on the evening of that day ought to have compared himself to Charles X., who did not desire to burn Paris; and with Louis Philippe, who did not wish to shed the blood of the people: and he ought to have done himself this justice, and claimed that he was a great politician! A few days afterward, M. Le général Th., formerly attached to one of Louis Philippe's sons, came to the Elysée. As far as Louis Bonaparte could see him, making in his mind the comparison which we have just indicated, he cried with an air of triumph to the general: "Well? M. Louis Bonaparte is actually the man who said to one of his former ministers, from whom we have it, '*If I had been Charles X., and if in the days of July I had taken Laffite, Benjamin Constant, and Lafayette, I would have had them shot like dogs.*'" The 4th of December Louis Bonaparte would have been torn in the evening from the Elysée, and the law would have triumphed, if he had been one of these men who hesitate before a massacre. By good luck for him, he had none of that delicacy. A few corpses more or less, what difference does that make? Come, kill! Kill at hazard! Saber, shoot, cannonade, crush, grind! Terrify me this odious city of Paris! The coup d'état was leaning over, this great murder raised it up again. Louis Bonaparte had failed to destroy himself by his felony, he saved himself by his ferocity. If he had only been Faliero it would have been all up with him; happily he was Cæsar Borgia. He went to swim with his crime in a river of blood; a less guilty man would have been drowned. He crossed it. That is what they call his success. To-day he is on the other bank, trying to dry himself, all streaming with the blood which he takes for the purple, and demanding the empire.

CHAPTER II.

A SUCCESSION OF CRIMES.

AND there is this malefactor! And one would not applaud thee, O Truth! when, in "the eyes of Europe, in the eyes of the world, in the presence of the people, before the face of God; while calling honor, the oath, faith, religion, sacredness of the human life, the right, the generosity of all souls, wives, sisters, mothers, civilization, liberty, the Republic, France to witness; before his valets, his Senate, and his Council of State; before his generals, his priests, and his agents of police; those who represented the people, for the people are reality; those who represented intelligence, for intelligence is light; those who represented humanity, for humanity is reason; in the name of this people enchained, in the name of intelligence proscribed, in the name of humanity outraged; before this heap of slaves who cannot or who dare not say a word, thou dost lash this brigand of order like a dog! Ah, let somebody else pick out moderate words. Yes, I am clear and hard, I am without pity for this merciless man, and I glory in it. Let us go on. To what we have just recounted add all the other crimes, to which we shall have more than one occasion to return, and whose history we will recount in detail, if God grant us life. Let us add the incarcerations en masse, aggravated by ferocious circumstances, the prisons overflowing.* The sequestration† of the goods of the proscribed in ten departments, especially in Nievre, in l'Allier, and in les Basses-Alpes; let us add the confiscation of the goods of Orleans, with that morsel given to the clergy. Schinderhannes always took the part of the clergy. Add the mixed commission, and the commission called that of clemency;‡ the courts-martial, com-

---

* The *Bulletin des Lois* publishes the following decree, under the date of 27th March: "Seeing that the law of the 10th of May, 1838, classes the ordinary expenses of the prisons of the departments among those which ought to be inscribed upon the budgets of the departments: Considering that such is not the character of the expenses occasioned by the arrests which have taken place following the events of December: considering that the facts, because of which these arrests were multiplied, were connected with a plot against the safety of the State, the suppression of which was of consequence to all society, and that for that reason it is best to make the public treasury meet the excess of expenditure which resulted from the *extraordinary* increase of the numbers imprisoned, it is decreed: There is opened to the Minister of the Interior, on the funds of the budget of 1851, an extraordinary credit of 250,000 francs, to be applied to the payment of the expenses resulting from the arrests effected in consequence of the events of December."

† Digne, the 5th of January, 1852.—"The colonel commanding during the state of siege in the departments of the Basses-Alpes—Appoints—After ten days' delay, the goods of those inculpated, who have taken flight, will be sequestered, and administered by the director of the domains in the department of Basses-Alpes, conformably with the laws civil and military, etc.—Fririon." One could cite ten similar proclamations of martial law. The first of the malefactors who committed this crime of confiscation of goods, and who set the example of this kind of arrests, is called Eynard. He is a general. Since the 18th December he put under sequestration the goods of a certain number of citizens from Moulins, "because," said he, cynically, "the examination which has been commenced leaves no doubt as to the part which they took in the insurrection and the pillaging of the department of Allier."

‡ The number of condemnations entirely carried out (they had reference

bined with the duty of the examining magistrates and multiplying the abominations; the people exiled by batches; the expulsion of a part of France out of France; from no more than a single department, Hérault, three thousand two hundred banished or transported. Add this shocking proscription, comparable with the most tragic desolations of history, which, for tendency, for opinion, for honestly differing from this government, for a word of a free man, spoken even before the 2d of December, takes, seizes, arrests, tears the laborer from his field, the workman from his trade, the freeholder from his house, the physician from his patients, the notary from his study, the councillor-general from his administration, the judge from his tribunal, the husband from his wife, the brother from his brother, the father from his children, the child from his parents, and marks all foreheads with a sinister cross, from the highest to the most obscure. No one escapes him. A man in rags, with his beard long, enters my room one morning at Bruxells. "I have just arrived," says he. "I have made the journey on foot. It is two days since I have eaten anything." You give him some bread. He eats. I say to him: "Where do you come from?" "From Limoges." "Why are you here?" "I do not know. They chased me from my home." "What are you?" "I am a sabot-maker." Add Africa, add Guiana, add the

---

most generally to transportations) were found, at the date of the reports, as follows:—

    Arrested by M. Canrobert 3876
         "   M. Espinasse 3625
         "   M. Quenlin Bauchart . 1634

                Total 9735

atrocities of Bertrand, the atrocities of Martinprey, those of
Canrobert and Espinasse, the cargoes of women dispatched
by General Goyon, the representative Miot dragged from
casemate to casemate, the barracks where there are a hundred and fifty under the sun of the tropics, huddled promiscuously, with filth, with vermin, and where all these innocent people are dying, far from their friends, in fever, in
misery, in horror, in despair, wringing their hands. Add
all those unfortunates delivered to the gendarmes, bound
two and two, stowed away in the spare-decks of the *Magellan*, of the *Canada*, or of the *Duguesclin;* cast away to
Lambessa, cast to Cayenne, without knowing what they
wanted with them, without being able to guess what they
had done. This one, Alphonse Lambert, from l'Indre,
torn from his bed, dying; that other, Patureau Francœur,
vine-dresser, transported, because in his village they had
wished to make him president of the Republic; this
other, Valette, carpenter at Chatearouse, transported for
having, six months before the 2d of December, on a day of
capital punishment, refused to set up the guillotine. Add
the hunt after men in the villages, the beating of Viroy in
the mountains of Lure, the beating of Pellion in the Bois
de Clamecy with fifteen hundred men; order re-established
at Crest, two thousand insurgents, three hundred killed;
marching columns everywhere; Charles Sauvan at Marseilles cries "Vive la République!" A grenadier of the
54th fires on him, the ball entering at the loins and going
out at the stomach. Vincent, from Bourges, is assistant of
his commune; he protests, as a magistrate, against the
coup d'état; they track him in his village; he flies, they
pursue; a cavalry man cuts off two of his fingers with a

saber-stroke, another cuts open his head. He falls. They transport him to Fort d'Ivry before dressing his wounds. He is an old man of seventy-six years of age. Add such facts as these: In Cher, the representative Viguier was arrested. Arrested, what for? Because he is a representative, because he is inviolable, *because the suffrage of the people* has made him sacred. They cast Viguier into prison. One day they allowed him to be absent for one hour to attend to business which absolutely required his presence. Before going out, two gendarmes, named Pierre Guérêt and Dubernelle, the latter a brigadier, seized upon Viguier; the brigadier joined his hands in such a way that the palms were pressed together, and bound them tightly with a chain; the end of the chain hung down; the brigadier made the chain go around once more by main force at the risk of breaking or bruising his wrists by the pressure. The hands of the prisoner became blue and swelled. "You are torturing me by this," says Viguier, quietly. "Hide your hands," says the gendarme, chuckling, "if you are ashamed." "Wretch!" replied Viguier, "you are the man that this chain dishonors, not I." Viguier traversed in this plight the streets of Bourges that he had frequented for twenty years, between two gendarmes, raising his hands, showing his chains. The representative Viguier is seventy years of age. Add the summary fusillades in twenty departments. "Every one who resists," wrote M. St. Arnaud, minister of war, "is to be shot in the name of society, in legitimate defence."*

---

* Here is this odious dispatch, just as it appeared in the *Moniteur*:—
"All armed insurrection has ceased in Paris, on account of rigorous suppression. The same energy will have the same effect everywhere.

"Six days sufficed to crush the insurrection," General Levaillant sent word. (He was commanding during martial law in Var.) "I have made good captures," De St.-Etienne sends word to the commandant at Viroy; "I have shot without seizure eight individuals; I am hunting the ring-leaders in the woods." At Bordeaux, General Bourjoly enjoins upon the marching columns to have all individuals shot who were found with arms in their hands. At Forcalquier, it is still better. The proclamation of martial law runs as follows: "The city of Forcalquier is under martial law; citizens *who have not taken part* in the events of the day, who have arms, are summoned to deliver them up on pain of being shot." The marching column of Pézénas arrived at Servian; a man tried to escape from a surrounded house; they shot him dead. At Entrains they made twenty-five prisoners; one tried to save himself by swimming, they fired on him, a ball hit him, he disappeared under the water; they shot the others. To these cursed things add these *infamous* things: at Brioude, in Haute-Loire, a man and a woman thrown into prison for having worked in the field of one who had been proscribed; at Loriol, in Drôme, Astier of the rural guard, condemned to twenty years' work, of forced work, for having given asylum to fugitives; add, and the pen trembles to write this, the death penalty re-established, the political guillotine again set up, horrible sentences; citizens condemned to

---

Bands which are engaged in pillage, rape, and arson put themselves beyond the protection of the law. With such one does not use argument, nor give any summons to disperse; one attacks them and disperses them. Everybody who resists ought to be *shot* in the name of society, in legitimate defence."

death on the scaffold by the janizary judges of courts-martial; at Clamecy, Millelot, Jouannin, Guillemot, Sabatier and Four; at Lyons, Courty, Romegal, Bressieux, Fauritz, Julien, Roustain, and Garan, adjunct of the mayor of Cliousat; at Montpelier, seventeen for the affair of Bédarrieux: Mercadier, Delpech, Denis, André, Barthez, Triadou, Piérre Carriére, Galzy, Calas called le Vacher, Gardy, Jacques Pages, Michel Hercules, Nar, Vène, Frié, Malaterre, Beaumont, Pradal; the six last, by good luck, contumacious; and at Montpelier four others: Choumac, Vidal, Cadelard, de Pagès.

What is the crime of these men? Their crime is yours, if you are a good citizen, it is mine, who write these lines. It is obedience to the 110th article of the Constitution. It is armed resistance to the outrage of Louis Bonaparte; and yet this council "orders that the execution shall take place in the *ordinary form*, on one of the public places of Bèziers" for the four last, and for the seventeen others on one of the public squares of Rédar-rieux." The *Moniteur* announces it. It is true that the *Moniteur* also at the same time announces that the collation at the last ball at the Tuileries was prepared by three hundred stewards, in the style rigorously prescribed by the ceremonial of the ancient imperial house. Unless a universal cry of horror stops this man, all these heads will fall. At this very hour in which we write here is what has just happened at Belley:

A man from Bugez, near Belley, a workman named Charlet, had ardently sustained the candidateship of Louis Bonaparte up to the 10th of December, 1848. He had distributed bulletins, contributed, canvassed, hawked; the election was for him a triumph; he believed in Louis Napoleon; he took as serious the socialistic writings of the man of Ham and his humanitarian and republican bills; on the 10th of December there were a good many of these honest dupes, who are to-day the most indignant of opponents. When Louis Bonaparte was in power, when one saw the man at work, the illusions vanished. Charlet, a man of intelligence, was one of those whose republican probity revolted, and little by little, in proportion as Louis Bonaparte sank more and more into reaction, Charlet detached himself from him; he passed thus from adhesion the most confident, to opposition the most loyal and active.

It is the history of many other noble hearts. On the 2d of December Charlet did not hesitate. In presence of all the combined attempts in the infamous act of Louis Bonaparte, Charlet felt the law stir in him; he said that he ought to be so much the more severe since he was one of those whose confidence had been the most betrayed. He understood truly that there was but one duty for a citizen, a strict duty, and one which was indistinguishable from the right to defend the Republic, to defend the Constitution, and to resist by all possible means the man whom the left, and his crime still more than the left, had outlawed. The refugees from Switzerland passed the frontier in arms, crossed the Rhone near Anglefort and entered the department of Ain. Charlet joined them. At Seyssel the little band encountered the custom-house people. The latter, willing or misled accomplices of the coup d'état, wished to oppose their passage. An engagement took place, one custom-house agent was killed. Charlet was taken.

The coup d'état brought Charlet before a court-martial. They accused him of the death of the custom-house officer, which, after all, was only an accident in the fight. In any case Charlet was guiltless of this death; the man had fallen pierced by a ball, and Charlet had no arm but a sharpened file. Charlet did not recognize the group of men who pretended to judge him as a tribunal. He said to them: "You are not judges; where is the law? the law is on my side." He refused to answer.

Interrogated on the fact of the death of the employee, he could have cleared up everything with a word; but to descend to an explanation would have been in a certain degree to accept the tribunal. He did not desire it; he kept silence. "These men condemned him to death according to the ordinary form of criminal executions." The condemnation pronounced, they seemed to forget him; days weeks, months, ran by. On all sides in the prison they said to Charlet: "You are saved." The 29th of June, at daybreak, the city of Belley saw a dismal thing. The scaffold had come out of the earth during the night, and was standing erect in the middle of the public square. The inhabitants accosted each other, pale as death, and asked each other: "Have you seen what is on the square?" "Yes." "For whom?" It was for Charlet. The sentence of death had been referred to M. Bonaparte; it had slumbered for a long time at the Elysée; they had other business; but one fine morn, after seven months, after everybody had forgotten about the engagement at Seyssel, and the slain custom-house officer and Charlet, M. Bonaparte, having probably wanted to put something between the fête of the 10th of May and that of the 15th of August, signed the order for the execution. On the 29th of June, scarcely a few days ago, Charlet was taken from his prison. They told him that he was going to die. He remained calm. A man who is on the side of justice does not fear death, for he feels that there are two things belonging to him: the one, his body, which they may kill; the other, justice, whose arm they do not bind, and whose head does not fall under the knife. They wished to have Charlet ride in a cart. "No," said he, to the gendarmes, "I will go on foot; I can walk, I am not afraid." The crowd was great when he passed. Everybody in the city knew him and loved him; his friends tried to catch a look from him. Charlet, with his arms tied behind his back, bowed to many on the right and left. "Good-bye, Jacques! good-bye, Pierre!" said he, and smiled. "Good-bye, Charlet," they answered, and all wept. The gendarmes and the troops of the line surrounded the scaffold. He mounted it with a quiet and firm step. When they saw him standing erect on the scaffold, a shuddering seized the crowd; the women uttered cries, the men shook their fists. While they were buckling him on the platform he looked at the knife and said: "When I think that I have been a Bonapartist!" and then raising his eyes to heaven, he cried, "Vive la République!" A moment after his head fell. There was mourning in Belley, and in all the villages of Ain. "How did he die?" they asked. "Bravely." "God be praised!"

It is in this fashion that a man has just been killed. Thought succumbs, and sinks in horror in presence of a fact so monstrous. This crime, added to the other crimes, completes them, and seals them with a sort of sinister seal. It is more than a completion of them, it is a crowning of them. One feels that M. Bonaparte ought to be content. To have, it matters not whom, shot in the night in obscure places, in solitude, at the Champs de Mars, under the arches of the bridges, behind a deserted wall, at hazard, pell-mell, unknown specters, even the number of whom one does not know; to have the nameless killed by the nameless, and that all this should go away into the darkness, into nothingness, into forgetfulness; in fact, it is little satisfactory to our vanity; one has the air of hiding himself, and truly one hides himself effectively; it is mediocre. People who have scruples have the right to tell you: "You see plainly that you also are afraid; you would not dare to do these things in public; you recoil before your own acts." And in a certain measure they seem to be right. To musket people by night, that is a violation of all laws, divine and human; but it is not sufficiently insolent. One does not feel himself triumphant after it. Something better is possible. The full day, the public square, the legal scaffold, the regular apparatus of social vengeance, to deliver innocent men to that, to make them perish in that manner. Ah! that is different; speak to me of this! To commit a murder in full noon, in the very middle of a village, by means of a machine called a court-martial, by means of another machine slowly built by a carpenter, put together, bolted, screwed, and greased at leisure; to say, it will be at such an hour; to bring two baskets and say: "This will be for the body, this will be for the head;" the hour arriving, to take the victim, bound with cords, assisted by a priest, to proceed to the murder with calmness. To charge the registrars to prepare an accurate record of it; to surround the murder with the gendarmes and the drawn saber, in such a manner that the people who are there shudder, and no longer know what they are looking at, and doubt if these men in uniform are a brigade of gendarmes or a band of brigands, and ask themselves, while watching the man who lets the knife go, whether he is the executioner or whether he is not rather an assassin! This is what is bold and firm; this is a parody on a legal proceeding very shameless and very tempting, and worth the trouble of carrying out; this is a grand and splendid blow on the cheek of justice. Very well! To do that seven months after the struggle, coldly, uselessly, as a slip of memory that one repairs, as a duty that one accomplishes, it is shocking, it is complete; one has an air of being in the right which stupefies the conscience, and which make honest men shudder. Terrible comparison, and one which contains the whole situation. Here are two men, a workman and a prince. The prince commits a crime, he enters the Tuileries: the workman does his duty, he mounts the scaffold.. And who is it who erects the scaffold for the workman? it is the prince. Yes, this man who, if he had been conquered in December, would only have escaped the death penalty by the omnipotence of progress, and by an application, surely too generous, of the inviolability of human life. This man, this Louis Bonaparte, this prince who adopts in his policy Poulmann's and Soufflard's style of doing things, it is he who rebuilds the scaffold! and he does not tremble! he does not grow pale! and he does not perceive that it is a fatal ladder which is there, that one is able to desist from raising it, but that once raised, one is no longer able to throw it down; and that he who sets it up for others finds it harder for himself! It recognizes him, and says: "You have put me here! I have waited for you." No! this man does not reason; he has wants, he has caprices; it is necessary that he should satisfy them. These are the desires of a dictator.

Omnipotence would be insipid if one did not season it in this style. Come, cut off Charlet's head, and the heads of the others; M. Bonaparte is prince-president of the French Republic; M. Bonaparte has sixteen millions a year, forty-four thousand francs a day; twenty-eight cooks for his personal service, as many aids-de-camp; he has the right of fishing in the ponds of Saclay and St. Quentin, and of hunting in the forests of Laign, d'Ourscamp, and of Carlemont, and in the woods of Champagne and Barbeau; he has the Tuileries, the Louvre, the Elysée, Rambouillet, Saint Cloud, Fontainebleau, Versailles, Compiègne; he has his imperial box at all the plays, fête, and gala-day, and music every day; the smile of M. Sibour,* and the arm of Mme. la Marquise de Douglas to enter a ball-room,—all that does not suffice him, he still must have the guillotine. He must have a few of these red baskets among the baskets of Champagne. Oh! let us hide our faces with our hands! This man—this hideous butcher of right and of justice—had still his apron on his stomach and his hands in the smoking entrails of the Constitution, and his feet in the blood of all the slaughtered laws, when you, judges, you, magistrates, men of the law, men of the right * * * But I stop; I will find you again, later on, with your black robes and your red robes, with your robes of the color of ink and your robes the color of blood, and I will find them again, also: I have already chastised them, and will chastise them again—those others,

---

* Then Archbishop of Paris.

your chiefs, these jurist sustainers of the ambush, these prostituted men, this Delangle, this Baroche, this Suin, this Royer, this Mongis, this Rouher, this Troplong, deserter of the laws, all those names which no longer express anything else than the quantity of contempt possible to man. And if he has not sawed these victims between two planks, like Christiern II.; if he has not buried these people alive, like Ludovic the Moor; if he has not built the walls of his palace out of living men and stones, like Timour-Beig, who was born, says the legend, with hands clinched and full of blood; if he has not ripped up the stomachs of pregnant women, like Cæsar, Duke de Valentinois; if he has not had women kicked by horses in the breast, *testibusque viros*, like Ferdinand of Toledo; if he has not roasted alive, burned alive, boiled alive, skinned alive, crucified, impaled, quartered, don't blame him for it, it is not his fault: it is because the century obstinately refuses to let him do it. He has done all that was humanly or inhumanly possible; the nineteenth century—century of sweetness, the century of decline, as the absolutists and the papists say—being given, Louis Bonaparte has equalled in ferocity his contemporaries, Haynau, Radetzky, Filangieri, Schwartzenberg, and Ferdinand of Naples, and has even surpassed them. A rare merit, and one of which it is necessary to keep account; as also of one difficulty in addition: the scene transpired in France. Let us render him this justice: in the times in which we live, Ludovic Sforza, le Valentinois, the Duke of Alva, Timour, and Christiern II., would have done nothing more than Louis Bonaparte. In their epoch, he would have done all that they have; in ours, at the moment of constructing and erecting gibbets, wheels, racks, cranes for torture by the kicking and plunging of horses, living towers, crosses, and piles of wood, they would have stopped as he has, in spite of them and mysteriously to them, before the secret and invincible resistance of the moral centre, before the invisible force of progress accomplished, before the formidable and mysterious refusal of an entire century, which arises at the north, at the south, at the east, at the west, around tyrants, and tells them, No !

CHAPTER III.

WHAT 1852 MIGHT HAVE BEEN.

But without this execrable "necessity," the 2d of December, as the accomplices, and following them the dupes, call it, what would have taken place in France? My God! this. Let us go back a few steps and briefly recall the situation as it was before the coup d'état.

The party of the past, under the name of the party of order, resisted the Republic, in other words resisted the future. Let one oppose it or not, let one consent to it or not, every illusion laid aside, the Republic is the future of nations; it may be near or far, but it is inevitable. How shall the Republic be established? It can be established in two ways: by struggle or by progress.

The Democrats wish it by progress; their opponents, the men of the past, seem to wish it by struggle. As we have just recalled, the men of the past resist; they are bitterly obstinate; they strike the tree with the hatchet, imagining that this will arrest the sap which mounts. They are prodigal of force, puerility, and anger. Let us cast no bitter words at our ancient adversaries who have fallen together with us, the same day that we fell, and several honorably, as far as their intentions were concerned. Let us limit ourselves to proving that it was into this struggle that the majority of the Legislative Assembly of France had entered from the first days of their installation, since the month of May, 1849. This policy of resistance is a fatal policy. This struggle of man against God is necessarily vain ; barren in result, it is fruitful in catastrophes. What is to be will be ; it is necessary that what is to flow should flow, that what is to fall should fall, that what is to be born should be born, that what is to grow should grow ; but put obstacles in the way of these natural laws, trouble arises and disorder commences.

A sad thing it is, this *dis*order that they have named order. Bind up a vein, you have disease ; stop up a river, you have inundation ; bar the future, you have revolutions ; obstinately persist in keeping in the midst of you, as if it were living, the past, which is dead, you produce I do not know what moral cholera. The corruption expands, it is in the air, one breathes it ; entire classes of society, the office-holders, for example, are falling into rottenness. Keep corpses in your houses, the pestilence will break out. Fatally does this policy blind those who practice it. These men, who style themselves statesmen, are so far blind as not to see that they themselves, with their own hands and at great pains, and by the sweat of their brows, have caused the terrible events which they lament, and that those catastrophes which are falling down upon them have been caused by them. What would they say of a peasant who would make an embankment from one bank of a stream to the other, before his cottage door, and who, when the river became a torrent, and should pass over its banks, when it should sweep down his wall, when it should take off his roof, should cry, wicked river ! The statesmen of the past, these great constructors of dikes across streams, pass their time in crying, wicked people !

Take away Polignac and the proclamations of July, that

is to say, the dams, and Charles X. would be dead at the Tuileries. Reform, in 1847, the electoral law; that is to say again, take away the dam, Louis Philippe would be dead on the throne. Is that as much as to say that the Republic would not have come? No. The Republic, let us repeat it, is the future; it would have come but step by step, gain by gain, conquest by conquest, as a river which flows and not like a deluge which invades. It would have come in its hour, when all would have been ready to receive it; it would have come not certainly more likely to live, for from the present time it is indestructible; but more tranquilly, without possible reaction, without princes lying in ambush for it, without coups d'état behind it. The policy of resistance to the onward movement excels, let us again insist, in creating artificial inundations. Thus it succeeded in making of the year 1852 a sort of fearful crisis, and that always by the same process, by the means of a dam. Here is a railroad; the train will pass in an hour; throw a beam across the rails, when the train arrives it will be wrecked over it; you will have Fampoux; take away the beam before the arrival of the train, the train will pass without even a suspicion that there was a catastrophe awaiting it. This beam is the law of the 31st of May. The chiefs of the majority of the Legislative Assembly had cast it across 1852, and they cried: "It is thus that society will be broken up!" The left said to them: "Take away the beam, take away the beam, let universal suffrage pass freely." This is the whole history of the law of the 31st of May. These are things that an infant could comprehend, and that statesmen do not comprehend. Now let us answer at once the question which we have put:

Without the 2d of December, what would have come to pass in 1852? Suppress the law of the 31st of May, take away from the people their dam, take away from Bonaparte his lever, his arm, his pretext; let universal suffrage alone, take the beam off the rails, do you know what you would have had in 1852?

Nothing.

Some elections.

Some calm Sunday-like days, when the people would have come to vote; yesterday workman, to-day elector, to-morrow workman, always sovereign. You reply: Yes, elections! You speak of them quite at your ease. But the " red chamber" which would have issued out of those elections? Did they not announce that the Constitution of 1848 would be a " red chamber?" Red chambers, red specters, red croque-mitaines;* all these predictions go for what they are worth. Those who carry about these magic lanterns at the end of a stick, before the angry population know what they are about, and laugh behind the horrible rag that they wave. Under the long scarlet robe of the phantom to which they have given this name, 1852, we see the great boots of the coup d'état stick out.

---

* Nursery horror.

CHAPTER IV.

JACQUERIE.*

However, after the 2d of December, the crime once committed, it was very necessary to throw opinion off the scent. The coup d'état began exclaiming at jacquerie as the assassin exclaimed at the thief. Let us add, that a jacquerie had been promised, and that M. Bonaparte could not without some inconvenience fail at the same time in *all* his promises. What was the red specter except a jacquerie? It was quite necessary to give some reality to the specter. One could not burst out laughing rudely in the face of the people and say: "there was nothing! I have made you afraid of your own shadows." There has then been a "jacquerie;" the promises of the post-bills have been kept. The imaginations of those about one have given themselves scope; they have unburied the frights of Mother Goose, and more than one child, in reading the journal, will be able to recognize the ogre of the good fellow Perrault, disguised as a socialist. They have supposed; they have invented; the press being suppressed, it was very simple; to lie is easy, when one has in advance torn out the tongue of contradiction. They cried: "Alarm, bourgeois, without us you are lost. We have shot at you with grape, but it was for your good. Look, the Lollards were at your door, the Anabaptists were scaling your walls, the Hussites were knocking in your venetian blinds, the Hungry Boys were

---
* Rising of the peasants.

coming up your staircases, the Hollow Stomachs were looking greedily at your dinner. Look out, have not mesdames your wives been really violated. They have given the floor to one of the principal editors of *La Patrie*, named Froissard. —"I would neither dare write, nor recount the horrible and
"improper deeds that they were doing to the ladies. But
"among the other misdemeanors and villainous acts, they
"killed a chevalier and put him on a spit, and turned him
"at the fire and roasted him before his wife and her chil-
"dren. After ten or twelve had forced and violated the
"lady, they wished to make them eat of it (the corpse!)
"by force, and then killed them and made them die pain-
"ful deaths! These wicked people robbed and burned
"everything, and killed and forced and violated all
"ladies and virgins without pity or mercy, like mad dogs.
"Such hordes maintained themselves between Paris and
"Noyon, and between Paris and Soissons, and Ham and
"Vermandois, through all Coucy. These were the great
"violators and malefactors; and they estimate that in the
"bishoprics of Laon, of Soissons, and of Noyon, between
"the Comté de Valois, more than a hundred chateaux, and
"country residences of gentlemen and esquires, were en-
"tered, and they killed and robbed as many as they found.
"But *God* by his grace has provided such a remedy as
"ought to make one return many thanks." They only put God for my lord the prince-president. It was the least they could do.

To-day, after eight months have gone by, one knows how far to believe in this jacquerie. The facts have at last come out into full day. And where? How? Before the very tribunals of M. Bonaparte. The sub-prefects whose wives had been violated had never been married; the curates who had been roasted alive, and whose hearts the jacques have eaten, have written that they are in good health; the gendarmes around the corpses of whom they had danced have come to give evidence before the court-martial; the public coffers which had been pillaged have found themselves intact in the hands of M. Bonaparte, who has "saved" them; the famous deficit of five millions of francs from Clamecy, is reduced to two hundred francs spent for bread tickets. An official publication had said, on the 8th of December, "The curate, the mayor, "and the sub-prefect of Joigny, and several gendarmes " have been massacred in the most cowardly manner." Somebody answered in a letter, which was published, " Not "a drop of blood has been shed at Joigny, nobody's life "has been menaced there." Who wrote that letter? This same mayor of Joigny, *who had been massacred in a cowardly manner*. M. Henri de Lacretelle, from whom an armed band had extorted two thousand francs, in his chateau of Cormatin is still stupefied to this hour, not at the extortion but at the fabrication. M. de Lamartine, whom another band had wanted to rob, and probably to hang up to the lamp-post, and whose chateau of Saint-Point had been burnt, and who had written to secure indemnification from the government, learned all the entire circumstances from the journals. The following document was produced before the court-martial of la Nièvre, at which ex-colonel Martinprey presided.

"ORDER OF THE COMMITTEE.—Probity is a virtue of " Republicans. *Every thief or plunderer shall be shot.* Every "owner of arms who in twelve hours shall not have de-

"posited them at the mayor's office, or who shall not have
"given them up, shall be arrested and detained till the
"issuing of a new order. Every citizen found drunk shall
"be disarmed and imprisoned.
  "*Clamecy, 7th December,* 1851.
      "Vive la République Sociale.
      "The Revolutionary Socialist Committee."
  What you have just read is the proclamation of the
"Jacques," death to plunderers! death to thieves! Such
is the cry of these thieves and plunderers. One of these
Jacques, named Gustave Verdun-Lagarde, from Lot-et-Garonne, died in exile in Brussels, on the 1st of May, 1852, leaving a hundred thousand francs to his native city, to found there a school of agriculture. This divider* has divided indeed. There has not then been, and the honest card-house builders of the coup d'état agree to it to-day among their intimate associates, there has not been any "Jacquerie" it is true; but the turn has been served. There was in the departments what there was in Paris, legal resistance, the resistance prescribed to the citizens by the 110th article of the Constitution, and by what is above the Constitution, by natural right; there has been *legitimate defense* (this time the word is in its place) against the "saviors," the armed struggle of the right and the law against the infamous insurrection of power. The Republic, suppressed by an ambush, has seized the coup d'état by the collar, and had been also seized by her. That is all. Twenty-eight departments rose up: Aix, Aube, Cher, the Bouches-du-Rhône, la Cote-d'Or, la Haute-Garonne, Lotet-Garonne,

---

* The name partageux is applied to extreme communists, who favor a division of property.

le Loiret, la Marne, la Meurthe, le Nord, le Bas-Rhin, le Rhone, Seine et Marne, l'Yonne, did their duty worthily; l'Allier, les Basses-Alpes, l'Aveyron, la Drôme, le Gard, le Gers, l'Hérault, le Jura, la Nièvre, le Puy-de-Dôme, Saône-et-Loire, le Var et Vaucluse, did it intrepidly. They succumbed, as Paris did.

The coup d'état was ferocious there, as at Paris. We have just cast a summary glance on its crimes.

It is this resistance—legal, constitutional, virtuous, this resistance in which heroism was on the side of the citizens, and atrocity on the side of power, it is that which the coup d'état has called jacquerie. Let us repeat it. A little of the red specter was useful. This jacquerie was invented for two ends; it served in two ways the policy of the Elysée; it offered a double advantage: on the one hand to make people vote "*yes,*" on the "*plebiscitum*"—to make them vote under the saber and in the face of the specter—to silence the intelligent, to scare the credulous—terror for the latter, fear for the former, as we shall explain it soon, all the success and the entire secret of the vote of the 2d of December is there;—on the other hand, to give a pretext for proscriptions. 1852 did not, then, contain in itself any real danger. The law of the 31st of May, killed morally, was dead actually before the 2d of December. A new assembly, a new president, the Constitution purely and simply put in practice, some elections; nothing more. Take away M. Bonaparte, and that is 1852.

But it was necessary that M. Bonaparte should go away. There was the obstacle. From thence came the catastrophe. So, this man, one fine morning, took the Constitution, the Republic, the law, France, all, by the throat. He gave to the future a stab from behind; he trod under his feet the right, good sense, justice, reason, liberty; he has arrested inviolable men, sequestered innocent men, banished illustrious men; he has seized the people in the persons of their representatives; he has swept the boulevards of Paris with grape-shot; he has made his cavalry wade in the blood of old men and women; he has shot without a summons to disperse, he has shot without judgment; he has filled Mazas, la Concièrgerie, Sante-Pélagie, Vincennes, the forts, the cells, the casemates, the dungeons, with prisoners, and the cemeteries with corpses; he has had the woman who carried the bread to her concealed husband put in St. Lazare; he sent to the galleys for twenty years the man who gave refuge to a proscribed person; he has torn up all the codes and violated all the injunctions; he has made the transported rot by thousands in the horrible holds of the hulks; he has sent to Lambessa and Cayenne a hundred and fifty children, from twelve to fifteen years old. He who was more comical than Falstaff has become more terrible than Richard III. And why all this? Because there was a plot, as he said, against his power; because the year which was ending had entered into a traitorous understanding with the year which was commencing, in order to overthrow him; because the 45th article perfidiously concerted matters with the calendar to put him out; because the second Sunday of May wished to depose him; because his oath had the audacity to plot his fall; because his word of honor conspired against him. The morning after the triumph, they relate that he said: "The second Sunday of May is dead!" No! It is worth which is dead; it is honor which is dead; it is the name of the emperor which is dead. How the man who is in the Chapelle St. Jerome ought to start up, and what despair he ought to manifest! Here is unpopularity which mounts around the great figure, and it is this fatal nephew who has put the ladder in position. Here are the great souvenirs standing in the background, and the evil souvenirs returning. One dares hardly speak any more of Jena, of Marengo, of Wagram. What are you speaking of? Of the Duc d'Enghien, of Jaffa, of the 18th Brumaire? One forgets the hero, and one sees only the despot. Caricature commences to torture the profile of Cæsar, and then, what a personage at the side of him! There are people already who confound the uncle with the nephew, to the joy of the Elysée, and to the shame of France. The author of the parody takes the airs of the head of the profession. Alas! on this immense splendor there was necessarily this immense blot! Yes, worse than Hudson Lowe. Hudson Lowe was only a gaoler,—Hudson Lowe was only an executioner. The man who really assassinates Napoleon is Louis Bonaparte: Hudson Lowe only killed his life; Louis Bonaparte kills his glory. Ah, the miserable man! he takes everything, he uses everything, he soils everything, he dishonors everything. He chooses for his ambush the month, the day, of Austerlitz. He returns from Satory as one returns from Aboukir. He makes I know not what night-bird issue from the 2d December and perch upon the flag-staff of France, and he says: "Soldiers! there is the eagle." He borrows Napoleon's hat and Murat's plume. He has his own imperial etiquette, his own chamberlains, his aids-de-camp, his courtiers. Under the emperor they were kings; under him they are lackeys. He has his policy all to himself; he has his own

13th of Vendemaire, he has his own 18th Brumaire, all to himself. He compares himself with his uncle. At the Elysée Napoleon the Great has disappeared, they say ; the uncle Napoleon, the man of destiny, has outdone Géronte.* The complete one is not the first, it is this one. It is evident that the first did not come except to make the bed for the second. Louis Bonaparte, surrounded with valets and mistresses, desecrates, to satisfy the wants of his table and alcove, coronation, consecration, the Legion of Honor, the Camp of Boulogne, the Column Vendôme, Lodi, Arcola, Saint Jean-d'Arc, Eylau, Friedland, Champaubert. . . . . . Ah, Frenchmen ! look at this swine, covered with mire, who is wallowing in the skin of a lion !

---

* A type of pretentious insignificance.

BOOK FIFTH.—PARLIAMENTARISM.

CHAPTER I.

ONE day, sixty-three years ago, the French people—possessed by one family for eight hundred years ; oppressed by the barons up to the time of Louis XI., and since Louis XI. by the parliaments, that is to say, to employ the just expression of a great lord of the eighteenth century, "Eaten first by the wolves and then by the lice ;" penned up in provinces, in castellaries, in generalities, in bailiwicks, and in the jurisdictions of seneschals ; worked, pressed, taxed, cut, skinned, shorn, shaved, clipped, and villified at will ; fined indefinitely at the good pleasure of the masters ; governed, led, driven, foundered, dragged, tortured ; beaten with rods and branded with hot irons for a false oath ; sent to the galleys for a rabbit killed on the lands of the king ; hung for five sous ; furnishing their millions to Versailles and their skeletons to Montfaucon ; loaded with prohibitions, regulations, with patents, with letters royal, with edicts pecuniary and rural, with laws, with codes, with customs ; crushed by duties on salt, by aides, by quit-rents, by mort-mains, by excises, by dues, by tithes, by tolls, by duty-labor, by bankruptcies ; clubbed with a stick that they call scepter ; sweating, panting, whining, always walking, crowned, but at the knees ; in short, more a beast than a nation—suddenly held themselves up, wished to become men, and took into their heads to demand accounts from the monarchy, to ask accounts from Providence, and to settle for these eight centuries of misery. It was a great effort.

8*

CHAPTER II.

THEY chose a vast hall, which they surrounded with seats raised in rows above each other, and then they took planks, and with these planks they built in the middle of the hall a kind of platform. When the platform was made, what they at that time called the nation—that is to say, the clergy in red and violet surplices, the nobility in white plumes and with swords at their sides, the bourgeoisie dressed in black—came to sit on these steps. Scarcely were they seated before they saw an extraordinary figure ascend the platform and there stand erect. "What is this monster?" said some. "What is this giant?" said others. It was a singular being, unexpected, unknown, suddenly emerging from the darkness, and struck with fear and fascinated all. A hideous disease had given him a sort of tiger's head; all the uglinesses seemed to have been deposited on this mask by all the vices. He was, like the bourgeoisie, dressed in black—that is to say, in mourning. His lifeless eye cast dimness on the assembly. He resembled reproach or menace. All viewed him with a sort of curiosity mingled with horror. He raised his hand: they were silent. Then they heard come out of that face a sublime voice. It was the voice of the new world which spoke by the mouth of the old world. It was '89 who raised itself erect, and which summoned, and accused, and denounced, before God and man, all the fatal dates of monarchy. It was the past, august sight; the past, bruised with chains, marked on the shoulder, a worn-out slave, an old galley-slave, the unfortunate past, which was calling with great cries for the future, the liberating future. That is what this unknown man was, that is what he was doing on that platform.

At his speech, which at moments was a thunder, prejudices, fictions, abuses, superstitions, errors, intolerance, ignorance, infamous exactions, barbarous penalties, decrepid authorities, worm-eaten magistracies, worn-out codes, rotten laws—all that was to perish, was seized with trembling and began to crumble. That formidable apparition left a name in the memory of men; they ought to have called it the Revolution: they call it Mirabeau.

CHAPTER III.

FROM the day when that man put foot on that platform, that platform was transfigured. The French tribune was founded.

The French tribune! It would require a book to say what that word contains. The French tribune has been for sixty years the open mouth of the human mind: of the human mind saying everything, mingling everything, combining everything, making everything fruitful, things good, things evil; the true, the false, the just, the unjust, the high, the low, the horrible, the beautiful, the dream, the fact; passion, reason, love, hatred; the material, the ideal, but, in short, for this is its sublime and eternal work, making night in order to draw out of it day, making chaos to draw out of it life, making revolution to draw out of it the Republic. What has passed on that tribune, what it has seen, what it has done, what tempests have assailed it, what events it has given birth to, what men have shaken it with their clamors, what men have sanctified it with their speech how can one recount, after Mirabeau,—Vergniaud, Camille Desmoulins, Saint Just, that severe young man, Danton, that heinous tribune, Robespierre, that incarnation of the immense and terrible year? There one has heard some of those wild interruptions: "Ah, then, you!" exclaims an orator of the Convention, "are you going to cut short my speech to-day?" "Yes," answers a voice, "and your neck to-morrow." And those superb apostrophes! "Minister of Justice," said General Foy to an iniquitous keeper of the seals, "I condemn you as you go out of this precinct and look at the statue of l'Hôpital!"* There everything has been pleaded, we have just said: evil causes as well as good ones,—the good only have been gained definitively. There, in presence of resistances, of denials, of obstacles, those who wish the future as those who wish the past have lost patience; there, it has happened to the truth to become violent and to the lie to become furious; there, all extremes have arisen. At this tribune the guillotine has had its orator, Marat, and the inquisition its own, Montalembert. Terrorism in the name of public saftey, terrorism in the name of Rome; gall in the two mouths, anguish in the audience. When one spoke, you expected to see the gleam of the knife; when the other spoke, you thought you heard the crackle of the wood-pile. There, parties have fought, all with rancor, a few with glory. There, the royal power violated the popular right in the person of Manuel, become august in the eyes of history by this violation. There, appeared, disdaining the past which they served, two melancholy old men—Royer Callard, haughty worth; Chateaubriand, bitter genius. There, Thiers, shrewdness, has striven against Guizot, strength, there, they have closed, they have grappled, they have fought, they have worked evidence like a sword. There, during more than a quarter of a century, hatreds, excitements, superstitions, egotisms, impostures, howling, whistling, barking,

---

* Statue of Justice.

standing up erect, twisting themselves, crying always the same calumnies, showing always the same closed fist, spitting since Christ the same saliva, have gone on eddying like a storm-cloud around thy calm face, Truth!

CHAPTER IV.

ALL that was living, ardent, fruitful, tumultuous, grand. And when all had been pleaded, debated, examined, dug into, penetrated, said, contradicted, what would issue from the clash? Always the spark. What would issue from the cloud? Always light. All that the tempest could do was to agitate, shake the ray, and change it into lightning. There they have laid down, analyzed, thrown light upon, and almost always settled questions—questions of finance, questions of credit, questions on labor, questions on circulation, questions on salaries, questions of State, questions of territory, questions of peace, questions of war. There they have pronounced, for the first time, those words which contained an entire new society—the rights of man! There one has heard resounding for fifty years the anvil on which superhuman forgers were forging pure ideas; ideas, those swords of the people, those lances of justice, those weapons of the right. There penetrated suddenly by sympathetic emotions, as live coals grow red in the wind, all those who have a hearth within their natures, mighty advocates like Ledru-Rollin and Berryer, great historians like Guizot, great poets like Lamartine, found themselves instantly and naturally great orators. That tribune was a place of force and of virtue. It lived, it inspired; for men thoroughly believe that these emanations issued from it, and all devotedness, all self-denial, all energies, all intrepid instincts. As for us, we honor all courage, even in the ranks opposed to us.

One day the tribune was enveloped in darkness; it seemed as if the abyss had opened around it. One heard in this darkness something like the roaring of a sea, and suddenly, in this livid night, at this edge of marble which the strong hand of Danton was clutching, they saw appear a pike with a bleeding head upon it. Boissy D'Anglas saluted it. That day was a menacing day; but the people do not overthrow the tribunes; the tribune belongs to it, and it knows it. Place a tribune in the center of the world and, before long, at the four corners of the earth, the Republic will arise. The tribune beams for the people; they are not ignorant of it. Sometimes the tribune provokes them, and makes them foam; they strike her with their wave, and even cover her, as on the 15th of May, and then they retire majestically, like the ocean, and leave her standing like the lighthouse. Overthrow the tribune when one is the people! It is folly, it is not a paying business, except for tyrants.

The people rose up, were irritated, were indignant. A certain generous error had seized them, a certain delusion was leading them astray; they were mistaken on a fact, on an act, on a measure, on a law; they grew angry; they abandoned that superb calm in which their strength lay; they rushed upon the public squares with a deep, rumbling sound and a terrible spring. It was a riot, an insurrection, civil war; a revolution, perhaps. The tribune was there. A beloved voice arose, and said to the people: "Pause, look, listen, judge! *Si forte virum quem conspexere, silent;* this was true in Rome, and it was true also in Paris." The people paused. O tribune! pedestal of strong men! from thence came eloquence, law, authority, patriotism, devotedness, and great thoughts; bridles for the people, muzzles for lions. In sixty years, every kind of mind, every variety of intelligence, every species of genius have successively had the floor in this place—the most resonant on earth. From the first Constituent Assembly to the last, from the first legislative body to the last, across the convention, the councils, and the chambers, count the men, if you can! It is an Homeric enumeration. What figures contrast between Danton and Thiers! What figures which resemble each other, from Barrére to Baroche, between Lafayette and Cavaignac! To the names which we have already mentioned, Mirabeau, Vergniaud, Danton, Saint-Just, Robespierre, Camille, Desmoulins, Manuel, Foy, Royer-Collard, Chateaubriand, Thiers, Guizot, Ledru-Rollin, Berryer, Lamartine, add these other names, different, perhaps their enemies, savants, artists, statesmen, military men, lawyers, democrats, monarchists, liberals, socialists, republicans, all famous; a few illustrious, having each his own halo: Barnave, Cazalés, Maury, Mounier, Thouret, Chapelier, Pétion, Buzot, Brissot, Sieyés, Condorcet, Chenier, Carnot, Lanjuinais, Pontécoulant, Cambacérès, Talleyrand, Fontanes, Benjamin Constant, Casimir Périer, Chauvelin, Voyer d'Argenson, Lafitte, Dupont (from l'Eure), Camille, Jordan, Lainé, Fitz-James, Bonald, Villèle, Martignac, Cuvier, Villemain, the two Lameths, the two Davids—the painter in '93, the sculptor in '48, Lamarque, Mauguin, Odilon Barrot, Arago, Garnier-Pagés, Louis Blanc, Mark Dufraisse, Lammenais, Emile de Girardin, Lamoricière, Dufaure, Crémmieux, Michel (from Bourges), Jules Favre. . . . What talents! What varied powers of adaptation! What services rendered! What struggles of all realities against all errors! What brains at work! What expense to the advantage of progress, of knowledge, of philosophy, of passion, of conviction, of experience, of sympathy, of eloquence! What prolific warmth spent! What an immense train of light! And we do not name them all. To make use of an expression which they borrow sometimes from the author of this book: "We have passed by some and better ones." We have not mentioned even that valiant legion of young orators who have risen upon the left in these late years: Arnauld (from l'Ariége), Bancel, Chauffour, Pascal Duprat, Esquiros, de Flotte, Farcounet, Victor Hennequin, Madier Montjau, Morellet, Noël Parfait, Pelletier, Sain, Versigny. Let us dwell upon them. Beginning with Mirabeau, there was in the world, in human society, in civilization, a culminating point, a central place, a hearth, a summit. This summit was the tribune of France; admirable guiding-mark for the generations in their march, dazzling peak in peaceful times, beacon in the obscurity of catastrophes. From the opposite ends of the intelligent universe, the nations fixed their gaze on this height from which the human mind sent out its rays; when any sudden darkness enveloped them, they heard a great voice coming thence which spoke to them in the shadow: "*Admonet et magnâ testatur voce per umbras.*" A voice which suddenly, when the hour had come, a cock-crowing announcing the day, the cry-of-the-eagle calling to the sun, sounded like a clarion of war or a trumpet of judgment, and made those heroic dead nations,—Poland, Hungary, Italy, stand erect, shake off their grave-clothes, and search for swords in their sepulchers! Then, at this voice of France, the splendid heaven of the future opened, the old blind and terrifying despotisms bent their foreheads into the darkness below, and one saw appear, with her feet upon the cloud, with her forehead amongst the stars, with her flaming sword in her hand, and with her great wings stretched into the open azure, Liberty, archangel of nations!

CHAPTER V.

This tribune was the terror of all tyrannies and of all fanaticisms, and the hope of every one who was oppressed under heaven. Whoever put foot on this summit felt distinctly the pulsation of the great heart of humanity. There, provided that he was a willing man, his soul grew great within him and cast its beams without him; something universal took possession of him and filled his mind as the blast fills the sail; as soon as he stood on those four planks he was stronger and better, he felt himself in this sacred minute live the collective life of nations; there came to him good words for all men; he perceived on the other side of the assembly grouped at his feet, and often full of emotion, the people attentive, serious, with ear stretched and with fingers on their lips; and on the other side of the people, the human race thoughtful, seated in a circle and listening. Such was this grand tribunal, from the height of which a man spoke to the world.

From this tribune, ceaselessly in vibration, sorts of sonorous waves were departing, immense oscillations of feeling and ideas, which, wave on wave, and from people to people, went to the confines of the earth and aroused those intelligent billows called human souls. Often one did not know why a certain law, a certain structure, a certain institution, tottered yonder, further than the frontiers, further than the seas: the papacy on the other side of the Alps, the throne of the czar at the end of Europe, slavery in America, the death-penalty everywhere. The tribune of

France had started! At certain hours a start of this tribune was a trembling of the earth. The tribune of France spoke: everybody who thinks here below closely concentrated his attention; the words spoken went away into obscurity, across space, at hazard, it made no difference where. "It was only wind—it was only sound," said barren minds, which live on irony; and the next day, or three months afterward, or a year later, something fell on the surface of the globe, or something rose, "Who did that?" This noise that had vanished, this wind which had passed. That noise, that wind, was the Word. A sacred force. From the Word of God the creation issued; from the word of man the social order of peoples.

CHAPTER VI.

ONCE mounted on this tribune, the man who was there was no longer a man—he was that mysterious worker which one sees in the evening, at twilight, walking with great steps in the furrows, and launching into space, with a gesture of command, the germs, the seeds, the future harvest, the riches of the next summer, bread of life.

He goes, he comes, he returns; his hand opens and shuts, fills and empties. The somber plain is stirred, deep nature opens, the unknown abyss of creation commences its labor, the dews, in suspense, descend; the sprig of foolish oats shivers, and thinks that the ear of wheat will succeed it; the sun, hidden behind the horizon, likes what man does, and knows that his rays will not be lost. Holy and marvelous work!

The orator is the sower. He takes in his heart his instincts, his passions, his beliefs, his sufferings, his dreams, his ideas, and casts them in handfuls in the midst of men. Every brain is a furrow to him. A word fallen from the tribune always takes root somewhere, and becomes a thing. You say: "It is nothing: it is a man who is speaking;" and you raise your shoulders. Short-sighted minds! It is a future which is germinating—it is a world which is breaking the shell.

CHAPTER VII.

Two great problems are pending on the world: war ought to disappear and conquest ought to continue. These two necessities of increasing civilization seem to exclude one another. How satisfy one without extinguishing the other? Who could resolve these two problems at once? What did resolve them? The tribune. The tribune is peace and the tribune is conquest. Conquest by the sword! who wishes any? No one: the peoples are countries. Conquests by ideas! who wishes them? The world: the peoples are humanity.

Now, two brilliant tribunes ruled the nations: the English tribune attending to business, and the French tribune creating ideas. The French tribune had elaborated since '89 all the principles which make up the essence of politics, and she had commenced to elaborate since 1848 all the principles which constitute the essence of the social order. A principle once drawn from limbus and brought out into the light, it cast it to the world armed at all points, and said to it: "Go!" The conquering principle entered the open country, met the custom-house officers at the frontiers, and passed in spite of the watch-dogs; met the sentinels at the gates of the cities, and passed in spite of the instructions; took the railroad, went on board the packet, wandered over the continent, crossed the sea, overtook the travelers on the high-roads, sat down at the hearths of families, slid between friend and friend, between brother and brother, between man and wife, between master and slave, between people and king; and to those who asked it: "What are you?" it answered: "I am Truth!" and to those who asked it: "From whence came you?" it answered: "From France." Then the man who had asked the questions held out his hand to it, and it was better than a province,—it was an intelligence annexed. From this time forth, between Paris, the metropolis, and this man isolated in his solitude, and this city lost in the depths of woods or on table-lands, and this people bowed down under the yoke, a current of thought and of love was established. Under the influence of these currents, certain nationalities were growing feeble, certain were growing strong and were rising. The savage felt himself less savage, the Turk less Turk, the Russian less Russian, the Hungarian more Hungarian, the Italian more Italian. Slowly and by degrees the French mind, furthering the universal progress, was assimilating the nations to itself.

Thanks to this admirable French language, composed by Providence, with a marvellous balance, having consonants enough to be pronounced by the peoples of the north, and vowels enough to be pronounced by the peoples of the south; thanks to this language, which is one of the powers of civilization and humanity; little by little, and by its own light alone, this high, central tribunal of Paris was conquering the peoples and making them France. The material frontier of France did what it could; but there were no treaties of 1815 for the *moral* frontier. The moral frontier was retiring ceaselessly, and was going on enlarging itself day by day; and before a quarter of a century, perhaps, they would have said of the French world what they said of the Roman world.

This is what the tribune was. This is what it did for France: a prodigious lobby of ideas, a gigantic apparatus of civilization, continually raising the level of intelligence in the entire universe, and setting free, into the midst of humanity, an enormous quantity of light. It is this which M. Bonaparte has suppressed.

CHAPTER VIII.

YES, M. Bonaparte has overthrown this tribune. This power, created by the pains of our great revolutionary labours, he has broken, ground, crushed; he has torn it at the points of his bayonets, trodden it under the feet of his horses. His uncle uttered an aphorism: "The throne is a plank covered with velvet;" he has uttered his: "The tribune is a plank covered with a cloth, on which one reads: *liberty, equality, fraternity.*" He has thrown the plank, and the cloth, and the liberty, and the equality, and the fraternity into the bivouac fire. A shout of laughter from the soldiers, a little smoke, and the story is told. Is it true? Is it possible? Did it come to pass in this way? Has such a thing actually happened? To cut off Cicero's head and to nail his two hands on the rostrum, took one brute who had an axe and another who had nails and a hammer.

The tribune was three things for France: a means of exterior initiation; a method of interior government; a glory.

Louis Bonaparte has suppressed initiation. France was teaching the peoples, and conquering them by love. What was the use of it? He has suppressed the method of government—his own is of more value. He has breathed upon the glory and extinguished it; certain breaths have this property. Nevertheless, to make an attempt upon the tribune is a crime in the family. The first Bonaparte had already committed it, but the glory which he brought to France to replace it, was at least glory, not ignominy. Louis Bonaparte is not satisfied with overthrowing the tribune, he has made it ridiculous. It is an effort, like the other. It is indeed the lesser, when one cannot say two words together, when one only harangues with the copy-book in one's hand, when one is a stammerer in speech and intelligence, let him make a little fun of Mirabeau! General Ratapoil says to General Foy: "Hold your tongue, babbler! What is that,—the tribune?" Exclaims M. Bonaparte–Louis: "That is 'parliamentarism!" What's that you say about parliamentarism? Parliamentarism pleases me. Parliamentarism is a pearl." The dictionary is enriched. This academician of the coup d'état makes words. It is a fact, one is not a barbarian for nothing. One will let drop a barbarism from time to time. He also is a sower; that sprouts in the brain. of the silly. The uncle had his "ideologists." The nephew has "parliamentarists." Parliamentarism, gentlemen; parliamentarism, ladies. That answers for everything. You hazard this timid observation: "It is perhaps sad, that one has ruined so many families, transported so many men, proscribed so many citizens, filled so many hand-barrows, dug so many graves, shed so much blood, ..." "Ah, indeed," replies a coarse voice, with a Dutch accent, "you regret, then, the 'parliamentarism?' Stand aside, parliamentarism is a God-send. I give my vote to M. Louis Bonaparte for the first arm-chair vacant at the institute. What! One must encourage this science of coining. This man issues from the charnel-house, he comes out of the morgue; this man with his hands smoking like a butcher—he scratches his ear, smiles, and invents terms like Julia d'Angennes. He marries the mind of the Hôtel de Rambouillet to the odour of Montfaucon. It is a rare gem. We shall both vote for him: Shall we not, Monsieur de Montalembert?"

CHAPTER IX.

THEN "parliamentarism"—that is to say, the security of citizens, the liberty of discussion, the liberty of the press, individual liberty, the scrutiny of taxes, transparency in the receipts and expenses, the safety-lock of the public strong-box, the right to know what they do with your money, the firmness of credit, the liberty of conscience, the freedom of worship, the security of property, the appeal against confiscations and unjust exactions, the security of the individual, which is the counterpoise to arbitrary power; the dignity of the nation and the splendour of France, the robust morals of free peoples, public initiative, movement, life,—all that is no more. Effaced—annihilated —vanished! And this deliverance has only cost France something like twenty-five millions, divided among fifteen or twenty saviours, and forty thousand francs' worth of brandy for each brigade! Certainly it was not dear; these gentlemen of the coup d'état have done the thing at a discount. To-day it is done—it is perfect—it is complete. The grass is sprouting at the Bourbon palace. A virgin forest is commencing to grow; between the Bridge of Concord and Bourgogne square one sees in the brushwood the sentry-box of the sentinel. The Corps Legislatif pours out its urn into the reeds, and glides to the feet of that sentry-box with a sweet murmur. To-day, it has ended. The great work is finished. And the result of the thing? Do you know that Messrs. So-and-so have built city-houses and country-houses simply on what they made on the belt railroad?

Attend to business, take your ease, and get stomach. It is no longer the question how to be a great people, how to be a powerful people, how to be a free nation, how to be a hearth shedding light. France no longer has an eye single to that. There is a success. France votes Louis Napoleon, carries Louis Napoleon, fattens Louis Napoleon, views Louis Napoleon, admires Louis Napoleon—and stupidly stops here. The end of civilization is attained. To-day, no more noise, no more hubbub, no more talk, parliament or parliamentarism: The Corps Legislatif, the Senate, the Council of State, are mouths sewed up. One has no longer to fear reading an able piece in the morning on waking. It's all up with the man who thought, who reflected, with the man who created, with the man who spoke, with the man who shone, with the man who was the centre of splendour in this great people. Courage, Frenchmen! Hold up your heads, Frenchmen! You are no longer anything; this man is everything. He holds your intelligence in his hand as a child holds a bird; the moment he pleases he will wring the genius of France's neck. It would be one hubbub the less. In the meanwhile—let us repeat it in chorus —"No more parliamentarism! no more tribune!" Instead of all these great voices which were dialogueing for the enlightenment of the world, which were one idea, another fact, another right, another justice, another glory, another faith, another hope, another science, another genius, which were instructing, which were charming, which were reassuring, which were consoling, which were encouraging, which were fertilizing,—instead of all these sublime voices, what is this which you hear in this black night which covers France? the noise of a spur which jingles and of sabre which trails on the pavement. "Hallelujah!" says M. Sibour; "Hosannah!" responds M. Parisis.

BOOK SIXTH.—THE ABSOLUTION.

CHAPTER I.

THE FIRST FORM OF ABSOLUTION: THE 7,500,000 VOTES.

THEY tell us: "You do not consider! All these acts which you call crimes are henceforth 'acts accomplished,' and in consequence respectable. All has been accepted, all has been adopted, legitimized, covered up, absolved. Accepted! adopted! legitimized! covered up! absolved!" By what? By a vote. What vote? The seven million five hundred thousand votes! Actually. There has been a plebiscite, and a vote, and 7,500,000 yeas. Let us say a word about it.

CHAPTER II.

A BRIGAND stops a stage-coach at the corner of a wood. He is at the head of a determined band. The travellers are more numerous, but they are separated, disunited, penned up in the compartments, half asleep, surprised in the middle of the night, suddenly seized, and without arms. The brigand orders them to get out, not to utter a cry or breathe a word, and to lie down with their faces to the ground. A few resist,—he blows out their brains. The others obey, and lie down on the pavement, silent, motionless, terrified, pell-mell with the dead, and as helpless as the dead. The brigand, while his accomplices put their feet on their backs, and hold their pistols at their temples, rifles their pockets, forces their trunks, and takes every valuable that they have. The pockets empty, the trunks pillaged, the coup d'état finished, he says to them: "Now, "in order to put myself in line with justice, I have written "on a paper that you acknowledge that all that I have "taken from you belongs to me, and that you yield it to "me of your own free will. I mean that this should be "your legal statement. They are going to place in the "hand of each of you a pen, and without saying a word, "without making a gesture, without quitting the position in "which you are, with your belly on the ground, and with "your faces in the mud, you will stretch out your right "hands and you will all sign this paper. If any one budges "or speaks, here is the mouth of my pistol. But, however, "you are free." The travellers stretch out their hands and sign. That done, the brigand lifts up his head and says: "I have seven million five hundred thousand votes."

CHAPTER III.

M. Louis Bonaparte is the president of that stage-coach. Let us recall a few principles. In order that a political ballot may be valid, three conditions are absolutely necessary. First, that the vote should be free; second, that the vote should be enlightened; and third, that the returns should be genuine. If one of these three conditions is wanting the ballot is void. What will be the case if the whole three at once are absent? Let us apply these rules. First, that the vote be free. What was the freedom of the vote of the 20th December? We have just described it; we have expressed this liberty by a striking figure. We might spare ourselves the pains of adding anything to it. Let every one of those who voted try to recollect, and ask himself under what moral and material violence he deposited his ballot in the box. We could cite such a district as that of Yonne, where out of five hundred heads of families four hundred were arrested, and the rest voted "yes;" such a district as that of Loiret, where, out of six hundred and thirty-nine heads of families, four hundred and ninety-seven were arrested or banished; the one hundred and forty-two who escaped voted "yes." And what we say of Yonne and Loiret we must say of all the departments. From the 2d of December every city had its swarm of spies; every town, every village, every hamlet had its informer. To vote "no" was prison, or exile, or Lambessa.

In the villages of a certain department they carried to the doors of the mayoralties (an eye-witness told us) ass-loads of affirmative votes. The mayors, flanked by the rural guards, sent them back to the peasants. They had to vote. At Savigny, near Saint Maur, on the morning of the vote, the enthusiastic gendarmes declared that the man who voted "no" should not sleep in his bed. The gendarmes entered on the gaoler's book, in the station-house of Valenciennes, M. Parent, junior, substitute of the justice of the peace of the district of Bouchain, for having induced the inhabitants of Avesne-le-Sec to vote "no." The nephew of the representative Aubry (from Nord), having seen affirmative votes distributed by agents of the prefect in the great square of Lille, went down on that square the next day and distributed negative votes; he was arrested and sent to the citadel. As to the vote of the army, a part voted in their own interest. The rest followed mechanically.

As to the freedom of even this vote of the soldiers let us hear the army itself speak. Here is what a soldier of the 6th of the line, commanded by Colonel Garderens de Boisse, wrote : " For the company the vote was a roll-call. " The sub-officers, the corporals, the drummers, and the " soldiers, placed in rank according to the roll, were called " by the quarter-master, in the presence of the colonel, " the lieutenant-colonel, the chief of battalion, and of the " officers of the company, and the exact moment each " man called answered 'present,' his name was written " down by the sergeant-major. The colonel said, rubbing " his hands, 'Faith, gentlemen, this goes swimmingly.' " When a corporal of the company to which I belonged " approached the table where the sergeant-major was "sitting, and begged him to give him the pen that he might with his own hand write his name on the negative register, which was to have remained blank, 'What!' cried the colonel, 'you who are proposed for quartermaster, you who are going to be named for the first vacancy, you formally disobey your colonel, and that before your company! Yet, if this refusal that you make at this moment were only an act of insubordination, it would be bad enough; but you do not know, wretch, that by your vote you are asking for the destruction of the army, the burning of your father's house, the entire annihilation of society! You are putting your hand to a dirty trick? What! X——! you whom I want to push forward, you come to-day to tell me such a thing as that?' The poor devil, as one might well know, let himself be written down like the others."

Multiply this colonel by six thousand, and you have the pressure brought to bear by the functionaries of all orders—military, political, civil, administrative, ecclesiastical, judiciary, of the customs, municipal, educational, commercial, consular, throughout France, all bearing upon the soldier, the citizen, and the peasant. Add, as we have already indicated above, the false jacquerie reported of the districts and the real Bonapartist terrorism, the government weighing heavily, by hideous delusions, on the feeble, and by dictatorship on the refractory, and setting in motion two terrors at once; and we have the truth. It would require a separate volume to recount, expose, and sift to the bottom the innumerable details of that immense extortion of signatures that they call the vote of the 20th of December. The vote of the 20th of December has thrown the honour, the originality, the intelligence, and the moral life of the nation to the earth. France went to this vote as the herd goes to the slaughter. Let us pass on.

Secondly: That the vote should be enlightened. Here is a first principle. Where there is no liberty of the press there is no vote. The liberty of the press is the condition, *sine qua non* of universal suffrage. A radical nullification of all ballotting takes place on the absence of the liberty of the press. That liberty involves as a necessary corallary the liberty of assemblage, of posting, and of canvassing; all liberties that right begets, and preliminary to all, the liberty of informing one's self before voting. To vote is to govern and to judge. Imagine a blind pilot at the helm; a judge with ears stopped up and with eyes put out. Liberty, then! Liberty to inform one's self by every means, by inquiry, by the press, by speech, by discussion. This is the express guarantee and the vital condition of universal suffrage. In order that a thing may be done validly it is necessary that it should be done knowingly. Where there is no light there is no act. These are axioms. Outside of these axioms everything is null, *ipso facto*. Now, let us see: did M. Bonaparte, in his ballot of December 20th, obey these axioms; has he fulfilled these conditions of a free press, free assemblage, free discussion, free postage, free colportage, free inquiry? A great shout of laughter answers, even at the Elysée. So you are forced yourself to agree, that it is thus that they made use of "universal suffrage." What? I know nothing of what has happened! They have killed, cut throats, mowed down men with grape-shot, assassinated, and I am ignorant of it! They have confiscated, tortured, expelled, exiled, transported, and I scarcely catch a glimpse of it! My mayor and my curate tell me: "Those people there, whom they are taking off bound with cords, are old offenders!" I am a peasant, I cultivate a corner of land at a remote point in a province; you suppress the journal; you stifle the information as to what takes place; you hinder the truth from reaching me; and you make me vote! What? in the deepest night! while I am groping! you rush out abruptly from the dark, with a sabre in your hand, and you tell me: "Vote!" and you call that a ballot. Certainly, a ballot "free and unsolicited," say the sheets of the coup d'état. Every rakish trick has worked for that vote. A mayor of a village, a kind of Escobar wild stock, put out into open field, said to his peasants: "If you vote yes, it is for the Republic; if you vote no, it is against the Republic." The peasants voted. And then let us bring to light another phase of this rascality, which they call the plebiscite of the 20th of December. How was the question put? Was there any possible choice? Did they—and this was certainly the least that the man of the coup d'état ought to have done, in a ballot so strange as this, in which every great principle was put once more at stake—did they allow each party the chance to vote for its candidate? Did they permit the legitimists to make efforts in behalf of their exiled prince and the ancient honour of the Lilies? Were the Orleanists permitted to turn toward that proscribed family which the valiant services of two soldiers, Messrs. de Joinville and d'Aumale, have honoured, and which that grand soul, the Duchess of Orleans, renders illustrious? Did they offer to the people, who are not a party, but who are the people, that is to say, the sovereign, did they offer to them that true

Republic, before which all monarchy is vanishing as night vanishes before day ; that Republic which is the evident and irresistible future of the civilized world ; the Republic without dictatorship ; the Republic of harmony, of science, and of liberty ; the Republic of universal suffrage, of universal peace and welfare ; the initiatrix of peoples, and liberatrix of nationalities ; that Republic which, after all, in spite of all that they may do, will have, as the author of this book has elsewhere said, France to-morrow, Europe the day after? Did they offer that? No! Here is how M. Bonaparte presented the thing. There was in this ballot two candidates. The first, M. Bonaparte. The second, the Abyss. France has had to choose. Admire the address of the man, and also notice a little his humility. M. Bonaparte has given himself for opposite dancer in this cotillon, whom? M. de Chambord? No. M. de Joinville? No. The Republic? Still less. M. Bonaparte, like those pretty creoles who set off their beauty by means of some frightful Hottentot, has given himself for competitor in election a phantom, a vision, a Nuremburg socialism, with teeth, and claws, and a coal of fire in its eyes ; the ogre of Little Poucet, the vampire of St. Martin's gate, the hydra of Théramène, the great sea serpent of the *Constitutionnel*, which the shareholders have had the good grace to lend him ; the dragon of the Apocalypse, the Tarasque,* the Dree,* the Gra-Oulli,* a fright. Aided by a Ruggieri, M. Bonaparte made on this pasteboard monster an effect of red Bengal fire, and said to the terrified voter : "There is nothing possible but this and me ; choose !" He said, "Choose between beauty and the beast ; the

---
* Nursery horrors.

beast is communism, the beauty is my dictatorship. Choose! No alternative! nothing between society overthrown, your house burned, your farm pillaged, your cow stolen, your field confiscated, your wife violated, your children butchered, your wine drunk by others, yourself eaten alive by those great open jaws which you see there, or me Emperor! Choose. Me or Croque-mitaine."* The bourgeois, terrified, and in consequence a child; the peasant, ignorant, and in consequence a child; preferred M. Bonaparte to Croque-mitaine. That is his triumph. Let us say, however, that out of ten million voters it seems that two million five hundred thousand would have liked Croque-mitaine much better. After all, M. Bonaparte has only had 7,500,000 votes then; and in this way, freely, as is seen, knowingly as is seen, what M. Bonaparte has the goodness to call universal suffrage has voted. Voted what? The dictatorship, autocracy, servitude, the Republic hurried into a despotism, France made a dominion of the Pasha, chains on all hands, the seal on all lips, silence, degradation, fear, the spy the soul of all! They have given to a man—to you—omnipotence and omniscience! They have made of this man the constituent, the sole legislator, the alpha of right, the omega of power. They have decreed that he is Minos, that he is Numa, that he is Solon, that he is Lycurgus! They have incarnated the people in him and the nation, the state and the law, and for ten years! What, for me a citizen, to vote not only my own renunciation, my own overthrow, my own abdication, but the abdication for ten years of the universal suffrage of new generations, over which I have no con-

---

* Nursery horrors.

troul, whose rights you, a usurper, force me to usurp. A thing which, of itself, let it be said in passing, would suffice to strike with invalidity this monstrous ballot, if all nullifications were not already heaped up and mingled in it! What! you make me do this, vote that all is over, that nothing now remains, that the people are negroes; you actually tell me, that seeing that you are sovereign, you are going to give yourself a master; seeing that you are France, you are going to become Hayti!* What abominable mockery!

That is the vote of the 20th of December, this sanction, as M. de Morny says, this absolution, as M. Bonaparte declares. Truly, in a little time from now, in a year, in a month, in a week perhaps, when all that we now see shall have vanished, we shall be somewhat ashamed of having done it, be it only for a moment, this infamous counterfeit of a vote, which they called the vote of the seven million five hundred thousand, the honour of discussing it. It is, however, the only foundation, the only prop, the only rampart, of the prodigious power of M. Bonaparte. This vote is the excuse of cowards, the buckler of dishonoured consciences. Generals, magistrates, bishops, all forfeitures, all prevarications, all complicities in fraud shelter their baseness behind this vote. France has spoken; say they: *Vox populi, vox Dei;* universal suffrage has voted; all is covered by a ballot. That a vote! that a ballot! One spits on it and passes on.

Thirdly: *that the figures should be accurate.* I admire that number, 7,500,000. It ought to have had a good effect that morning, through the fog, in letters of gold three feet high, over the front gate of Notre Dame. I admire that

---

* An allusion to Soulouque.

number. Do you know why? Because it looks so modest. 7,500,000! Why 7,500,000? That is few. No one used to refuse M. Bonaparte good measure. After what he had done on the 2d of December, he had a right to more. Truly, who would have cavilled at him? Who would have hindered him from putting down eight millions, ten millions, a round number? As for myself, I was deceived in my hopes. I counted on a unanimous vote. Coup d'état, you are modest. What! they have done all that we have just recalled and recounted; they took an oath, and they perjured themselves; they were the guardians of the Constitution, and they destroyed it; they were the servants of a Republic, and they betrayed it; they were the agents of a sovereign assembly, and they violently broke it up; they have made of the military order a poignard to slay military honour; they have used the flag of France to wipe up mud and shame; they have handcuffed the African generals, made the representatives of the people travel in prison-carriages; they have filled Mazas, Vincennes, Mont Valerien, and St. Pelagie with inviolable men; they have shot almost at the muzzles of their guns, on the righteous barricade, the legislator, clothed in that scarf which is a sacred and venerable mark of the law; they have given to a certain colonel whom we could name one hundred thousand francs to tread his duty under foot, and to each soldier ten francs a day; they spent in four days forty thousand francs for brandy on each brigade; they covered the carpet of the Elysée with the gold of the bank, and said to their friends: "Take it!" They murdered M. Adde in his own house, M. Belval in his own house, M. Debaecque, M. Labilte, M. de Couverselle, M. Monpelas, M. Thirion de Montauban, each in his own house; they have slaughtered on the Boulevards and elsewhere, shot one does not know where or whom : they have committed many murders, of which they have the modesty only to avow ninety-one; they have actually changed the pits of the Boulevard trees into basins full of blood; they have shed the blood of the infant with the blood of the mother, and mingled with all the champagne of the gendarmes; they did all this and gave themselves this trouble, and when they ask of the nation, "Are you satisfied," they only get 7,500,000 yeas! Truly, the thing has not been paid for.

Devote yourself then to saving a society! Ah, the ingratitude of nations! In fact, three millions of mouths have actually answered no! Who was it, then, who said that the savages of the South Sea called Frenchmen the Yes-yeses?

Let us speak seriously, for irony drags heavily in these tragic matters. People of the coup d'état, nobody believes in your seventy-five hundred thousand votes. Stop, there is too much franchise, avow it. You have been a little Greek, you are cheating. In your balance of the 2d of December you have counted too many votes and too few corpses!

Seven million five hundred thousand! What number is that? Where does it come from? Out of what does it issue? What do you want us to make of it? Shall we make it seven millions, eight millions, ten millions? What difference does it make? We yield you everything, and we contest everything.

The seven millions you have, plus the five hundred thousand; the main amount, plus the odd numbers; you say it is so, prince; you affirm it; you swear; but who proves it? Who counted the votes? Baroche. Who scrutinized the ballot? Rouher. Who registered it? Pietri. Who summed it up? Maupas. Who verified it? Troplong. Who proclaimed it? You. That is to say, that baseness counted it, dullness scrutinized it, rakish trickery registered it, forgery added it, venality verified it, and falsehood proclaimed it.

Well.

On this M. Bonaparte goes up to the capitol, orders M. Sibour to thank Jupiter, puts a blue and gold livery on the Senate, a blue and silver one on the Corps Legislatif, green and gold on his coachman, lays his hand on his heart, declares that he is the fruit of "universal suffrage," and that his "legitimacy" has come out of the ballot urn. That urn is a goblet.

CHAPTER IV.

WE declare it then, purely and simply the 20th of December, 1851, eighteen days after the 2d, M. Bonaparte poked his hand into the conscience of every man, and stole from each his vote. Others steal pocket-handkerchiefs; he stole the empire. Every day, for just such pranks, a sergeant of police seizes a man by the nape of the neck, and takes him to the station-house. Let us be understood, however. Is what we have said as much as to say that we pretend that no one really voted for M. Bonaparte, or voluntarily said "Yes?" or freely and knowingly accepted the man? Far from it: M. Bonaparte had on his side the mob of office-holders, the twelve hundred thousand parasites of the budget, with their tenants and dependents; he had the corrupt, the compromised, the cunning, and, at their backs, the idiots. A worthy mass!

He had in his favour my lords the cardinals, the bishops, the canons, the curates, the vicars, the archdeacons, the deacons, the subdeacons, the prebendaries, the church-wardens, the sextons, the beadles, the porters of the parish, and the monastics—"the men of religion," as they are called. Yes, we do not make any difficulty in acknowledging it, M. Bonaparte has had in his favour all the bishops who sign themselves after the style of Veuillot and Montalembert,* and all the "men of religion." Precious race! old, but much recruited since the landlord terrors of 1848.

---

* Two strong Catholics; the latter, Count Montalembert.

They are the kind of men who pray in these terms: "O my God! make the shares of Lyons go up." "Sweet Lord Jesus, make me realize twenty-five per cent. on my Naples-Rothschild certificates." "Holy apostles, sell my wines." "Blessed martyrs, double my governments." "Holy Mary, Mother of God, spotless Virgin, Star of the Sea, Garden enclosed, hortus conclusus, deign to cast a favourable eye on my little business, situated at the corner of Tirechappe and Quincampoix streets." "Tower of Ivory, make the shop opposite run down." These voted really and incontestably for M. Bonaparte: first class, the office-holder; second, the fool; third, the Voltairian-landlord-manufacturer-priest class.

Let us own it: the mind of man, and the bourgeois intellect in particular, has singular puzzles. We know it, and we have no desire to hide it: from the shopkeeper to the banker, from the little tradesman to the exchange-broker, a good number of men of business and manufacturers in France—that is to say, a good number of those men who know perfectly well what a well-placed confidence is, a deposit faithfully kept, a key placed in sure hands—voted, after the 2d of December, for M. Bonaparte. The vote accomplished, you might have spoken to one of these business-men—the first you met, taken at hazard—and this is the dialogue that you would have exchanged with him:—

"You have nominated Louis Bonaparte President of the Republic?"

"Yes."

"Would you take him for your cash-boy?"

"Certainly not."

CHAPTER V.

AND that is the ballot. Let us repeat it, and dwell on it, and not get tired. *"I cry a hundred times the same things,"* says Isaiah, *"in order that they may hear once."* That thing there is the ballot, that is the plebiscite, that is the vote, that is the sovereign decree of "universal suffrage," under the shadow of which these men who are holding France to-day shelter themselves, and out of which they make themselves titles of authority, and a diploma of government, while in the mean time they are commanding, and domineering, and judging, and reigning; their arms plunged to the elbows in gold, and their feet to the knees in blood. Now, and to make an end of it, let us make one concession to M. Bonaparte. No more quibbles. His ballot of the 20th of December was free, it was enlightened; all journals printed what they pleased. Who has said the contrary? Slanderers! They opened the electoral assemblages; the walls disappeared, covered up with the posted notices; the passers-by in Paris swept with their feet, on the Boulevards and in the streets, a snow-storm of election tickets—white, blue, yellow, red; they said what they wanted to say, wrote what they wished to write; the number of votes is honestly returned. It was not Baroche who counted, it was Barême. Louis Blanc, Guinard, Felix Pyat, Raspail, Caussidière, Thoré, Ledru-Rollin, Stephen Arago, Albert, Barbès, Blanqui, and Gent, were the sifters of the votes. It was they who announced the seven million five hundred thousand votes. Be it so. We concede all that. But after that, what is the conclusion which the coup d'état makes of it? He rubs his hands and asks no more: that satisfies him. He supposes that all is hushed up and ended, and that he has nothing further to do—that he is "absolved."

Halt there!

The true vote, the genuine returns, that is not the critical side of the question. There remains the moral side. There is, then, a moral side? Yes, prince, and that is the true side, the great side. Let us examine it.

10

CHAPTER VI.

It is necessary first, M. Bonaparte, that you should have some knowledge as to what the human conscience is. There are two things in this world; learn this new idea; and they call them good and evil. It is necessary that it should be revealed to you that to lie is not righteous, to betray is evil, to murder is worse. It is in vain that these are useful, they are forbidden. By whom? you will ask me. We shall explain it to you further on; but let us proceed. Man, know also this other peculiarity, is a thinking being, free in this world, to give account in the other. Strange thing, and one which will surprise you, he was not made only to enjoy, to satisfy every whim, to move at the chance impulse of his appetites, to crush whatever happens to be before him as he walks, sprig of herb, or oath sworn; nor to devour, whatever presents itself when he is hungry. Life is not his prey; for example, in order to pass from nothing a year to two hundred thousand francs, it is not allowable to take an oath which one does not intend to keep; and to pass from two hundred thousand francs to twelve millions, it is hardly right to break up the Constitution and laws of one's country, and to rush from ambush upon a sovereign assembly, to slaughter Paris, to exile ten thousand persons, and to proscribe forty thousand. I continue to help you penetrate this singular mystery. Unquestionably it is agreeable to have one's lackeys in white silk stockings; but to arrive at this great result, it is not permitted to suppress the glory and the thought of a people, to overthrow the central tribune of the civilized world, to fetter the progress of the human race, and to pour out waves of blood. That is forbidden. By whom? do you again ask? you, who see before you nobody who forbids you anything. Patience, you will soon know what!—here you start back, and I understand it,—When one has on one side his interests, his ambition, his fortune, his pleasure, a fine palace to keep on the Faubourg St. Honoré, and on the other side the jeremiads and the furious cries of women whose husbands they are taking off, of mothers whose sons they are seizing, of families whose fathers they are tearing away, of children whose bread they have stolen, of people whose liberty they have confiscated, of society whose prop, the laws, they have drawn away; what! that when these bawlings are on one side, and interest on the other, it is not to be permitted to disdain these uproars, to let all these people shout on, to tread on the obstacle, and to go perfectly natural over everything to that spot where one sees his fortune, his pleasure, and the fine palace of the Faubourg St. Honoré. That is the plan of the strong man. What! It is necessary to be engrossed with thinking on the fact that three or four years ago, one knows no longer when, one knows no longer where, one day in December, when it was very cold, and rained, and one had to quit a chamber in an inn to lodge one's self better, that one uttered, one no longer knows on what suggestion, in a badly lighted hall, before eight or nine hundred imbeciles, who believed one, these eight letters: "I swear it!" What! when one meditates a great act, it is necessary to pass one's time in asking one's self about what evil might possibly result from what one does; to give one's self any uneasiness because this man here will be devoured by vermin in these casements, that other there will rot in the hulks, this other die at Cayenne, that other be killed by the bayonet, that one crushed with paving-stones, that other will have been fool enough to get himself shot; that these will be ruined, those exiled, and all the men that one ruins, exiles, shoots, massacres; all who rot in the hulks, die in Africa, are honest men who shall have done their duty! A man must stop at these things! What! a man has wants, he has no money; he is a prince, chance places power in his hands; he uses it, he authorizes lotteries, he has the ingots of gold shown in the thoroughfare Jouffroy; the pockets of all the world open, one draws out what one can; you give some to your friends, devoted companions, to whom one owes a recognition, and as there arrives a moment when public indiscretion mixes itself up with the affair, and this infamous liberty of the press wishes to pierce the mystery, and justice imagines that it concerns her, it would be necessary to quit the Elysée, leave power, and go stupidly to seat one's self between two men-at-arms on the bench of the sixteenth chamber. Come then, is it not more simple to seat one's self on the throne of the emperor? Is it not simpler to crush the liberty of the press? Is it not simpler to crush justice? Is it not shorter to put the judges under one's feet? They do not ask for anything better, after all! They are all ready! and it would not be permitted, it is forbidden!! Yes, my lord, that is forbidden! Who opposes it? Who does not permit it? Who forbids it? M. Bonaparte, one is master; one has eight millions of votes for his crimes, and twelve millions of francs for his privy purse; one has a senate, and M. Sibour within it; one has armies, cannon, fortresses, Troplongs* flat on their stomachs, Baroches on all fours; one is despot, all powerful. A certain man who is lost in the darkness, a passer-by, unknown, stands before you, and says: "Thou shall not do that." This some one, this mouth that speaks in the shade, that one does not see, this unknown insolent is—the human conscience? That is what the human conscience is. It is some one, I repeat, that one does not see, and who is stronger than an army, more numerous than seven million five hundred thousand votes, higher than a senate, more religious than an archbishop, more intelligent in the question of right than M. Troplong, more prompt to outstrip it matters not what justice than M. Baroche, and which thee and thou's Your Majesty.

---

* Minister of Justice.

CHAPTER VII.

LET us examine these novelties a little. Learn then, M. Bonaparte, this further: What distinguishes a man from a brute is the idea of good and evil. Of that good and that evil of which I spoke to you just now. There is the abyss. The animal is a complete being. What makes the grandeur of man is, that he is an incomplete being; it is to feel one's self in a multitude of points outside of the finite. It is to perceive something on that side of one, something on this. That something which is on either side of man is the mysterious; is—to employ those weak human expressions which are always imperfect, and never express more than one side of a thing—is the moral world. This moral world man bathes in, is steeped in, as much, nay more, than in the material world. He lives in what he feels more than in what he sees. In vain does the creation beset him, in vain does want assail him, in vain does enjoyment tempt him, in vain does the brute which is in him torment him; a sort of perpetual aspiration to another region casts him irresistibly outside of the created world, outside of want, outside of enjoyment, outside of the brute. He is always, at each instant, throughout all, catching glimpses of the higher world, and he fills his soul with this vision, and regulates his actions by it. He does not feel complete in this life below. He carries in himself, so to speak, a mysterious copy of this prior and later world, and perfect world, with which he ceaselessly, and in spite of himself, compares this imperfect present world, and himself and his infirmities, and his appetites, his passions, and his actions. When he sees that he is approaching this ideal model, he is joyful; when he sees that he is departing from it, he is sad. He profoundly understands that there is nothing useless or inadmissible in this world, nothing which does not come from something, and does not lead to something. The just, the unjust, the good, the evil, good works, bad actions, all fall into the gulf; but they do not perish, they go away into the infinite to be the accusation or the benediction of those who have done them. After death one finds them again, and the whole are summed up. To lose one's self, to vanish, to be annihilated, to cease to be, is no more possible for the moral than the material atom. Behold in man this grand double consciousness of liberty and responsibility. It is given to him to be good or to be wicked. That will be an account to settle. He can be guilty; and striking and terrible fact, and one on which I insist, in that lies his grandeur. There is nothing equal to it for the brute. For him there is nothing but instinct; to drink when thirst comes, to eat when hungry; to breed in the season, to sleep when the sun goes down, and to awake when it arises; to do the reverse if he be a night animal. The animal has only one kind of obscure self, which no moral gleam lights up. All his law, I repeat it, is instinct. Instinct, a sort of rail on which fatal nature draws the brute. No liberty, then no responsibility, and in consequence no other life. The brute does neither good nor evil; he is ignorant of either. The tiger is innocent. If you only happened to be as innocent as he is! At some moments, one is tempted to believe, that having no more inward light than he has, you have no more responsibility. Indeed there are times when I pity you. Who knows? You are perhaps only an unfortunate blind force. Mons. Louis Bonaparte, you do not possess the idea of good and evil. You are perhaps the only man in all humanity without it. That places a bar between you and the human race. Yes, you are impregnable. It is that which constitutes your genius, they say. I agree that in any case it is that which now constitutes your power. But do you know what issues from this kind of power? Action?—yes. Justice?—no. Crime tries to cheat history about its name. It comes and says: "I am success." Thou art crime! you are crowned and masked! Down with the mask! down with the crown! Ah! you are losing your paint, you are losing your appeals to the people, your plebiscite, your ballots, your certificates, your additions, your executive commissions, announcing the whole; your red or green streamers, with this number on gilt paper: 7,500,000. You will make nothing by getting up this scene. There are things about which one cannot change universal opinion. The human race, taken in mass, is an honest man. Even around you they judge you. There is no one among all your establishment, among those decorated with lace, as among those in the embroidered uniform, valet of the stable or valet of the senate, who does not say in a low tone what I say aloud. What I declare publicly, they whisper; that is all the difference. You are omnipotent: they bow down, nothing more. They salute you with blushes on their brows. They *feel* that they are vile, but they *know* that you are infamous. Stop! since you are in the mood to give chase to those whom you call the revolters of December; since it is on them that you let loose your hounds; since you have installed a Maupas and created a minister of police especially for that, I denounce to you this rebellious and unsubdued insurgent, the universal conscience. You give money, but it is the hand that receives, not the conscience. Conscience! While you are about it, enter it on your lists of exiles. It is an obstinate opponent,— opinionated, tenacious, inflexible,—and one that makes trouble everywhere. Chase it out of France for me. You will be let alone forever after. Do you want to know how it treats you, even in the houses of your friends? Do you wish to know for what reason an honourable knight of St. Louis, eighty years old, a great enemy of "demagogues" and a partizan of yours, voted for you on the 20th of December? "He is a wretch," said he, "but he is *a necessary wretch!*" No! there are no necessary wretches. No! the criminal is never useful; crime is never good. Society saved by treason? Blasphemy! We must leave it to the archbishops to say such things. Nothing good has evil for foundation. The just God does not impose on humanity the necessity of wretches. There is nothing necessary in this world but justice and truth. If that old man had looked less at life and more at the tomb, he would have seen that. This speech is surprising on the part of an old man; for there is a light from God which illumines souls near the tomb and shows them the true. Never do right and crime meet. The day when they should be coupled the words of the human language would change their meaning, all certainty would vanish, and social darkness would spread over all. When, by chance, such a thing has been seen at times in history,—when, by chance, it happens for a moment that crime has the force of law,—something trembles in the very groundwork of humanity. *"Jus que datum sceleri!"* cries Lucian, and this line crosses history like a cry of horror.

Then, even by the avowal of those who voted for you, you are a "wretch." I take away "necessary." You cannot alter this. "Well, be it so," you will say; it is the truth; but one gets himself "absolved" by universal suffrage. Impossible! How! impossible? Yes, impossible. I am going to put the thing under your very nose.

CHAPTER VIII.

You are captain of artillery at Berne, M. Louis Bonaparte. You have necessarily a touch of algebra and geometry. Here are some axioms of which you have probably some idea: two and two make four; a straight line is the shortest distance between two points; the whole is greater than the part. Now, make 7,500,000 votes declare that two and two make five; that a straight line is the longest distance; that the whole is less than the part. Make eight millions declare it, ten millions, a hundred millions; you have not advanced one step. Well, now, this is going to surprise you: there are axioms in good character, in honesty, in justice, just as there are axioms in geometry; and moral truth is no more at the mercy of a vote than algebraic truth. The idea of good and evil is not to be decided by universal suffrage. It does not belong to a ballot to make the false true, and injustice just. They do not put human conscience to vote. Do you understand now? See this lamp, this little, obscure light, forgotten in a corner, lost in the shadow. Look at it—admire it. It is scarcely visible; it burns all alone. Make seven million five hundred thousand mouths blow at it at once: you will not put it out; you will not even make the flame stagger. Make the hurricane blow on it: the flame continues to rise straight and pure toward heaven. That lamp is conscience. That flame is that which sheds light in the midst of the night of exile on this sheet of paper on which I am writing at this moment.

CHAPTER IX.

THUS, then, whatever your numbers may be, forged or not, extorted or not, true or false, it makes little difference ; those who live with the eye fixed on justice say, and will continue to say, that crime is crime, that perjury is perjury, that treason is treason, that murder is murder, that blood is blood, that mire is mire, that a villain is a villain ; and that such as think to copy Napoleon on a small scale are copying Lacenaire on a large one ; they say that and they will repeat it in spite of your numbers, seeing that seven million five hundred thousand votes weigh nothing against the conscience of one honest man, seeing that ten millions, that a hundred millions of votes, the very unanimity of the human race itself ballotting *en masse*, does not count before this atom, this particle of God, the soul of the just, seeing that universal suffrage, which has all sovereignty on political questions, has no jurisdiction over moral ones.

I lay out of this question for the moment, as I said just now, your election proceedings—the bandages put on people's eyes, the gags placed in their mouths, the cannon on the public squares, the drawn sabres, the spies swarming, silence and terror conducting the voter to the urn like the malefactor conducted to the post ; I lay out that. I suppose I repeat to you true universal suffrage, free, pure, real universal suffrage, sovereign of itself as it ought to be ; newspapers in all hands, men and facts questioned and sifted, post-bills covering the walls, speech everywhere, light everywhere!

Well, to such universal suffrage submit peace and war, the effective force of the army, credit, the budget, public charity, the death penalty, the life-tenure of the judges, the indissolubility of marriage, divorce, the civil and political condition of woman, free education, the constitutions of municipal corporations, the rights of labour, the salary of the clergy, free trade, railroads, the circulation, colonization, taxes, all problems whose solution does not draw in their train its own abdication; for universal suffrage can do everything except abdicate; submit *them* to it; it will solve them magisterially, with possible error, doubtless, but with all the amount of certainty which is possible to man. It will solve them magisterially. Now, try to make it decide the question whether John or Peter did right or wrong in stealing an apple on a farm. There it stops. There its effort proves abortive. Why? Is it because the question is too low? No; it is because it is too high. All that constitutes the proper organization of societies, whether you consider them as territories, as corporations, as a state, or as a country; all political, financial, social matters depend upon universal suffrage, and obey it. *The smallest atom of the least moral question defies it.* The ship is at the mercy of the ocean. The star is not!

They said of M. Leverrier, and of you, M. Bonaparte, that you were the only two men who believed in their stars. You believe in your star most truly; you are looking for it above your head. Well! this star which you are looking for outside of yourself, other men have in themselves. It sends out its rays under the arch of their skull; it lights and guides them; it makes them see the true colors of life; it shows them the good and the evil in the obscurity of human destiny, the just and the unjust, the real and the false; it reveals to them ignominy and honour, rectitude and felony, virtue and crime. This star, without which the human soul is only night, is moral truth. This light failing you, you were deceived. Your ballot of the 20th December is only to a man who thinks a sort of monstrous artlessness. You applied what you call "universal suffrage" to a question which is no connection with universal suffrage. You are not a politician—you are a malefactor. What ought to be done with you has no reference to universal suffrage. Yes, artlessness! I insist on it. The bandit of Abruzzes, with hands scarcely washed, and having blood yet in his nails, goes to ask absolution of the priest; you have asked absolution from the vote; only you have forgotten to confess; and when you asked the vote to absolve you, you placed your pistol at its temple. Ah, desperate wretch! to "absolve" you, as you say, is out of the power of the people; it is out of the power of man. Listen.

Nero, who had invented the society of the Tenth of December, and who, like you, employed it to applaud his comedies, and even, still like you, his tragedies; Nero, after having bored his mother through the bosom with a knife, would have been able himself also to convoke his *universal* suffrage, which still further resembled yours in that it was not troubled by the license of the press; Nero, pontiff and emperor, surrounded by judges and priests prostrating themselves before him, would have been able, laying one of his bloody hands on the warm corpse of the empress and raising the other to heaven, to take all Olympus to witness that he had not shed her blood; and to adjure his universal suffrage to declare, in the face of gods and men, that he, Nero, had not killed that woman; his universal suffrage, discharging its functions about as yours did, in the same light and the same liberty, would have been able to affirm by seven million five hundred thousand votes that the divine Cæsar Nero, pontiff and emperor, had done no evil to the woman who was dead! Know, sir, that Nero would not have been "absolved;" it would have been enough that one voice, one single voice upon the earth, the most humble and the most obscure, should have lifted itself in the midst of that profound night of the Roman empire, and cried in the darkness, "Nero is a parricide;" this would have sufficed in order that the echo, the eternal echo of the human conscience, should repeat forever, from people to people, and from century to century, "Nero killed his mother!" Well, that voice which protests in the darkness, is mine. I cry to-day, and do not doubt it, the universal conscience of humanity repeats with me: "Louis Bonaparte has murdered France! Louis Bonaparte has killed his mother!"

BOOK SEVENTH.—THE ABSOLUTION.

SECOND FORM OF ABSOLUTION: THE OATH.

CHAPTER I.

A REDOUBLED OATH.

WHAT is Louis Bonaparte? He is living perjury, mental reservation incarnate; he is felony in flesh and bone; he is false swearing, having on the hat of a general and having himself called my lord.

Well, what does he demand of France, this ambushman? An oath. An oath! Assuredly, after the 20th of December, 1848, and the day of the 2d December, 1851, after the dissolution of the assembly by the armed hand, after arresting and hunting and tracking the inviolable representatives, after the confiscation of the Republic, after the coup d'état, one ought to expect a cynical and honest shout of laughter on the part of this malefactor with regard to an oath, and that this Sbrigani should say to France: "It is very droll; do not speak any more about such stupidities as that." Not at all: he wishes an oath. Thus, mayors, judges, spies, prefects, generals, city guards, rural guards, commissioners of police, functionaries, senators, councillors of state, legislators, clerks; a herd, it is said, he wishes it; this idea has passed through his head; he intends it thus ; it is his pleasure. Come, make haste, defile, you in an enregistering office, you in a prætorium, you under the eyes of your brigadiers, you at the minister's house ; you, senators, at the Tuileries, in the parlour of the marshals ; you, spies, at the prefecture of police ; you, chief-presidents and procurers-general, in his ante-chamber. Make haste ! by carriage, on foot, by horse ; in your robes, in your scarfs, in costume, in uniform, in mourning ; gilded, spangled, plumed ; with your swords at your sides, with gala-cap on your forehead, the priestly band on your necks, with belts on your stomachs ; arrive ! some before the plaster busts, some before the man himself; well done ! there you are ; you are all up to the mark ; nobody fails him. Look him well in the face ; concentrate your thoughts ; search in your conscience, in your loyalty, in your shame, in your religion ; take off your glove, raise your hand, and make oath to his perjury, and swear fidelity to his treason.

Is it done? Yes. Ah ! what an infamous farce ! Then Louis Bonaparte takes the oath seriously. True, he trusts to my word, to thy word, to yours, to ours, to theirs ; he believes everybody's word except—his own. He requires that about him they should swear, and he orders that they should be loyal. It pleases Messalina to surround herself with virgins.

Admirably well ! He wishes that they should have honour. "You will consider it an understood thing, Saint Arnaud, and you will consider it," said Maupas. Let us go to the bottom of these things, however : there are two kinds of oaths. The oath which freely, solemnly, in the face of God and men, after having received a commission full of confidence from 6,000,000 citizens, one takes in full national assembly, to the constitution of one's country, to the law, to the right, to the nation, to the people, to France—that is nothing, that does not bind ; one can play with that, and laugh at it, and tear it to pieces some fine morning under the heel of one's boot ; but an oath that one takes under the cannon, under the sabre, under the eye of the police, to keep the employment which enables him to live, which gives one bread, to preserve the rank which is one's property ; the oath which, to save one's head and the head of his children, one takes to a cheat, to a rebel, to the violator of the laws, to the murderer of the Republic, to a backslider from all righteous conduct, to the man who himself has broken his oath,—oh ! that oath is sacred ! Don't let us joke : the oath that one takes to the 2d of December, nephew of the 18th Brumaire, is doubly holy. What I admire is absurdity, to receive as cash and as sound coin these *Juro* of the official herd ; not even to dream that one has destroyed all scruples, and that he would not be able to secure a single word that can be relied on ! One is prince and one is traitor ! To set an example at the head of the State, and to imagine that it will not be followed ! To sow lead and fancy that one is going to reap gold ! Not even to perceive that all consciences model themselves in such a case on the conscience above, and that the false oath of the prince makes all oaths bad money !

CHAPTER II.

INEQUALITY IN THE PRICES.

AND then, of whom do you require these oaths? Of this prefect? he has betrayed the State. Of this general? he has betrayed the flag. Of this magistrate? he has betrayed the law. Of these functionaries? they have betrayed the Republic. Curious thing, and one which makes philosophy consider, this heap of traitors from which issues this heap of oaths! Then let us insist on this beauty of the second of December. M. Bonaparte—Louis, believes in people's oaths! he believes in the oaths that they take even to *him!* When M. Rouher takes off his glove and says "I swear it;" when M. Suin takes off his glove and says "I swear it;" when M. Troplong puts his hand on his chest at the spot where the third button of senators is situated, and the hearts of other men, and says "I swear it," M. Bonaparte feels the tears in his eyes, adds up with emotion all these loyalties, and contemplates these beings with tenderness. He confides! he believes! O abyss of candour! Most certainly the innocence of scoundrels sometimes dazzles honest men. One thing, nevertheless, astonishes the benevolent observer, and puts him a little out of humour; that is the capricious, disproportionate manner in which the oaths are paid for; it is the inequality of the price that M. Bonaparte puts on this merchandise. For instance, M. Vidocq, if he were still chief of the Service of Safety, would have six thousand francs wages a year; M. Baroche has twenty-five thousand. It follows from this that the oath of M. Vidocq would not bring him in but sixteen francs sixty-six centimes a day, whilst the oath of M. Baroche brings him in two hundred and twenty-two francs twenty-two centimes a day. This is evidently unjust. Why this difference? An oath is an oath; an oath is composed of a glove taken off and eight letters.

What does M. Baroche's oath possess which M. Vidocq's does not? You will tell me that it depends upon the difference in the functions; that M. Baroche presides at the Council of State, and that M. Vidocq would be only chief of the Service of Security. I answer that these are chance differences; that M. Baroche would probably excel in directing the Service of Security, and that M. Vidocq* would make a very good president at the Council of State. That is not a reason. Are there then different qualities of oaths? Is it as it is with masses? Are there then, also, masses at fifty cents and masses at ten cents, which, as the curate said, are only fit for the ignoramuses? Have they oaths at their several prices? Is there in this commodity of oaths superfine, extra fine, fine, and half fine? Are the first of better materials than the others? are they more solid, less full of tow and cotton? Are they better dyed? Are there oaths all new, and which have not been worn; oaths worn at the knees, oaths patched, oaths worn down at the heels; is there, in short, any choice? Let them tell us of it; the thing is worth while, we are the ones who pay. This observation is in the interest of the taxpayers. I ask M. Vidocq's pardon for having made use of his name. I acknowledge that I had no right to do it. After all, M. Vidocq might have refused the oath.

---

* He was a celebrated detective, assuming marvellous disguises and mingling with thieves.

CHAPTER III.

OATH OF THE MEN OF LETTERS AND SCIENCE.

PRECIOUS item: M. Bonaparte wished Arago to swear. Know it, astronomy has to make oath. In a well regulated State, like France or China, all is office, even science. The mandarin of the institute depends upon the mandarin of the police. The great telescope, with parallactic* feet, owes homage to M. Bonaparte. An astronomer is a kind of sky policeman. The observatory is a sentry-box, like any other. It is necessary to keep an eye on the good God, who is above, and who seems sometimes not to be completely submissive to the Constitution of the fourteenth of January. Heaven is full of disagreeable allusions, and ought to be well looked after. The discovery of a new spot on the sun constitutes, evidently, a case for censorship. The prediction of a high tide may be seditious. The announcement of an eclipse of the moon may be treasonable. We are something of a moon at the Elysée. Astronomy is almost as dangerous as a free press. Do they know what is taking place in those tête-à-têtes between Arago and Jupiter? If it was M. Leverrier, all right, but a member of the provisionary government! take care, M. de Maupas! † it is necessary that the bureau of longitudes

---

* That is, widely separated.
† Minister of police.

should swear not to conspire with the stars, and above all not with those foolish blunders of celestial coups d'état which they call comets. And then we have already said, one is a fatalist when one is Bonaparte. The great Napoleon had a star; the little one ought certainly to have a nebulus of them; astronomers are certainly somewhat astrologers. Gentlemen, make oath. It is needless to say that Arago refused. One of the virtues of the oath to M. Bonaparte is that according as you refuse it or accord it, this oath takes away or gives to you talents, merits, adaptabilities. You are professor of Greek and Latin, make oath, or else they will drive you from your chair; you no longer know any Latin or Greek. You are professor of rhetoric, make oath, or else tremble! the orations of Theramene and the dream of Athalia are forbidden to you; you wander about the rest of your days without ever being able to re-enter. You are professor of philosophy, make oath to M. Bonaparte, or else you will become incapable of comprehending the mysteries of the human conscience, and of explaining them to young people. You are professor of medicine, make oath, without which you will no longer know how to try the pulse of a fever patient. But if the good professors go away, there will be no more good scholars! In medicine particularly this is serious. What will become of the sick? Of whom? The sick. That is a matter of great interest. But we have something besides the sick to think of. The matter of importance is that medicine should make oath to M. Bonaparte. Otherwise either seven million five hundred thousand votes have no sense, or it is evident that it is better to have your leg cut off by an ass who has made oath, than by Dupuytren, if he is refractory.*

Ah! one wishes to laugh at it, but all this weighs on the heart. Are you a young and rare and generous spirit like Deschanel, a firm and correct intelligence like Despois, a reason serious and energetic like Jacques, an eminent writer, a popular historian like Michelet, make oath, or die of hunger. They refuse. Silence, and the darkness which they stoically enter, know the rest.

---

* If they have sense, and Dupuytren is not among them, then Dupuytren has no sense. He was one of the greatest surgeons of the age.

CHAPTER IV.

CURIOSITIES OF THE THING.

ALL morality is denied by such an oath, all shame swallowed up, all modesty defied. There is no reason why one should not see unheard-of things; one sees them. In such a city as Evreux,* for example, the judges who made oath judge the judges who refused it.

---

* The president of the tribunal of commerce at Evreux refuses the oath. Let us permit the *Moniteur* to speak:

" M. Verney, the former president of the tribunal of commerce at
" Evreux, was cited to appear on Thursday last before the correctional
" judges of Evreux, on account of events which took place on the 29th of
" April last within the bounds of the consular precinct. M. Verney is
" detained on the charge of exciting hatred and contempt of the govern-
" ment. The judges in the first instance dismissed Verney with an admo-
" nition. Appeal *a minimæ* of the procurer of the Republic. Judgment
" of the Court of Appeals of Rouen.

" The court, seeing that the prosecutions have for their only object the
" repression of the crime of exciting hatred and contempt of the govern-
" ment; seeing that this crime would result, according to the accusation
" from the last paragraph of the letter written by Verney to the procurer
" of the Republic at Evreux, on the 26th of April last, and which was couched
" in these terms: ' But it would be too serious to claim for a much longer
" time what we believe to be the right. The magistracy itself would take
" it kindly of us not to expose the robe of the judge to succumb under the
" farce which your dispatch announces to us.'

" Seeing that *censurable as may have been the conduct of Verney in this*

Ignominy seated on the tribunal makes honour sit on the stool; conscience sold censures conscience honest; the woman of the town lashes the virgin. With this oath one treads from surprise to surprise. Nicolet is only a booby beside M. Bonaparte. When M. Bonaparte has gone the rounds of his valets, his accomplices, and of his victims, and pocketed the oath, he turned with good nature toward the valiant chiefs of the army of Africa, and held with them pretty nearly this language: "Apropos, you know, I have had you arrested in your beds during the night by my people; my spies have entered your houses with the sword uplifted; I have even decorated them since for this feat of arms; I have had you menaced with the gag, if you utter a cry; I have had you taken by the throat by my galley sergeants; I have had you put in Mazas in the thieves' cell, and at Ham in my own cell; you have yet on your wrists the marks of the cord with which I have bound you. Good-morning, gentlemen; God have you in his holy keeping; swear fidelity to me."

Changarnier looked fixedly at him, and answered: "No,

" *affair*, the court cannot see in the terms in this part of his letter the
" crime of exciting to the hatred and contempt of the government, since
" the order in virtue of which force was to be employed to hinder the
" judges who had refused to take the oath from sitting, did not emanate
" from the government.

"Seeing that there is not room, therefore, to make the penal law apply
" to him by these facts, confirms the judgment on which the appeal is
" made without *costs*.

" The Court of Appeal of Rouen has for its first president Franck-Carré,
" former procurer-general of the Court of Peers in the prosecution at Co-
" logne; the same who addressed these words to M. Louis Bonaparte:
" ' You have tampered with the loyalty of citizens and distributed money
" to buy treason.' "

traitor!" Bedeau answered: "No, forger!" Lamoricière answered: "No, perjurer!" Leflo answered: "No, bandit!" Charras gave him a slap in the face. At the present moment the face of M. Bonaparte is red, not with shame, but with the blow.

Another variety of oath. In the casemates, in the fortresses, in the hulks, in the penal colonies of Africa, there are prisoners by thousands. Who are those prisoners? We have said, they are republicans, patriots, soldiers of the law, innocent men, martyrs. What they suffer, generous voices have already denounced; one catches a glimpse of it; we ourselves, in the special book upon the second of December, shall succeed in tearing off the veil. Well! Do they want to know what happens? Sometimes, in the extremity of suffering, exhausted of strength, bending under miseries, without covering for the feet, without bread, without clothing, without shirts, burning with fever, gnawed with vermin, poor workmen torn from their workshops, poor peasants torn from their plows, mourning a wife, a mother, children; a family widowed or orphaned, without bread at hand, and perhaps without shelter, heaped together, sick, dying, in despair, a few of these unhappy creatures give up, and consent to "ask pardon." Then they bring them to sign a letter, already made out, and addressed to "My Lord, the Prince-President." This letter we publish, exactly in the shape in which Quentin Bauchart acknowledges it:

"I, the undersigned, declare on my honour that I accept with thankfulness the pardon which is extended to me by Prince Louis-Napoleon, and I engage to have nothing to do with secret societies, to respect the laws, and to be *faith-*

ful to the government which the country has given me by the vote of the 20th and 21st of December, 1851."

Let no one mistake the meaning of this grave fact. This is not clemency granted, it is clemency implored. This formula, "Ask your pardon of us," means: "Accord us our pardon." The assassin, leaning over the assassinated, with his knife raised, cries to him: "I have arrested you, seized you, thrown you to the ground, stripped you, robbed you, pierced you with stabs; then you are under my feet; your blood is pouring out from twenty wounds; tell me that *you repent*, and I will not absolutely kill you." This *repentance* of the innocent, exacted by the criminal, is nothing but the form which takes him out of his inward remorse. He imagines himself to be assured in this manner against his own crime.

To whatever expedients he may have recourse to shake off the thought of it,—however much he may make the seven million five hundred thousand little bells of his "plebiscitum" ring in his ears,—the man of the coup d'état thinks at moments; he catches vague glimpses of a to-morrow, and struggles against the inevitable future. He needs a legal purge, a discharge, a withdrawal, a receipt. He asks it of the conquered, and at need he puts them to the torture to obtain it. At the bottom of the conscience of every prisoner, of every transported and of every proscribed man, Louis Bonaparte feels that there is a tribunal there, and that this tribunal gives notice of his trial; he trembles; the hangman has a secret fear of his victim, and, under the form of a pardon accorded to this victim, he has his own acquittal signed by this judge. He hopes thus to call off the attention of France, who is herself a living conscience and an attentive tribunal, and who, he thinks—the day of his sentence having arrived, and she having seen him absolved by his victims—will herself give him pardon. He is mistaken; let him pierce the wall at another point,—he will not escape by this.

CHAPTER V.

THE FIFTH OF APRIL, 1852.

HERE is what they saw at the Tuileries on the 5th of April, 1852. Toward eight o'clock in the evening, the ante-chamber was filled with men in red robes; grave, majestic, speaking low; holding in their hands black velvet caps trimmed with gold lace; the most of them with white hair. They were the presidents and counsellors of the courts of cassation, the first presidents of the courts of appeal, and the procurers-general; all the high magistracy of France. These men remained in this ante-chamber. An aid-de-camp introduced them and left them there. A quarter of an hour passed, and then a half-hour, and then an hour; they went and came, backward and forward, talking among themselves, looking at their watches, waiting for the ringing of a bell. At the end of an hour they perceived that they had not even arm-chairs to sit down on. One of them, M. Troplong, went into another ante-chamber, where the valets were, and complained. They brought him a chair. At last a folding-door opened; they entered a saloon pell-mell. There a man in a black frock was standing leaning against a mantel-piece. What did these men in red robes come to do at the house of this man in a black coat? They came to make oath to him. It was M. Bonaparte. He nodded to them; they bowed down to the earth, as was proper. Before M. Bonaparte, at a few paces, there was standing his chancellor, M. Abattucci, late liberal deputy, now minister of justice of the coup d'état. They began. M. Abattucci made a discourse, and M. Bonaparte a speech. The prince pronounced, looking at the carpet, a few drawling and disdainful words: he spoke of his "legitimacy;" after which the magistrates swore. Each one raised his hand in his turn. While they were swearing, M. Bonaparte, with his back half turned, chatted with some aids-de-camp grouped behind him. When it was finished, he turned his back altogether, and they went away, shaking their heads, ashamed and humiliated, not for having done a base act, but because they had not had chairs in the antechamber.

As they went out, this dialogue was heard: "There," said one of two, "there is an oath which it was necessary to take." "And which it will be necessary to keep," replied a second. "Like the master of the house," added a third.

All this is abject; let us pass on. Among the first presidents who swore fidelity to Louis Bonaparte, there were a certain number of the late peers of France, who, as peers, had condemned Louis Bonaparte to perpetual imprisonment. But why look so far back? Let us pass further on. Here is what is better. Among these magistrates there were seven men named thus: Hardouin, Moreau, Pataille, Cauchy, Delapalme, Grandet, Quesnault. These seven men composed, before the 2d of December, the high court of justice; the first, Hardouin, president; the two last, substitutes; the four others, judges. These men had received and accepted from the Constitution of 1848 a commission couched in the following terms:

"Art. 68. Every measure by which the President of the

"Republic dissolves the national assembly, prorogues it or "places obstacles in the way of the execution of its decrees, "is a crime of high treason. The judges of the high "court shall assemble immediately, on pain of forfeiture; "they shall convoke the jury in the place which they shall "designate, in order to proceed to the trial of the president "and his accomplices; they shall constitute themselves the "magistrates charged with fulfilling the functions of the "public ministry."

On the 2d of December, in presence of the flagrant outrage, they had commenced the process, and named the procurer-general, M. Renouard, who had accepted, to proceed against Louis Bonaparte on the crime of high treason. Let us join this name, Renouard, to the seven others. On the 5th April they were—the whole eight of them—in the ante-chamber of Louis Bonaparte! What they did there we have just seen.

Here it is impossible not to pause. These are dismal ideas on which it is necessary to have the strength to dwell; these are sewers of ignominy that it is necessary to have the courage to sound. See this man. He was born by chance —by misfortune—in a little paltry room, in a paltry house, in a den, they know not where, they know not of whom. He has come out of the dust to fall into the bog. He had only just enough of a father and a mother to enable him to be born, after which all forsook him. He crawled the best that he could. He grew up with naked feet, naked head, in rags, and without knowing what to do to live. He does not know how to read, he does not know that there are laws over his head; he scarcely knows that there is a heaven. He has no hearth, no roof, no family, no belief, no book. He is a blind soul. His intelligence has never opened, for intelligence, like flowers, only opens to the light; and he is in darkness. However, he has to eat. Society has made a brute beast of him; hunger has made a carniverous beast. He waits for foot-passengers at the corner of the wood, and tears away their purses. They take him and send him to the galleys. So far so good. Now, see this other man. It is no longer the red cap—it is the red robe. This one believes in God, reads Nicolle, is a jansenist, and devout, goes to confession, goes to get the blessed bread. He is well born, as they say; nothing is wanting to him, nothing has ever been wanting to him; his family have lavished everything on his childhood—cares, lessons, counsels, Greek and Latin literature, masters. He is a grave and scrupulous personage. Also, they have made a magistrate of him. Seeing this man pass his days in the meditation of all the great texts, sacred and profane, in the study of right, in the practice of religion, in the contemplation of the just and unjust, society has placed in his keeping those which are the most august and most venerable objects which it possesses, the book and the law. It has made him judge and punisher of treason. It has said to him: "A day may come, an hour may sound, which the chief with material force shall tread law and right under its feet; then thou, man of justice, thou shalt arise, and thou shalt strike with thy rod the man of power. For that, and expecting this perilous and supreme day, it heaps thee with benefits, and clothes thee with purple and ermine." That day is actually approaching; that hour unique, solemn, severe, that grand hour of duty. The man in the red robe begins to stammer the words of the law; suddenly he perceives that it is not justice which prevails, that it is treason which is carrying him away; and then, he, this man who has passed his life in illuminating, penetrating himself with the pure and holy light of right, this man who is nothing if he is not the despiser of unjust success, this man of letters, this scrupulous man, this religious man, this judge to whom they have confided the keeping of the law, and in a certain degree of the universal conscience, turns toward the triumphant perjurer, and with the same mouth, with the same voice with which, if the traitor had been conquered, he would have said, "Criminal, I condemn you to the galleys," says, "My lord, I swear fidelity to you." Take a balance. Put this judge in one scale, and that galley-slave in the other, and tell me on which side it goes down.

CHAPTER VI.

OATH EVERYWHERE.

SUCH are the things which have been seen in France on account of the oath to M. Bonaparte. They have sworn here, there, everywhere; at Paris, at the east, at the west, at the north, at the south; it has been in France during all a great month, a tableau of arms stretched out, and of hands raised up; final chorus: *Let us swear, etc.* The ministers swore before the president, the prefects before the ministers, the mob before the prefects.

What is M. Bonaparte doing with all these oaths? Is he making a collection of them? Where does he put them? It has been remarked that the oath has never been refused except by functionaries who are not remunerated; the counsellors-general, for example. In reality, it is to the budget that they have taken oath. One heard, on the 29th of March last, a certain senator implore in a high voice against the omission of his name, which was in a certain sense an accidental modesty. M. Sibour,* archbishop of Paris, swore; M. Franck Carré,† procurer-general at the Court of Peers in the affair of Boulogne, swore; M. Dupin,‡ president of the National Assembly on the second of December, swore. Oh, my God! it is enough to make one wring his hands with shame! It is, however, a holy

---

* As Senator.
† As first President of the Court of Appeals.
‡ As President of an agricultural precinct.

thing, this oath! The man who makes an oath is no longer a man, he is an altar; God descends on him. Man, that infirmity, that shadow, that atom, that grain of sand, that drop of water, that tear fallen from the eyes of destiny; man so little, so weak, so uncertain, so ignorant, and so restless; man who goes on in trouble and doubt, knowing little of yesterday and nothing of to-morrow; seeing just enough of his path to place his foot before him, the rest darkness; man trembling if he looks before him, sad if he looks behind him; man enveloped in these immensities and these obscurities, time, space, being, and lost in them; having a gulf within him, his soul, and a gulf without him, heaven; man who, at certain hours, bends down with a sort of sacred horror beneath all the forces of nature, under the sound of the sea, under the shivering of the trees, under the shadow of the mountains, under the beaming of the stars; man, who cannot raise his head by day without being blinded by the light, by night without being crushed by the infinite; man, who knows nothing, who sees nothing, who hears nothing, who, perhaps, carried away to-morrow, to-day, this moment, by the wave which passes, by the wind which blows, by the flintstone which falls, by the hour which rings; man, endowed for a day, this shivering, tottering, miserable being, the coral of chance, the plaything of the minute which is flying by, collects himself suddenly, before the enigma which they call human life, feels that there is in him something grander than the abyss, honour; stronger than fatality, virtue; deeper than the unknown, faith; and alone, feeble, and naked, he says to all this awful mystery which holds him, and which envelopes him: "Do with me what thou wilt, but as for me, I will do this, and I shall not do that ;" and bold, serene, tranquil, creating with a word a fixed point in this sombre instability which fills the horizon ; as the sailor casts an anchor in the ocean, he casts his oath into the future. Oh, oath! Wonderful confidence of the just man in himself! Sublime permission to affirm, given by God to man! It is finished. There is no more of it. One more splendour of the soul has vanished!

BOOK EIGHTH.

CHAPTER I.

PROGRESS INVOLVED IN THE COUP D'ÉTAT.

AMONG us, democrats, the event of the 2d of December struck many sincere minds with stupor. It has disconcerted some, discouraged others, filled several with consternation. I have seen some who cried : *Finis Poloniæ!*

As for myself, since at certain moments it is necessary to say I, and to speak before history as a witness, I proclaim that I have seen this event without apprehension. I say more, there are moments when in presence of the 2d of December I declare myself satisfied. When I succeed in abstracting myself from the present, when it happens to be possible for me to turn away my eyes for an instant from these crimes, from this blood poured out, from all these victims, from all the proscribed, from these hulks where the imprisoned have the rattle already in the throat, from those frightful galleys at Lambessa and Cayenne, where they die quickly, from that exile, in which they die slowly, from that vote, that oath, this immense heap of shame put upon France, and which goes on increasing every day— when, forgetting for a few moments the melancholy thoughts which habitually beset my mind, I succeed in enclosing myself within the severe indifference of the politician, and in no longer considering the deed, but the consequences of the deed; then, among many disastrous results, no doubt, advance, real, considerable, enormous advance, appears to me, and in such a moment, if I am always one of those whom the 2d of December makes indignant, I am no longer one of those whom it afflicts. The eye is fixed on certain aspects of the future. I am able to say to myself of it : "The act is infamous, but the fact is good."

They have tried to explain the inexplicable fact of the victory of the coup d'état in a hundred fashions :—Equilibrium took place between the different resistances, which were possible, and they mutually neutralized each other;—the people were afraid of the bourgeoisie, the bourgeoisie were afraid of the people;—the faubourgs hesitated before the restoration of the majority, fearing, wrongfully nevertheless, lest their victory might place that right which is profoundly unpopular in power;—the shopkeepers recoiled before the red Republic;—the people did not understand; the middle classes were evasive;—the former said, "whom are we going to have enter the legislative palace?" the latter said, "whom are we going to see in the Hôtel de Ville?"—finally, the rude repression of June, 1848, the insurrection crushed by cannon-shots, the quarries, the casemates, the transportations; living and terrible recollection;—and then : if one had been able to beat the recall !—if a single legion had turned !—if M. Sibour had been M. Affre, and had cast himself before the balls of the prætorians !—if the high court had not allowed itself to be chased away by a corporal !—if the judges had done as the representatives, and if one had seen the red robes in the barricades as one saw the scarfs! if one single arrest had failed ! if a regiment had hesitated ! if the massacre of the Boulevard had not taken place, or had gone ill for Louis Bonaparte! etc., etc. All that is true, however, it is that which has been which was to be. Let us say it again, under this monstrous victory, and in its shadow, an immense and definite advance had been made. The 2d of December has succeeded, because in more than one point of view, I repeat it, it was well, perhaps, that it should succeed. All explanations are correct, and all are vain. The invisible hand is mingled with it all. Louis Bonaparte has committed the crime ; Providence has brought about the result. It was really necessary that what he calls order should be brought to light in his logic. It was necessary that men should know well and know forever, that in the mouths of the men of the past that word, Order, signifies false oath, perjury, pillage of the public money, civil war, courts-martial, confiscation, sequestration, transportation, proscription, volleys of musketry, police censorship, the dishonour of the army, the reducing the people to a cipher, the abasement of France, a mute Senate, a tribune overthrown, the press suppressed, the policy of the guillotine, the throttling of liberty, the strangling of right, the violation of laws, the sovereignty of the sabre, massacre, treason, ambush. The sight which one has under his eyes is a useful sight. What one sees in France since the 2d of December, is the orgy of disorder. Yes, Providence is in this result. Consider it further. Fifty years ago the Republic and the Empire were filling all imaginations, the first with its reflection of terror, and the last with its reflection of glory. Of the Republic, one saw only 1793 ;' that is to say, formidable revolutionary necessities, the furnace; of the Empire, one only saw Austerlitz. Hence a prejudice against the Republic, and a prestige for the Empire. But what is the future of France? Is it the Empire? No, it is the Republic. It was necessary to overthrow that situation, to suppress the prestige in that which could not revive, and to suppress the prejudice against that which is to be. Providence has done it. It has destroyed these two mirages. February has come, and has taken terror away from the Republic; Louis Bonaparte has come, and has taken the prestige from the Empire.

From this time forth, 1848, fraternity, is laid down upon and covers up 1793, terror; Napoleon the Little is superposed upon Napoleon the Great.

The two great things, one of which terrified, and the other of which dazzled, draw back by one plan. One no longer perceives 1793 except across that which gives it justification, and Napoleon except across his caricature; the foolish fear of the guillotine is dissipated, the vain imperial popularity has vanished.

Thanks to 1848, the Republic no longer terrifies; thanks to Louis Bonaparte, the Empire no longer fascinates. The future has become possible. These are the secrets of God. And further, the *word* Republic no longer satisfies; it is the *thing* Republic that we need. Well, we shall have the thing with the word. Let us develope this.

CHAPTER II.

WHILE waiting for those marvellous but certain simplifications which will one day bring about the union of Europe and the democratic confederation of the Continent, what will be the form of that social edifice in France of whose indistinct yet luminous features the thinker catches a glimpse at present, across the darkness of dictatorships?

That form will be this: the commune sovereign, management by an elected mayor; universal suffrage everywhere, subordinate to the national unity only in that which touches general acts. That is for the administration. The council of prosecuting officers and the committees of prud'hommes* regulating the private differences of associations and of industries; the jury, the examining magistrate of facts, enlightening the judge, the magistrate deciding upon the right of facts; the judge elected. That is for justice. The priest outside of everything except the church, living with his eye fixed on his book, and on heaven; a stranger to the budget, ignorant of the State, known only to his faithful, having no longer authority, but having liberty. That is for religion. War limited to the defence of territory; the nation, the national guard, divided into three sections, able to arise as one man. That is for power. The law always, the right always, the vote always; the sabre nowhere.

---

* Discreet men selected to arbitrate.

But, to this future, to this magnificent realization of the democratic ideal, what have been the obstacles?

There were four material obstacles; here they are: the standing army, the centralized administration, the clergy in secular office, the magistracy irremovable.

CHAPTER III.

WHAT, these four obstacles are, what they were, even under the Republic of February, even under the Constitution of 1848, the evil that they were producing, the good that they were hindering, what past they were making permanent, and what excellent social order they were postponing, the writer on the laws of nations was catching a glimpse of, the philosopher knew; the nation, with reference to it, were totally ignorant.

Those four institutions, enormous, ancient, solid, propped up one against the other, mingled at their base and at their summit, crossing like a forest of grand old trees, with their roots under our feet, and their branches over our heads, stifled and crushed everywhere the scattered germs of new France. Where there would have been life, movement, association, local liberty, spontaneity in the communes, there was administrative despotism; where there would have been intelligent vigilance, armed when needed, on the part of the patriot and the citizen, there was the passive obedience of the soldier; where the living Christian faith might have struggled to burst out, there was the Catholic priest; where there might have been justice, there was the judge. And the future was there under the feet of suffering generations; it could not come forth out of the earth, but which was waiting.

Did they know that among the people? Had they any misgivings of such a thing? Did they divine it? No. Far from it, in the eyes of the great majority, and of the middle classes in particular, these four obstacles were four supports. Magistracy, army, administration, clergy, were the four virtues of order, the four social forces, the four holy columns of the ancient French formation. Attack that, if you dare! I do not hesitate to say it: in the state of blindness which prevailed in the best minds, with the methodic march of healthful progress, with our assemblies, of which no one will suspect me of being a detractor, but which, when they are at once honest and timid, a thing which often happens, only allow themselves willingly to be governed by their own average—that is to say, their mediocrity; with their committees for initiating proceedings, their delays, and their ballotings, if the 2d of December had not come to bring its thundering demonstration, if Providence had not interfered in it, France would have remained indefinitely condemned to an irremovable magistracy, to administrative centralization to the standing army, and clerical office-holders. Assuredly, the power of the tribune and the power of the press combined, those two great forces of civilization, I am not the man to try to oppose and diminish them; but nevertheless, see how much effort would have been necessary, of every kind, in every sense, and under all forms, by the tribune and by the journal, by the book and by speech, in order to shake the universal prejudice favourable to those four fatal institutions! How much, in order to succeed in *overthrowing* them; to make evidence gleam before all eyes; to conquer interested resistance, passionate or totally unintelligent; to enlighten profoundly public opinion, consciences, the official powers; to make the quadruple reform penetrate into ideas, and then into laws! Count the speeches, the writings, the newspaper articles, the rough drafts of laws, the counter-drafts, the amendments, the amendments to amendments, the reports, the reports of the minorities, the facts, the incidents, the attacks, the discussions, the affirmations, the contradictions, the stories, the steps in advance, the steps in retreat, the days, the weeks, the months, the years, the quarters of a century, the half centuries, that would be necessary.

CHAPTER IV.

I SUPPOSE on the benches of an assembly, the most intrepid of thinkers, a brilliant mind, one of those men who, when they stand erect upon the tribune, rise into enthusiasm, grow suddenly grand, become colossal there, surpass by a whole head those massive semblances which mask realities, and see distinctly the future over the high and sombre wall of the present. This man, this orator, this seer, wishes to warn his country; this prophet wishes to enlighten the statesmen; he knows where the rocks are; he knows that society will fall to pieces just on account of these four props for support: administrative centralization, the standing army, an irremovable judiciary, a salaried priesthood; he knows it, he wishes that all should know it. He ascends the tribune; he says: "I denounce to you four great public perils. Your political system carries within it that which will kill it. It is necessary to transform the administration from foundation to roof, the army, the clergy, and magistracy; to suppress here, to retrench there, to re-make everything, or to perish by these four institutions which you take as the elements of permanence, and which are the elements of dissolution." They murmur. He exclaims: "Your centralized administration! do you know what it may become in the hands of a perjured executive power? An immense treason, executed at one moment over all the face of France, by the office-holders, without exception."

Murmurs break out anew, and with more violence. They

cry: "Order!" The orator continues: "Do you know what your standing army can become on any given day? An instrument of crime! Passive obedience is the bayonet forever charged at the heart of the law. Yes, here even, in this France, which is the initiative power of the world, in this land of the tribune and the press, in this native home of human thought; yes, an hour may sound when the sabre shall reign; when you, inviolable legislators, will be seized by the collar by corporals; when our glorious regiments will be transformed in the interests of one man, and, to the shame of the people, into gilded hordes and prætorian bands; when the sword of France will be something which strikes from behind, like the poignard of the Italian assassin; when the blood of the first city of the world will splash the golden epaulettes of your generals."

The murmur becomes a tumult. They cry: "Order!" on all sides. They interrupt the orator: "You have just insulted the administration, now you outrage the army." The president calls the orator to order. The orator resumes: "And if there should arrive a day in which a man, having in his power the five hundred thousand office-holders who constitute the administration, and the four hundred thousand soldiers who compose the army,—if it should happen that this man should tear up the Constitution, violate all laws, infringe all oaths, outrage all rights, commit all crimes, do you know what your irremovable magistracy— the defender of the right, the guardian of laws—would do? It would turn traitor!"

The clamours hinder the orator from completing his sentence. The tumult becomes a tempest. "This man respects nothing. After the administration and the army he drags the magistracy in the mud. Reprimand! reprimand!" The orator is reprimanded, and it is inscribed upon the record of proceedings. The president declares to him that if he continues the assembly will be consulted and the floor will be denied him. The orator pursues: "And your salaried clergy! and your office-holding bishops! On the day when any pretender shall have employed the administration, the magistracy, and the army in all these outrages, —on the day when all these institutions shall drip with blood, shed by the traitor and for the traitor, placed between the man who shall have committed the crimes and the God who commands us to hurl anathemas at the criminal, do you know what they will do, your bishops? They will prostrate themselves, not before God, but before *man!*"

Can one imagine the whoops, the melée of curses, which such words would receive? Can one imagine the cries, the rebukes, the threats, the entire assembly arising en masse, the tribune scaled, and scarcely protected by the attendants?—The orator has successively profaned all the sacred arks, and he has ended by touching the holy-of-holies—the clergy! And then what does he suppose? What a herd of impossible and infamous hypotheses!— Does not one hear Baroche growl from this place and Dupin thunder? The orator would be called to order, censured, fined, excluded from the chamber for three days, like Pierre Léroux and Emile de Girardin; who knows? even, perhaps, expelled like Manuel. And the next day the indignant bourgeois would say: "Well done!" And from all quarters the journals of order would shake their fists at the SLANDERER. And in his own party, on his own bench at the assembly, his best friends would abandon him and would say : "It is his own fault; he has been wool-gathering ; he has supposed chimeras and absurdities!" And after his generous and heroic effort, he would discover that the four institutions attacked would be more venerable and infallible than ever, and that the question, instead of having advanced, would have been retarded.

CHAPTER V.

But Providence goes to work otherwise. He puts the things splendidly before your eyes, and tells you : see. A man comes some fine morning,—and what a man ! the first come, the last come ; without past, without future, without genius, without glory, without prestige, is he an adventurer? is he a prince? this man has simply his hands full of money, of bank notes, of shares, of railroad stock, of places, of decorations, of sinecures ; this man stoops to the functionaries, and says, "Functionaries, turn traitors." The functionaries turn traitors. All? Without exception? Yes, all. He addresses the generals and says : "Generals, massacre." The generals massacre. He turns to the irremovable judges, and says to them : "Magistracy, I infringe the Constitution, I perjure myself, I dissolve the sovereign Assembly, I arrest the inviolable representatives, I pillage the public treasury, I sequestrate, I confiscate, I banish whoever displeases me, I transport at caprice, I mow down with grape-shot without summons, I shoot without sentence, I commit every deed which it is proper to call crime, I violate everything which it is proper to call right. Look at the laws—they are under my feet." "We will pretend not to see," say the magistrates. "You are insolent," replies the man of Providence. "To turn away your eyes is to outrage me. I intend that you should aid me. Judges, you are going to-day to congratulate me, who am farce and crime; and to-morrow those who have resisted me, those who are honour, right, law, you will judge, and you will condemn." The irremovable judges kiss his boot and set to work to prepare the *affair of the troubles*. They make oath to him, into the bargain. Then he perceives in a corner the clergy, endowed, gilded, crosiered, coped, mitred, and he says to them: "Ah! you are there, archbishop. Come here! you are going to bless me all this." And the archbishop strikes up his Magnificat.*

---

* My soul doth magnify the Lord.

CHAPTER VI.

AH ! what a striking and instructive thing ! *Erudimini,* Bossuet would say. The ministers imagined that they were dissolving the assembly ! They were dissolving the administration. The soldiers fired on the *army* and killed it. The judges thought to judge and condemn innocent men ; they judged and condemned to death the irremovable magistracy. The priests thought to chant an hosanna over Louis Bonaparte ; they chanted a De profundis over the clergy.

CHAPTER VII.

WHEN God wishes to destroy a thing, he charges that thing itself with the duty. All bad institutions in this world end in suicide. When they have weighed long enough on men, Providence does with them as the Sultan does with his viziers. He sends them a cord by a mute; they execute themselves. Louis Bonaparte is the mute of Providence.

CONCLUSION.—FIRST PART.

CHAPTER I.

LITTLENESS OF THE MASTER, BASENESS OF THE SITUATION.

BE calm, history has got hold of him. Nevertheless, if it flatters M. Bonaparte's vanity to be seized by history; if he should by chance have an illusion in his mind on the subject of his worth as a political villain, and one would actually suppose it, let him remove it; let him not go on imagining, that because he has heaped horrors on horrors, that he will ever hoist himself to the height of the great historical bandits. We have been wrong, perhaps, in a few pages of this book, here and there, in comparing him with these men. No; although he may have committed enormous crimes, he will remain paltry. He will never be anything but the nocturnal strangler of liberty; he will never be anything but the man who has glutted the soldiers—not with glory, like the first Napoleon, but with wine; he will never be anything but the pigmy tyrant of a great people. The stamp of the individual is incompatible, thoroughly so, with grandeur, even grandeur in infamy. Dictator! he is a buffoon; let him make himself emperor—he will be absurd.

He will accomplish *this*. He will make the human race shrug their shoulders; that will be his destiny. Will

Napoleon the Little.

he be less vigorously punished on that account? No. Disdain takes away nothing from anger; he will be hideous, and he will remain ridiculous. That is all. History laughs, and strikes him with a thunderbolt.

The most indignant even will not save him from that. Great thinkers are delighted to chastise great despots, and sometimes even ennoble them somewhat in order to make them worthy of their fury; but what do you want the historian to make of this personage?

The historian will only be able to bring him before posterity, holding him by the ear. The man, once stripped of success—the pedestal taken away, the dust settled, the tinsel and the glitter and the great sabre taken off, the poor little skeleton stripped naked and shivering with cold—and can one imagine anything more wretched and piteous? History has its tigers. Historians, immortal keepers of ferocious animals, show the nations this imperial menagerie. Tacitus alone, that great exhibitor of beasts, has taken and shut up eight or ten of these tigers in the iron cages of his style. Look at them; they are frightful, grand, superb. Their spots make part of their beauty. This one is Nimrod, the hunter of men; this one is Busiris, the tyrant of Egypt; this is Phalaris, who had living men cooked in a brazen bull, in order to make the bull bellow; this is Antiochus, who tore off the skin from the heads of the seven Maccabees and had them roasted alive; this is Nero, the burner of Rome, who covered the Christians with wax and with tar and lighted them like torches; this is Tiberius, the man of Caprera; this is one Domitian; this one, Caracalla; this one is Heliogabulus; and this one is Commodus, who has this further merit in horror, that he was the son of Marcus Aurelius; these are the czars; these are the sultans; these are the popes; remark among them the tiger Borgia; here is Philip, called the Good, as the furies were called Eumenides; here is Richard III., sinister and deformed; here is Henry VIII., with his large face and great stomach, who, of the five wives that he had, killed two and disembowelled one; here is Christiern II., the Nero of the North; here is Philip II., the Demon of the South. They are frightful; hear them roar; examine them one by one. The historian brings them to you, drags them, furious and terrible, to the edge of the cage, opens their jaws for you, lets you see their teeth, shows you their claws; you can say of every one of them: "He is a royal tiger." They have really been taken on all the thrones. History walks them across the centuries. She prevents them from dying; she takes care of them. They are *her* tigers; she does not mingle them with jackals. She keeps the unclean animals apart. M. Bonaparte will be with Claude, with Ferdinand VII. of Spain, with Ferdinand II. of Naples, in the cage of the hyenas.

He is something of a brigand, and a good deal a rogue. One always smells in him the poor swindling prince, who lived on his wits in England; his actual prosperity, his triumph, his empire, and his inflation make no difference; that mantle trails over boots run down at the heels. Napoleon the Little; nothing more, and nothing less. The title of this book is good. The lowness of his vices injures the grandeur of his crimes. What could you expect? Peter the Cruel massacred, but he did not steal. Henry the Third assassinated, but he did not swindle. Timour crushed the children under the hoofs of horses, about as M. Bonaparte exterminated the women and old men on the Boulevard, but he did not lie. Listen to the Arabian historian: "Timour Beig Sahebkeran (master of the world, and of the century, master of the planetary conjunctions), was born at Kesch, in 1336. He cut the throats of a hundred thousand captives, and when he was besieging Siwas, the inhabitants, in order to bend him, sent a thousand little children to him, carrying each a Koran on his head, and crying: 'Allah! Allah!' He had the sacred books taken away with respect, and had the children crushed under the feet of his horses. He employed seventy thousand human heads, with cement, stone, and brick, to build towers at Heérat, at Sebzvar, at Tekrit, at Aleppo, at Bagdad. He detested falsehood. When he had given his word he could be trusted." M. Bonaparte is not of that stature. He has not the dignity which the great despots of the east and west mingled with their ferocity. The Cæsarian breadth is wanting. In order to make out a good appearance, and to present a suitable style among these illustrious cut-throats, who have tortured humanity for four thousand years, one must not cause the mind of a beholder to hesitate between a general of division and the man who beats the big drum at the Champs-Elysées. It is not necessary to have been a policeman in London; it is not necessary to have endured with downcast eyes, in full court of peers, the haughty contempt of M. Magnan; it is not necessary to have been called pickpocket by the English journals; it is not necessary to have been threatened with Clichy; it is not necessary, in a word, that there should be anything of the rascal in the man. Monsieur Louis Napoleon, you are ambitious, you aim high, but it is very necessary to tell you the truth. Well, what do you want us to make of it? It is in vain that you have realized, in your fashion, the wish of Caligula : "I could wish the human race had only one head, that I might behead them at a blow." It is in vain that you have banished the Republicans by thousands, as Philip the Third expelled the Moors, and as Torquemada drove away the Jews ; it is in vain that you have casemates like Peter the Cruel, hulks like Adrian, tortures like Michael le Tellier, and trap-dungeons like Ezzelin III.; it is in vain that you have been perjured, like Ludovico Sforza ; it is in vain that you have massacred and assassinated, en masse, like Charles IX. ; it is in vain that you have done each and all of these impressive things ; it is in vain that you have brought all those names to mind when one meditates on *your* name ; you are only a knave. "He is not a monster who desires to appear one."

CHAPTER II.

OUT of every agglomeration of men, out of every city, out of every nation, there breaks out fatally a centralizing power. Put this centralizing force at the service of liberty; have it regulated by universal suffrage, the city becomes a commune, the nation becomes a Republic. This centralizing force is not inherently intelligent—belonging to everybody, it belongs to nobody; it floats, so to speak, on the outside of the people. Until the day when, according to the true social formula, which is the least government possible, this force shall be reduced to be nothing but a police of the street and of the road, paving the high-roads, lighting the street-lamps, and watching the malefactors, until that day, this centralizing force, being at the mercy of many chances and ambitions, needs to be guarded and defended by institutions which are jealous, clear-sighted, well armed. It may be enslaved by tradition; it may be surprised by ruse. A man may throw himself upon it, seize it, bridle it, subdue it, and make it tread on the citizens. The tyrant is that man who, emerging from tradition, like Nicholas of Russia, or from ruse, like Louis Bonaparte, takes possession of this centralizing force of the people for his own profit, and disposes of it according to his own choice. This man, if he was from birth what Nicholas is, he is the social enemy; if he has done what Louis Bonaparte has done, he is the public thief. The first has nothing to do with regular and legal justice, with the articles of codes. He has behind him the spy and the garroter, hatred in his heart and vengeance in his hand, in his palace Orloff, and among his people Mouravieff; he may be assassinated by any member of his army, or poisoned by a member of his family; he runs the chance of the conspiracies of barracks, of the revolts of regiments, of secret military societies, of domestic plots, of sudden and obscure diseases, of terrible blows, of great catastrophes. The second ought simply to go to Poissy. The first has what is necessary in order to die in the purple, and to end pompously and royally as monarchies and tragedies finish; the second ought to live— to live between four walls, behind gratings which permit him to be seen by the people, sweeping the courts, making brushes out of horse-hair or socks out of list, emptying tubs with a green cap on his head, with wooden shoes on his feet, and with straw in his wooden shoes. Ah! leading men of the old parties, men of the absolutism in France, you have voted en masse among the 7,500,000; outside of France you have applauded, and you have taken this Cartouche* for the hero of order. He is ferocious enough for that, I grant, but look at his height. Do not be ungrateful for your true colossi. You have dismissed too soon your Haynaus and your Radetzkys. Consider above all this comparison which offers itself so naturally to the mind. What is this lilliputian mandarin compared with Nicholas, czar, and Cæsar, emperor and pope—a power half Bible and half knout,† who damns and condemns, who commands 800,000 soldiers and 200,000 priests, holds in his right hand the keys of Paradise, and in his left the keys of Siberia, and possesses as his private property 60,000,000 of men—the souls as if he were God, the bodies as if he were the tomb.

---

* Eminent bandit. † A Russian scourge.

CHAPTER III.

UNLESS there shall be a catastrophe, sudden, imposing, and brilliant; if the actual situation of the French nation should be prolonged and become permanent, the great injury, the frightful injury would be the *moral* injury. The Boulevards of Paris, the streets of Paris, the fields and the cities of twenty-eight departments in France, were strewn, on the 2d of December, with slaughtered and prostrate citizens; one saw before the thresholds fathers and mothers with their throats cut, children sabred, women with dishevelled hair wet with blood, ripped open by grape-shot; one saw people who were begging for their lives massacred in the houses, some shot in heaps in their cellars, others dispatched with the bayonet on their beds, others brought down by a ball on the flagstone of their hearth : all sorts of bloody hands are still imprinted, even at this present hour, here on a wall, there on a door, there on an alcove; after the victory of Louis Bonaparte, Paris trod for three days in a reddish mud; a cap full of human brains was hung on a tree in the Boulevard des Italiens; I who write these lines, I saw, among other victims, on the night of the 4th, near the Mauconseil barricade, an old man with white hair stretched on the pavement, shot through the chest with an iron ball, and with his collar-bone broken; the gutter of the street which flowed under him bore away his blood. I saw, I touched with my hands, I helped undress a poor child of seven years of age, killed, they told me, in Tiquetonne-street; it was pale, its head moved backward and forward from one side to the other while they were taking off its clothing; its half-opened eyes were fixed, and while stooping near its half-opened mouth one seemed to hear it still murmur: Mother! Well! there are things more heart-rending than this slain child, more mournful than that old man killed with grape-shot, more horrible than that rag filled with human brains, more frightful than these pavements red with carnage, more irreparable than the loss of these men and women, these fathers and mothers slaughtered and assassinated,—it is the *honour of a great people* which has vanished. Most certainly, those pyramids of the dead that they saw in the cemeteries after the wagons that came from the Champs de Mars were unloaded; those immense open ditches, that they filled in the morning with human bodies, making haste because the light was gaining upon the twilight, these were shocking; but what is more frightful still, is to think that at the present hour the peoples are left in darkness, and that for them France, that great moral splendour, has disappeared! What is more heart-rending than skulls cleft by the sabre, bosoms ploughed through with bullets, more disastrous than houses violated, than murder filling the streets, than blood poured into the gutters, is to think that now they are saying to themselves among all the peoples of the earth: You know well, that nation of nations, that people of the 14th of July, that people of the 10th of August, that people of 1830, that people of 1848, that race of giants which crushed the fortresses, that race of men whose face gave light, that country of the human race which produced heroes, which made all the revolutions, and brought forth all the children; that France, whose name once meant liberty, that kind of soul of the world which shed its beams over Europe, that light—well! somebody has walked over it and extinguished it. There is no longer any France. It is all over. Look—darkness everywhere! The world is groping. Ah, it was so grand! Where are those times, those beautiful seasons mingled with storms, but splendid when all was life, when all was liberty, when all was glory? those times when the French nation, awaking before all, and standing erect in the darkness, with its forehead whitened by the day-break of the future already risen for her, said to the other peoples still on the ground, and in heaps, and scarcely moving their chains in their sleep: "Be quiet; I am doing what is necessary for all; I am digging the earth for all; I am the workman of God!" What deep sweetness! Look at this torpor, where there was once such power! Look at this shame, where there was once that pride! Look at the superb people, who were raising their heads, and who now abase it! Alas! Louis Bonaparte has done more than kill persons; he has diminished souls; he has lessened the heart of the citizen. It is necessary to belong to the race of the indomitable and invincible to persevere at this moment in the rough path of self-denial and of duty. I know not what gangrene of material prosperity is threatening to make public honour fall into rottenness. Ah! what good fortune to be banished, to be fallen, to be ruined, is it not honest workmen? is it not worthy peasants hunted from France, and who have no asylum, and who have no shoes? What happiness to eat black bread, to lie on a mattress thrown on the ground, to be out at elbows, to be beyond all that, and to those who say to you, "You are Frenchmen," to answer: "I am proscribed!" What misery is this joy of interests and cupidities, glutting itself in the trough of the 2d of December! Faith, let us live, let us attend to our business, let us job in zinc-stocks or in railroads, let us make money; it is not noble, but it is excellent; a scruple the less, a louis the more; let us sell our whole souls at this rate! They run, they rush, they make an ante-chamber, they swallow all shame, and if one cannot have a grant of a rood in France, or a grant of land in Africa, one asks for a place. A crowd of intrepid devotees besiege the Elysée, and group themselves around the man. Junot, near the first Bonaparte, braved the splashes of the shell; these, near the second, brave the splashes of mud. To partake of his infamy, what difference does that make to them, provided that they partake of his luck? It is a question as to who will make this sale of himself most impudently, and among these beings there are young people who have the pure and limpid eye, and every appearance of the generous age; and there are old men, who have only one fear, and that is lest the place solicited should not come in time, so that they may not be able to dishonour themselves before they die. One would give himself for a prefecture, another for a receipt, another for a consulate, another wants a tobacconist's shop, another wants an embassage; all want money, some more, some less, for it is of the salary, not of the duties that they think. Each one holds out his hands. All offer themselves. One of these days they will establish an assayer of conscience in money.

What! we have come to this! What, those very men who sustained the coup d'état, those very ones who were afraid of the red croquemitaine* and of the nonsense of the jacquerie in 1832; the very men who found this crime good, because, according to them it has drawn their stock, their notes, their cash, their portfolios, out of danger; these very men do not understand that material interests, floating on the waters, would be, after all, only a sad waif in the midst of an immense moral shipwreck, and that it is of a situation frightful and monstrous that they say: "All is saved, save honour!"† The words independence, enfranchisement, progress, popular pride, national pride, French greatness, one can no longer pronounce in France. Chut! These words make too much noise; let us walk on tiptoe, and speak low. We are in a sick man's room. What is this man? He is the chief, he is the master; everybody obeys him. Ah, all the world respects him, then? No, all the world despises him. O situation! And military honour, where is it? Don't speak any more, if you please, of what the army did on the 2d of December, but of what they submit to at the present moment, of that which is at their head and on their head. Do you think of it? Do they think of it? O army of the Republic! army whch has had for captains, generals paid four francs a day; army which has had for chiefs Carnot, austerity; Marceau, disinterestedness; Hoche, honour; Kléber, devotion; Joubert, worth; Dessaix, virtue; Bonaparte, genius! O French army, poor unfortunate, heroic army, led astray following the lead of such men as those! What will they do with it? Where will they bring it? In what way will

---

*Nursery horror.   †Parody upon the words of Francis I. when he was taken.

they employ it? What parodies are we destined to see and hear? Alas! what are these men who command our regiments and who govern? The master we are acquainted with. This one, who has been minister, was going to be "seized" on the 3d of December, that is why he *made* the 2d. This other is the "borrower" of the twenty-five millions from the Bank. This other is the man of the ingots of gold. To this other, before he was a minister, "a friend" said: "*Ah, you dupe us with your actions in the affair in question, that tires me. If there are to be swindles, count me in sure!*" That other, who has epaulets, has just been convicted of a sort of breach of trust. That other, who has also epaulets, received on the morning of the 2d of December, a hundred thousand francs to provide against possible events. He was only colonel : if he had been general he would have had more. This one, who is general, was a body-guard of Louis XVIII., and when he was on guard once behind the king's arm-chair during mass, he cut off a gold tassel from the throne and put it in his pocket. They dismissed him from the guards for that. Assuredly they could raise a column to these men also, *ex aere capto* (with the money taken). This other, who is general of a division, embezzled fifty-two thousand francs, to the certain knowledge of Colonel Charras, in the construction of the villages of Saint-Andre and Saint-Hyppolyte, near Mascara. This one, who is general-in-chief, was surnamed, at Gand, where they were acquainted with him, *General Five-hundred-francs*. This one, who is minister-of-war, owes it entirely to the clemency of Gen. Rullière that he was not brought before a court-martial. Such are the men. It is all the same. Forward! Drums beat, clarions sound, banners float. Soldiers!* from the height of those pyramids the forty thieves look down on you. Let us advance in this melancholy subject, and let us see all its sides. The mere sight of a fortune like that of M. Bonaparte placed at the summit of the State would be enough to demoralize a people. There are always,—in consequence of the defect of social institutions, which ought, before everything, to enlighten and to civilize,—there are always in a numerous population like that of France, a class which is ignorant, which suffers, which covets, which struggles, placed between the bestial instinct which impels to take and the moral law which invites to work. In the mournful and oppressed condition in which it is at present, this class, in order to maintain itself in righteousness and in wealth, needs all the pure and holy lights which are sent forth from the gospel; it needs that the mind of Jesus on the one side, and the mind of the French Revolution on the other, should address it in the same manly words, and show it, without ceasing, as the only lights worthy of the eyes of man, the high and mysterious laws of human destiny, self-denial, devotion, sacrifice, work which tends to material welfare, worth which tends to the inward welfare; even with this perpetual teaching, at once divine and human, this class, so worthy of sympathy and of fraternization, often succumbs. Suffering and temptation are stronger than virtue. Now, do you understand the infamous advice which the success of M. Bonaparte gives it? A man, poor, ragged, without resources, without work, is there in the shadow, at the corner of a street, sitting on a post; he is meditating and at the same time he is repelling a wicked

---

* Parody on Napoleon I. in Egypt.

action; at one moment he wavers, at another he holds himself upright; he is hungry, and he has a mind to steal; in order to steal it is necessary to make a false key, it is necessary to scale a wall, and then, a false key made and the wall scaled, he will be before the strong box; if any one awakes, if they resist him, it will be necessary to kill. His hair bristles, his eyes become haggard, his conscience, the voice of God, revolts within him, and cries to him: "Stop! that is wrong! those are crimes!" At this moment the chief of the State passes. The man sees M. Bonaparte, dressed as a general, with the red cord, and some lackeys in gold-laced livery, galloping toward his palace in a carriage with four horses; the unfortunate, uncertain before his crime, looks eagerly at this splendid vision, and the tranquillity of M. Bonaparte, and his gold epaulets, and the red cord, and the livery, and the palace, and the carriage with four horses, say to him: "Succeed!" He fastens on the apparition; he follows it; he runs to the Elysée; a guilded crowd rush after the prince. All sorts of carriages pass under that gate, and he catches a glimpse there of men happy and radiant. This one is an ambassador. The ambassador looks at him, and says to him: "Succeed." This one is a bishop. The bishop looks at him, and says: "Succeed." This one is a judge. The judge looks and smiles at him, and says: "Succeed." So, to escape the gendarmes, that is henceforth the whole law. To steal, to pillage, to poignard, to assassinate—these are only bad if one has the stupidity to get taken. Every man who meditates a crime has a constitution to violate, an oath to break, in a word, an obstacle to destroy. Choose your measures well. Be clever. Succeed. There are no crimes, but blunders. You put your hand into the pocket of a passer-by, in the evening, at night-fall, in a deserted place. He seizes you; you let go; he arrests you, and takes you to the station-house. You are guilty. To the galleys! You do *not* relax your hold. You have a knife on you; you stick it into the man's heart; he falls. There, he is dead; now, take away his purse, and go away. Bravo! it is a thing well done. You have shut the victim's mouth, the only witness who could speak. They have nothing to say to you. If you had done nothing but rob the man, you would have been wrong; kill him, you are right. Succeed; everything is in that. Ah, this is terrible! The day when the human conscience shall be put out of countenance, the day when success shall be more righteous than it, all will be over; the last moral gleam will reascend to heaven. It will be night in the soul of man. You will have nothing further to do but to devour yourselves, ferocious beasts! With moral degradation political degradation is joined. M. Bonaparte treats the people of France like a conquered country. He effaces the Republican inscriptions; he cuts down the trees of liberty, and makes fagots of them. There was a statute of the Republic on Bourgogne square, he put the mattock to it. There was a figure of the Republic crowned with ears of wheat on the coin; M. Bonaparte replaces it with the profile of M. Bonaparte. He has his bust crowned and harangued in the markets, as the bailiff Gessler had his cap saluted. Those clowns of the Faubourgs had the habit of singing in chorus, in the evening, returning from work. They sang the great Republican song, the "Marseillaise," the "Chant du Départ;" an injunction was laid on them to hold their tongues; the men of the Faubourgs will sing no more; there is amnesty only for obscenities and drunken songs. The triumph is such that one is no longer inconvenienced. Yesterday they were still hiding; they were shooting by night. It was from horror; but it was also from modesty. It was a remnant of respect for the people. They seemed to suppose that there were still enough alive to revolt if they saw such things. To-day they show themselves, they are no longer afraid; they guillotine in open day. Whom do they guillotine? Whom? The men of the law, and justice is there. Whom? The men of the people, and the people are there. That is not all: there is a man in Europe who strikes Europe with horror; this man has put Lombardy to the sack, he has erected the gallows for Hungary, he has had women lashed on the public squares—he called that to hand-whip them, and in his eyes it was clemency. After one of these executions, the husband of one of these women killed himself. The terrible letter in which the woman, Mme. Maderspach, recounts the deed, is still remembered. She says: "*My heart has turned to stone!*" At Brescia,—it is Gen. Pepe who relates the fact in his memoirs,—this man had the cannon rammed with the arms of women and the heads of infants in the style of bullets, and he sent these arms and these heads to the fathers and the husbands who were fighting in the barricades! Last year this man desired to visit England, as a tourist. While he was in London, he took it into his head to go into a brewery—the brewery of Barclay and Perkins. There he was recognized; a voice murmured: "It is Haynau." "It is Haynau!" repeated the workmen. It was an affrighting cry. The crowd rushed on the wretch, tore out his infamous white hair by handfuls, spit in his face, and flung him out of doors. Well, that old bandit in epaulets, this Haynau, this man who still wears on his cheek the immense insult of the English people, has been invited, it is announced, by my lord the prince-president, to visit him in France. It is quite right: London had done him an insult; Paris owes him an ovation. It is an amends. Be it so. We shall assist at that. Haynau recoiled from the maledictions and the whoops at the Perkins brewery; he will go for some flowers at the brewery St. Antoine. The Faubourg Saint Antoine will receive the order to be wise. The Faubourg St. Antoine, mute, motionless, passive, will see passing by, with an air of triumph, and chatting like two friends, in the old revolutionary streets, one in French uniform, the other in that of Austria, Louis Bonaparte, the butcher of the boulevard, giving his arm to Haynau, the lasher of women . . . . . . Go on, continue, add affront to affront, disfigure this France fallen upon her back on the pavement! Make her unrecognizable! crush the face of the people under your heel! Oh! inspire me with a plan, search for me, give me, find me, a means, whatever it may be, by the poignard, which I do not desire! A Brutus for this man! pshaw! he does not even deserve Louvel! Find me a means, whatever it may be, to hurl this man down, and to deliver my country! to cast this man down!—this man of subterfuge, this man of lies, this man of success, this man of misfortune!—a means, the first that presents, pen, sword, paving-stone, revolt by the people, by the soldiers; yes, whatever it may be, provided it is loyal and in open day, I take it, we all take it—we the proscribed,—if it can re-establish liberty, deliver the Republic, raise up our country from shame, and make this imperial ruffian, this prince pickpocket, this outsider among kings, this traitor, this master, this performer of Franconi! this manager radiant, immovable, satisfied, crowned with his happy crime, who goes and comes, walks peaceable across quivering Paris, and who has everything on his side—everything, the exchange, the shop, the magistracy, all influences, all cautious feelings, all prayers, from that in the name of the soldier's God to the Te Deum of the priest. Oh, I say, that there was some to make this successful wretch go again into his dust, into his oblivion, into his ditch! Surely when one has fixed his gaze too long on certain aspects of this sight, there are hours when a sort of vertigo would seize the strongest minds. But, nevertheless, does this Bonaparte do himself justice? Has he a gleam, an idea, a suspicion, any perception whatever of his infamy? Really one is forced to doubt it. Yes, sometimes, at the proud words which escape him, when one sees him address incredible appeals to posterity, into that posterity which will quiver with horror and with anger over him, when you hear him speak with coolness of his "legitimacy," and of his "mission," one would be almost tempted to believe that he had succeeded in taking himself into his own high consideration, and that his head was turned to that degree that he no longer perceives what he is, nor what he does. He believes in the adhesion of workmen, he believes in the good-will of kings, he believes in the feast of the Eagles, he believes in the harangues of the council, he believes in the benedictions of bishops, he believes in the oath that he has had sworn, he believes in the seven million five hundred thousand votes! He speaks to this hour, feeling himself in the humour of Augustus, of granting amnesty to the proscribed. Usurpation giving amnesty to honour! Cowardice giving amnesty to courage! Crime giving amnesty to virtue! He is so besotted with his success that he finds everything perfectly simple. Odd effect of drunkenness! Optical illusion! He sees this thing of the fourteenth of January gilded, splendid, radiant; the Constitution soiled with mud, stained with blood, ornamented with chains, dragged away in the midst of the shouts of Europe, by the police, the Senate, the Corps Legislatif, and the Council of State, bound anew with iron! He takes this hurdle, on which, standing erect, hideous and with a lash in his hand, he carries the bleeding corpse of the Republic, for a chariot of triumph, and wishes to have it pass under the arch de l'Etoile!

SECOND PART.

CHAPTER I.

MOURNING AND FAITH.

PROVIDENCE brings men, things, and events to maturity by the simple fact of universal life. It is sufficient in order that an old world should vanish, for civilization ascending majestically toward its solstice to beam on old institutions, old prejudices, old laws, old manners. This radiancy burns the past and devours it. Civilization enlightens, that is the evident fact, and at the same time it consumes, that is the mysterious fact. Influenced by it, slowly and without jolt, what is to decline declines, and what is to grow old grows old; wrinkles come to the things condemned, to the castes, to the codes, to the institutions, to the religions. This work of decrepitude, in a certain way, goes on of its own accord ;—fruitful decrepitude, under which new life springs up. Little by little the ruin is preparing ; deep crevices, that one does not see, branch out in the shadow and reduce to dust the interior of that venerable structure, which still looks massive on the outside ; and it is thus that some fine day, suddenly, this antique collection of worm-eaten facts, of which decrepid societies are formed, will become a deformity ; the edifice will become disjointed and unnailed, and bulge out. Then nothing has any further support. Let one of those giants which are natural to revolutions come suddenly on ; let this giant raise his hand and the story is told.

There is a certain hour in history when a push of Danton's elbow would make Europe totter.

Eighteen hundred and forty-eight was one of those hours. Old feudal Europe, monarchical, papal, patched up so fatally for France in 1815, tottered. But Danton missed. The sinking did not take place. They said a good deal, in the hackneyed phraseology which is employed in such cases, viz., that 1848 had opened a gulf. Not at all. The corpse of the past was on Europe ; is it there yet. 1848 opened a grave to throw that corpse in. It is this grave which they have mistaken for a gulf. In 1848 all that held to the past, all that was living on the corpse, saw this grave close by. Not only the kings on their thrones, the cardinals under their hats, the judges in the shadow of their guillotines, the captains on their war horses, were moved ; but whoever had any interest whatsoever in that which was going to disappear ; whoever was nursing in his own interest a social fiction ; whoever had an abuse to let or to lease ; whoever was guardian to a lie, doorkeeper to a prejudice, or contractor to a superstition ; whoever speculated, lent on usury, ground down, lied ; whoever sold with false weights, from those who altered balances to those who falsified the Bible ; from the bad shopkeeper, from those who manipulate the figures, to those who coin the miracles, all, from a certain banker Jew, who thinks himself somewhat of a little Catholic, to a certain bishop who becomes something of a Jew, all these men of the past leaned their heads against each other and trembled. That grave which was yawning, and where all fictions, their treasure, which had loaded down man for so many centuries had failed to fall, they resolved to fill. They resolved to wall it up, and to heap stone and rock upon it, and to set up on this heap a gibbet, and to hang on this gloomy and bloody gibbet that great culprit, Truth. They resolved to make an end, once for all, of the spirit of freedom and emancipation, and to tread down and compress forever the ascensional force of humanity. The enterprise was rude. What this enterprise was we have indicated already, more than once, in this book and elsewhere. To undo the work of twenty generations, to kill three centuries in the nineteenth century, namely, the sixteenth, seventeenth, and eighteenth,—that is to say, Luther, Descartes, and Voltaire—to stifle religious inquiry, philosophical inquiry, universal inquiry; to crush in all Europe that immense vegetation of free thought—a great oak here, a sprig of herb there; to marry the knout—Russian scourge—and the aspergile ;* to put more Spain in the south and more Russia in the north ; to resuscitate all that one can of the inquisition, and to stifle all that one can of intelligence; to stupefy youth—in other words, to besot the future ; to make the world assist at the auto-da-fé of ideas ; to throw the tribune over, to suppress the newspaper, the post-bill, books, speech, the cry, the murmur, the breath ; to make silence ; to pursue thought into the case of the printing-shop, into the composing-stick, into the lead type, into the stereotype and the stereotype-plate, into the lithographic-office, into the image, on the theatre, on the stage, into the mouth of

---

* Brush for holy-water.

the actor, into the copy-book of the schoolmaster, into the pack of the colporteur; to give to every one for faith, for law, for aim, and for God, material interest; to say to the peoples: eat, and think no more; to take the brain out of the man and put it in his stomach; to extinguish individual initiative, local life, national impulse, all the deep instincts that push man toward the right; to annihilate this I of nations that they call country; to destroy nationality among peoples divided and dismembered, the Constitutions in constitutional States, the Republic in France, liberty everywhere; to put the foot on human effort everywhere. In a word, to close this abyss which they call progress. Such was the plan, vast, enormous, European, which nobody conceived, for not one of those men of the old world had the genius for it; but which all followed. As to the plan in itself, as to this immense idea of universal pressure, whence does it come? Who could tell? They saw it in the air. It appeared beside the past. It enlightened certain souls, it showed certain routes. It was like a glimmer coming out of the tomb of Machiavelli. At certain moments in human history, at things which happen, it seems as if all the old demons of humanity—Louis XI., Philip II., Catharine de Medicis, the Duke of Alva, Torquemada—are somewhere there, in a corner, sitting around a table and holding council. One looks, one searches, and in place of Colossi one finds abortion, where one supposed the Duke of Alva, one finds Schwartzenburg, where one supposed Torquemada, one finds Veuillot. The ancient European despotism continues its march with those little men, and advances always; it resembles the Czar Peter on the road. "*One relays with what one finds,*" wrote he; "*when we had no more Tartar horses we took asses.*" In order to attain this object, the compression of everything and of everybody, it was necessary to set to work in a way obscure, winding, rugged, and difficult; they set to work at it thus. A few of those who entered into it there knew what they were about. Parties live on words; these men, these ringleaders that 1848 frightened and bantered, had, as we have said above, found their words; religion, family, property; they speculated with that vulgar address which is sufficient when one speaks to fear, on certain obscure aspects of what they called Socialism. The question was how to "save religion," property, and the family. "Follow the flag!" said they. The crowd of imbettered interests rushed there; they coalesced, they formed a front, they consolidated, they gathered a crowd around them. This crowd was composed of different elements. The landlord went into it because his rents had fallen; the peasant because he had paid the forty-five centimes; he who did not believe in God thought it necessary to serve religion, because he had been forced to sell his horses. They took from this crowd the force which it contained and made use of it. They made pressure with everything—with the law, with arbitrary power, with the assemblies, with the jury, with the magistracy, with the police, in Lombardy, with the sabre at Naples, with the galleys in Hungary, with the gibbet. In order to remuzzle intelligences, to put minds again in chains like escaped slaves, in order to hinder the past from disappearing, in order to hinder the future from being born, in order to remain kings, the powerful, the privileged, the fortunate, everything became good, everything became just, everything became legitimate. They fabricated for the wants of the struggle, and they scattered in the world a garroter's morality against liberty, a morality which Ferdinand put in practice at Palermo and Antonelli, at Rome, Schwartzenburg, at Milan, and at Pesth, and later, at Paris, the men of December, those wolves of state. There was a people among the peoples who were a sort of elder brother in this family of the oppressed, who were like a prophet in the tribe of man. That people had the initiative in all human movement. They went, they said "Come," and one followed them. How completely in addition to the fraternity of men which is in the gospel they taught the fraternity of nations. That nation spoke by the voice of its writers, of its poets, of its philosophers, of its orators as by one single mouth, and its words went away to the end of the world, to place themselves as tongues of fire on the foreheads of all peoples. It presided at the Lord's supper of the intelligent, it multiplied the bread of life to those who were wandering in the desert. One day a tempest had enveloped it; it trod on the abyss, and said to the frightened peoples: "What do you fear?" The wave of revolutions, raised up by it, grew smooth under its feet, and, so far from engulfing it, glorified it! The nations, sick, suffering, and infirm, pressed around it. This one was limping; the chain of the Inquisition, rivetted about its ankle, for three centuries had disabled it; it said to it, "Walk," and it walked. The other was blind. The old Roman papacy had filled its eyeballs with fog and with night; it said to it, "See." It opened its eyes and saw. "Cast away your crutches, that is to say, your prejudices," said it, "cast away your mists, that is to say, your superstitions, hold fast to your rights, raise your head, look at the heavens, look at the sun, contemplate God. The future is yours. Oh, peoples, you have a leprosy, ignorance ; you have a pestilence, fanaticism ; there is not one of you who does not have and does not spread one of those frightful diseases which they call a despot. Go, walk, break the bonds of wickedness ; I deliver you, I heal you !"

There was throughout all the land a clamour of recognition from peoples whom this word was making healthy and strong. One day it approached dead Poland ; it raised its finger and cried to her: "Arise!" Dead Poland arose. This people, the men of the past, whose fall it announced, derided and hated. By force of ruse and crooked patience and audacity they ended by seizing it, and finally succeeded in strangling it. For more than three years the world has assisted at an immense personal torment, at a frightful spectacle. For more than three years the men of the past—the scribes, the Pharisees, the publicans, the chief-priests have been crucifying, in the presence of the human race, the Christ of peoples, the people of the French. Some furnished the cross, others the nails, others the hammer. Falloux put on its forehead the crown of thorns. Montalembert pressed to his lips the sponge of gall and vinegar. Louis Napoleon is the wretch who pierced its side with the spear, and made it utter that last cry : "Eli! Eli! lamma sabachthani!" Now it is finished. The French race is dead. The great tomb is going to open for three days.*

---

* The translator cannot believe that the author meant here to utter blasphemy. The passage is only a very strong presentation of the common theological statement, that Christ suffers in the person of his people.

CHAPTER II.

LET us have faith. No, let us not allow ourselves to be crushed. To despair is to desert. Let us look at the future. The future—one does not know what tempests separate us from the port ; but the port, radiant, though distant, is in view ; the future, let us repeat it, is the Republic for all ; let us add, the future is peace with all. Let us not fall into the vulgar whim and dishonour the century in which we live. Erasmus called the sixteenth century the "excrement of times," *fex temporum ;* Bossuet thus characterizes the seventeenth century : "A time wicked and small ;" Rousseau stigmatizes the eighteenth century in these terms : "This great rottenness in which we live." Posterity has decided against these illustrious minds. She has said to Erasmus, "The sixteenth century is grand ;" she has said to Bossuet, "The seventeenth century is grand ;" she has said to Rousseau, "The eighteenth century is grand." The infamy of these centuries must have been real, yet these strong men were wrong in complaining. The thinker ought to accept with simplicity and calmness the centre in which Providence has placed him. The splendour of the human intelligence, the elevation of human genius does not shine less by contrast than by harmony with times. The stoical and profound man is not debased by baseness around him. Virgil, Petrarch, Racine, are great in their purple; Job is greater on his dunghill. But we can say it, we men of the nineteenth century, the nineteenth century is not a dunghill. Whatever may be the shames of the present instant, whatever may be the blows by which the shifting gear of events may strike us, whatever may be the apparent desertion or the momentary lethargy of minds, none of us democrats will disown this magnificent epoch in which we live, the masculine age of humanity. Let us proclaim this aloud, let us proclaim it in our fall and in our overthrow, this century is the grandest of centuries; and do you know why? because it is the sweetest. This century, the immediate and the first issue of the French Revolution, freed the slave in America, elevated the parias in Asia, extinguished the funeral-pile in India, and crushed the last firebrands at the martyr's stake in Europe; is civilizing Turkey, is causing the gospel to penetrate even to the refutation of the Koran, elevates woman, subordinates the right of might to the might of right, suppresses piracies, softens suffering, makes the galleys wholesome, throws the red branding-iron into the sewer, condemns the death penalty, takes the ball from the foot of the galley-slave, abolishes corporal punishment, degrades and dishonours war, takes the edge away from the Dukes of Alva and the Charles the Ninths, tears out the claws of tyrants.

This century proclaims the sovereignty of the citizen and the inviolability of life; it crowns the people and consecrates man. In art it has all varieties of genius: writers, orators, poets, historians, publicists, philosophers, painters, statuaries, musicians; majesty, grace, power, strength, brilliancy, depth, colour, form, style. It reinvigorates itself at once in the real and in the ideal, and carries in its hand those two thunderbolts, the true and the beautifuL In science it performs every miracle ; it makes saltpetre out of cotton, of steam a horse, of the voltaic pile a workman, of the electric fluid a messenger, of the sun a painter ; it waters itself with subterranean waters till it warms itself with central fire ; it opens on the two infinites those two windows, the telescope on the infinitely great, the microscope on the infinitely little, and it finds in the first abyss stars, and in the second insects, which prove God to it. It suppresses duration, it suppresses space, it suppresses suffering ; it writes a letter from Paris to London, and it has the answer in ten minutes ; it amputates a man's thigh while the man is singing, and smiling. It has only to realize—and it is close upon it—a progress which is nothing at the side of the other miracles which it has already done ; it has only to find the means to propel in a mass of air a bubble of air still lighter ; it has already secured the air-bubble, and it holds it imprisoned ; it has only to find the impelling force, only to make the vacuum before the balloon, for example, only to burn the air before it, as the rocket would ; it has only to resolve in some such way this problem, and it will resolve it ; and do you know what will happen then ? At that very instant frontiers will vanish, barriers will retire, everything which is a Chinese wall around thought, around commerce, around industry, around nationalities, around progress, will crumble ; in spite of censorship, in spite of the index, it will rain books and journals everywhere ; Voltaire, Diderot, Rousseau will fall in hail on Rome, on Naples, on Vienna, on St. Petersburg ; human speech is manna and the serf will pick it up in the furrow; fanaticisms will die, oppression will be impossible; man crawls along the earth, he escapes; civilization will make herself a flock of birds and fly away, and go whirling, and light joyously on all points of the globe at once. Stop! there she is, she is passing; point your cannon, old despotisms, she disdains you; you are only the bullet, she is the lightning; no more hatreds, no more interests mutually annulling one another, no more wars; a sort of new life, made up of concord and light, carries away and pacifies the world; the fraternity of peoples crosses space and communes in the eternal azure, men are mingled in the heavens. Until this last progress, see the point to which this century has brought civilization.

Formerly there was a world where one walked with slow steps, with back bent, with head hung down; a world in which Count Gouvon had himself served at table by Jean Jacques; in which the Chevalier de Rohan struck Voltaire with his cane; in which they delivered Daniel De Foe to the pillory; in which a city like Dijon was separated from a city like Paris by dangers which made it proper to make your will; thieves at all the corners of the woods, and ten days of stage-coach to endure; in which a book was a kind of infamy and filth, which the executioner burnt on the steps of the Palace of Justice; a world in which superstition and ferocity gave each other their hands; in which the pope said to the emperor: "*Jungamus dexteras, gladium gladio copulemus;*" in which one met at every step crosses on which amulets were hanging, and gibbets on which hung men; in which there were heretics, Jews, and lepers; in which houses had battlements and loop-holes; in which they closed the streets with a chain, the rivers with a chain, the camps themselves with a chain, as at the battle of Tolosa; in which they surrounded cities with walls, kingdoms with prohibitions and penalties; in which, except authority and force, which kept close together, everything was penned off, partitioned out, cut up, divided, hewn in pieces, hated and hating, scattered and dead; men dust, power block. To-day there is a world in which all is living, united, combined, paired, blended; a world in which reign thought, commerce, industry; in which politics, more and more developed, tend to blend with science; a world in which the last scaffolds and the last cannons hasten to cut off their last heads, and to vomit forth their last shells; a world in which light increases at every minute; a world in which distance has disappeared, in which Constantinople is nearer Paris than Lyons was a hundred years ago; in which America and Europe throb at the same heart-beat; a world, all circulation and all love, whose brain is France, whose arteries are railroads, and whose nerves are electric wires. Do you not see that simply to describe such a situation is to explain everything, to demonstrate everything, to resolve everything? Do you not see that the old world had, as a fatal fault, an old soul—tyranny, and that into the new world there is about to descend, necessarily, irresistibly, divinely, a young soul—liberty? That was the work which had created among men the nineteenth century, and which was continuing it splendidly, that century of baseness, decrease, and of decadence, as the pedants, the rhetoricians, the imbeciles call it, and all that unclean horde of bigots, of rogues, and knaves who slaver sanctimonious gall upon glory, who declare that Pascal is a fool, that

Voltaire is a fop, and Rousseau a brute, and whose triumph it would be to put a fool's cap on the human race. You speak of the Lower Empire? Seriously? Did the Lower Empire have behind it John Huss, Luther, Cervantes, Shakespeare, Pascal, Molière, Voltaire, Montesquieu, Rousseau, Mirabeau? Did the Lower Empire have behind it the taking of the Bastile, the Confederation, Danton, Robespierre, the Convention? Did the Lower Empire have America? Did the Lower Empire have universal suffrage? Did the Lower Empire have those two ideas, country and humanity; country, the idea which enlarges the heart; humanity, the idea which enlarges the horizon? Do you know that under the Lower Empire Constantinople was falling into ruins, and ended by having no more than 30,000 inhabitants? Is Paris as far gone as that?

Because you have seen a prætorian attack succeed, you declare yourselves the Lower Empire! That is said hastily, and loosely considered; but reflect, then, if you can. Did the Lower Empire have the compass, the galvanic battery, the printing press, the newspaper, the locomotive, the electric telegraph? So many wings, which carried man along, and which the Lower Empire did not have? Where the Lower Empire crept, the nineteenth century soars. Do you reflect? What! shall we see again the Empress Zoe, Romanus, Argyrus, Nicephorus the Logothete, Michael Calaphate? Come, then! Do you think that Providence repeats himself dully? Do you think that God is a tautologist? Let us have faith! Let us say something positive. Irony of itself is the beginning of baseness. It is in affirming that one becomes good; it is in affirmation that one becomes great. Yes, the emancipations of intelligences, and consequently the emancipations of peoples, was the sublime task which the nineteenth century was accomplishing in co-operation with France, for the doubly providential work of time and of men, of repining and of action, was blending itself in the common effort, and the great epoch had for its home the great nation. Oh, country! at this hour, in which thou art there bloody, lifeless, with thy head abased, thine eyes closed, with thy mouth open and yet no longer speaking, with the marks of the lash upon thy shoulders, with the nails of the boots of hangmen printed on thy body, naked and soiled and equal to a dead thing, an object of hatred, an object of derision; alas! it is at this hour, native land, that the heart of the proscribed overflows with love and respect for thee! There thou art, motionless! The man of despotism and oppression laughs and tastes the proud illusion of no longer fearing thee. Rapid joys. The peoples who are in the darkness forget the past, and only see the present and despise thee. Forgive them; they know not what they do. Despise thee! Great God, despise France! And who are they? What language do they speak? What books do they hold in their hands? What names do they know by heart? What is the post-bill pasted on the walls of their theatres? What form do their arts, their laws, their manners, their garments, their pleasures, their fashions, have? What is the great date for them as for us? '89! If they take France out of their souls, what will remain to them? O, peoples! though she be fallen, and fallen forever, do they despise Greece? Do they despise Italy? Do they despise France?

Look at those breasts; they are your nurse. Look at that womb; it is your mother. If she sleeps, if she is in lethargy; silence, and stand uncovered. If she is dead; on your knees!

The exiles are scattered; destiny has blasts that scatter men as a hand scatters ashes. Some are in Belgium, some in Piedmont, some in Switzerland, where they have no liberty; others are in London, where they have no roof. This one, a peasant, has been torn from his native enclosure; this one, a soldier, has no longer anything but the handle of his sword, for his sword they have broken; this one, a workman, does not know the language of the country; he is without clothes, and without shoes; he does not know whether he will eat to-morrow; this one has left a wife and children, beloved group, the object for which he labours, the joy of his life; this one has an old mother, with white hair, who is weeping for him; that one has an old father, who will die without having seen him again; this other, loved, he has left behind him an adored being, who will forget him; they raise their heads, they stretch out their hands to each other, they smile; there are no people who do not step aside with respect when they pass, and who do not view with profound tenderness, as one of the most beautiful sights which fortune can give to men, all these peaceful consciences, all these broken hearts.

They suffer, they are silent; in them the citizen has sacrificed the man; they look fixedly at adversity; they do not even cry under the pitiless rod of misfortune: "*Civis romanus sum;*" but in the evening, when one thinks, when all in the strange city puts on sadness, for what seems cold by day becomes funereal by twilight; in the night, when one does not sleep, souls the most stoical open to grief and dejection. Where are the little children? Who will give them bread? Who will give them their father's kiss? Where is the wife? Where is the mother? Where is the brother? Where are they all? And those songs that one used to hear in the evening in their native language, where are they?

Where is the wood, the tree, the path, the roof full of nests, the bell surrounded by tombs? Where is the street, where is the faubourg, the lamp lighted before your door, the friends, the workshop, the trade, the accustomed work? And the furniture sold at public notice, the auction invading the domestic sanctuary! Oh what farewells forever! destroyed, dead, thrown to the four winds, that moral being which they call the hearth of a family, and which is not only composed of prattlings, tendernesses, and of embraces, but also of hours, and habits, of the visits of friends, of the laughter of one, of the pressure of another's hand, of the view that one saw from such a window, of the place where a familiar object stood, of the armchair where your grandfather sat, of the carpet on which your first-born has played! Flown away are all those objects on which your life was imprinted! Vanished, the visible form of recollections! There are in grief inward and obscure, sides where the boldest courage bends. The orator of Rome bent his head without growing pale to the knife of the centurion Lenas; but he wept when he thought that his house would be destroyed by Clodius. The proscribed are silent; or, if they mourn, it is only among themselves. As they know each other, and know that they are doubly brothers, having the same country and the same proscription, they relate to each other their miseries. He who has money divides with those who have none; he who has firmness gives it to those who lack it. They exchange reminiscences, aspirations, hopes. They turn, with their arms stretched out into the shadow, toward what they have left behind them. Ah! how happy they are down there, those who think no longer of us! Each one suffers, and, at moments, becomes impassioned.

They engrave on all memories the names of all the hangmen. Each one has something that he curses: Mazas, the hulks, the casemates, the informer who betrayed the spy who lay in ambush, the gendarme who arrested, Lambessa where one has a friend, Cayenne where one has a brother; but there is one thing that they bless all and with one accord, it is thou, France! Oh! a complaint, a word against thee, France! No, no, no! One has never more of country in his heart than when he is in exile. They will do their whole duty with a tranquil forehead and an unshaken perseverance. Never to see thee again, that is their sorrow; never to forget thee, that is their joy.

Ah, what mourning! and after eight months it is in vain that one tells himself it is so; it is in vain that one looks around him and sees the spire of St. Michael instead of the Pantheon, and St. Gudule instead of Notre Dame; one does not believe it! So it is true; we cannot deny it, we must agree to it, we must recognize it, though one die of humiliation and despair, that which you see there on the ground is the nineteenth century—it is France! What! And this Bonaparte has done this ruin!

What! is it in the centre of the greatest people on earth, is it in the middle of the greatest century of history, that this personage has stood erect and triumphed, to make a prey for himself out of France? Great God! What the eagle dreaded to take in his talons, the parrot has taken in his claw! What! Louis XI. miscarried at it! Richelieu was broken upon it! Napoleon was not sufficient for it! In a day, from evening until morning, the absurd has been the possible. All that was axiom has become chimera. All that was lie has become actual fact. What! the most brilliant concourse of men! the most magnificent movement of ideas! the most formidable chain of events! what no Titan could have restrained, what no Hercules could have overthrown, the human stream in flood, the French billow advancing, civilization, progress, intelligence, revolution, liberty, *he* arrested one fine morning, purely and simply and neatly; he, this mask, this dwarf, this abortive Tiberius, this nothing!

God was marching on, Louis Bonaparte, with crest erect, put himself across the path and says to God: "Thou shalt go no further!" God stopped. And you imagine that that was so! and you imagine that this plebiscitum exists, that this Constitution of, I no longer know what day of January, exists, that this Senate exists, that this Council of State and this Corps Legislatif exist! You imagine that there is a lackey whose name is Rouher, a valet whose name is Troplong, an eunuch whose name is Baroche, and a sultan, a pacha, a master who is called Louis Bonaparte! You do not see what all this chimera is! You do not see that the 2d of December is only an immense delusion, a pause, a time of rest, a sort of curtain behind which God, the marvellous machinist, is preparing and constructing the last act, the supreme and triumphal act of the French revolution! You are looking stupidly at the curtain, at the thing painted on the coarse canvas, the nose of one, the epaulets of another, the great sabre of a third, the laced Cologne-water tradesmen that you call generals, those poosahs that you call magistrates, those good-natured men that you call senators; this mixture of caricatures and spectres, you take them for a reality! And you do not hear over there, in the shadow, that deep sound! You do not see some one who comes and goes! You do not see the curtain tremble at the breath of him who is behind it!

THE END.

www.ingramcontent.com/pod-product-compliance
Lightning Source LLC
Chambersburg PA
CBHW022105230426
43672CB00008B/1286